Kiwis, Canaries and Monkeys
500 Extraordinary Racing Stories

GRAHAM SHARPEN

RACING POST

This edition first published in Great Britain in 2011 by
Racing Post Books
Raceform, Compton, Newbury, Berkshire, RG20 6NL

1 3 5 7 9 10 8 6 4 2

ISBN 978-1-905156-97-9

Designed by Fiona Pike

Printed and bound in Great Britain by the MPG Books Group

www.racingpost.com/shop

INTRODUCTION

STRANGELY STRANGE, BUT ODDLY NORMAL!

'Strangely Strange But Oddly Normal' is a track by the Sixties folk group, Dr Strangely Strange. Perhaps the strangest thing about it is how much it reminds me of the folk song, Streets of London.

The other strange thing about it is that it has no connection whatsoever with horse racing, nor do the lyrics mention racing, yet, for me, the title so perfectly sums up a day at the races or so many of them that I have enjoyed over the years.

And that 'other-worldly' quality to the Sport of Kings has been the one which has most appealed to me, to the extent that I have written frequently about the way in which the normal rules of life and how it works so often cease to function on and around racecourses.

The forerunner to this book, *500 Strangest Racing Stories*, was published in 2007 and it proved to be my most successful title in over a quarter of a century of writing books about racing and betting.

The quirky, offbeat, unusual and eccentric racing yarns contained in the book clearly struck a chord with regular racegoers and fans of the sport alike.

The object of the exercise was to tap into the bizarre side of the Sport of Kings, to reflect the way in which every day at the races produces one or more incidents which, when recalled and discussed result in the mutual recognition and appreciation of anyone and everyone who has ever gone racing or backed a horse – and who invariably comes away with a story about SOMETHING which they'd never come across, seen or heard before.

It can be a nightmarish experience like that at Newbury in February 2011 when horses were tragically struck down in the parade ring; hilariously humorous as so many of these stories are, or it can be bafflingly bizarre – also more common than you might expect.

Now I have decided that the time is right for a follow up, because since experiencing, collecting and reporting the last half a thousand, I have discovered and uncovered as many more again.

I have mined a treasure trove of tales of racehorses and racecourses. Many of which animals and tracks quite possibly you have never heard of.

All of the stories will appeal to the racing fan's sense of the absurd, the different, the fascinating and the fantastical. I must thank all of those who responded to my tiresome requests for information out of the blue – particularly 'Aussie' Phil Percival, who supplied several great stories.

The racecourses include the familiar and the far flung – they range from Agua Caliente to Zarzuela; they include brilliantly, crazily named tracks like Whoop Up Downs, Fannie Bay, Bong Bong, Mingenew and Zobnatica. Another track, oddly named to British eyes and ears, Fukushima in Japan, was sadly affected by the horrendous earthquake and tsunami of March 2011.

Anyone with an affinity with, and affection for, racing and racetracks will just NEED to know what has happened on these tracks which cover every continent of the world and introduce you to an array of colourful, intriguing characters both equine and human.

Alongside the track stories you will be offered more strangely strange but oddly abnormal racing yarns to amaze, astonish, and amuse ...

Graham Sharpe, 2011

1 TRAGIC NEWBURY NIGHTMARE
Newbury

Racing was abandoned at Newbury on Saturday, February 12, 2011, when two horses collapsed and died under freak circumstances in the paddock prior to the opening race.

The executive of the Berkshire course decided human and equine safety was paramount as they were unable to ascertain the precise cause of the incident.

Fenix Two and Marching Song were about to be mounted by their jockeys on the grass on the far side of the parade ring when they both fell to the ground.

Connections of the stricken horses speculated that they may have suffered an electric shock of some kind.

Kid Cassidy recovered after briefly collapsing but was withdrawn at the start of the Bet Totepool On 0800 221 221 Novices' Hurdle, with jockey Robert Thornton reporting that the horse's rider, A P McCoy had told him that his mount had gone down to the start 'as if his tail were on fire' but then refused to budge once he reached the start. The Merry Giant was also affected, but took part in the race, only to finish tailed off, and was later reported to be "badly traumatised".

As the two dead horses lay under covers in the hastily cordoned-off area of the paddock, the race actually took place around 20 minutes late but after the runners were taken to the adjoining pre-parade ring to be unsaddled, the decision was taken to call the meeting off.

Newbury's joint managing director Stephen Higgins said: 'Ultimately we are guessing, but at the end of the day horses are very important but people are more important and we didn't want them accessing the area in question until we know what the issue is. We still don't know what happened, and when we do we will let everybody know. It is the racecourse's decision (to abandon) and we take responsibility for what happens on the racecourse'

Electrocution was the general consensus and Andy Turnell, trainer of Marching Song, and his assistant and part-owner Graham Thorner were particularly upset.

'It looks like they've been electrocuted,' said Turnell. 'My fellow seemed perfectly all right and I was about to leg him up but he just went straight down. To a layman with no evidence, you would say it was electrical. The lad who was with him was saying "I'm getting an electric shock off this horse".

'It can't be coincidence four horses have done the same thing and two have died, all in the same area. Three people said they were getting a shock off the horse. I hope we find out what it was but it doesn't bring the horses back.'

Several sources said that horses are more susceptible to electrical shocks than humans and that those wearing steel plates – as were the two fatalities – would be the most vulnerable.

Jonjo O'Neill, trainer of Fenix Two, said: "Mine reared up and we couldn't get him back, it was like he was stuck to the ground. It was the weirdest thing I've ever seen in my life."

Reports suggested that some of the runners who took part in the race appeared to have burn marks around their mouths when their tack was removed. This was not confirmed.

Police and the electricity board were informed.

Investigators from Southern Electric later carried out tests in the parade ring and reportedly discovered an ancient cable, which Newbury clerk of the course Richard Osgood said he had not been aware of despite thirty years at the track. A section of cable was removed.

Inevitably, as with Dick Francis' Devon Loch freak Grand National collapse, there was no shortage of fanciful theories put forward: 'There was talk of that bizarre Ascot stun gun affair,' wrote racing journalist Rodney Masters, who added of Marching Song that 'he squealed like no horse I've heard before. No exaggeration, believe me, it was blood-curdling.'

There were claims that a local farmer had reported his cattle suffering distress at a similar time. There were suspicions voiced about the installation of a large screen by the paddock. Trainer Keith Goldsworthy told stewards that lights in the track's Berkshire Stand had flickered erratically at the time.

William Muir, trainer of Island Sunset, told Newbury that when the horse raced there in September she 'got very upset and started to throw herself around' in the same area of the parade ring. Others recalled the 1983 death of Denys Smith-trained The Grey Bomber, electrocuted in a freak gallops accident.

The meeting was rescheduled for, and took place on, the following Friday afternoon with no further paddock problems. The day before that meeting took place it was announced that autopsies on the two dead horses confirmed that they had been accidentally electrocuted, and Southern Electric Power said they were satisfied there were now no electrical problems in the area from which they had removed the cable.

Marcus Townend of the *Daily Mail* asked, 'whether an old, forgotten cable was damaged by routine maintenance or had simply deteriorated?' while his colleague Martin Samuel wondered, 'had a similar accident occurred at a football ground, it would be interesting to note whether those in charge would have been forgiven so quickly.'

The *Racing Post* pointed out that 'there has been no explanation about how a section of cable close to where the pair (of horses) collapsed came to be live when it was thought to have been disconnected in 1992.'

Two days after the tragedy Michael Hanlon, Science Editor of the *Daily Mail* reported that there had been reports of similar incidents in a 2008 *Journal of Equine Veterinary Science* which 'blamed electrocution by buried cable as the probable cause in many cases of unexplained equine death'. It detailed a case at an un-named American course when one horse died and two others were badly affected. 'It was later found that a 220 volt cable had been buried under the area'.

Hanlon also highlighted a similar accident 'at a Spanish course a few years before.'

As this book went to press no comprehensive explanation of the tragedy had been forthcoming, and racing has continued quite normally ever since.

2 CHELTENHAM FERTILITYVAL Cheltenham

Cheltenham supremo Edward Gillespie is used to receiving queries about the course's famous Festival and the great races run at the track – but he was dumbfounded to be asked to help confirm the date on which a racegoer got pregnant to help her determine who the father of her baby was!

'The lady phoned me a couple of years back to ask me to check which day the Gold Cup was run on twenty years ago. Why? Because she'd met a bloke up here and gone back to his hotel, got pregnant but never revealed to her husband her suspicions that the baby was not his.

The husband had recently died and she was looking up her cycle from that year. She was delighted to hear the answer, as it proved the father of her son might be still around and he was 'really lovely'.

3 JUDGE WAS DEAD LOSS Brisbane

Racegoers and punters were celebrating as the favourite won by a clear length at an Ascot, Brisbane, meeting under jockey Ken Lee in 1940. However, they were astonished when the winning number went up as Eight, carried by obvious runner-up Thought Reader, rather than the favourite, Simonic's number – Three.

Lee, who went on to become a leading trainer, recalled, 'The crowd went wild and threatened to pull the grandstand down. Somebody went to the judge's box to find out what went wrong, and when they got there they found the judge was dead. He had obviously died of a heart attack.'

But that tragic event merely compounded the problem of the moment – as Lee explained, 'The judge's decision is final, and although there was a riot when the result stood, I didn't get the race'.

4 SHAKEN – AND QUITE STIRRED! New Zealand

Racehorse semen 'milkshakes' were the bizarre attraction on the menu at the 2011 annual Wildfoods Festival in New Zealand. The 'shots' were provided at 10 kiwi dollars a time by racehorse owner Lindsay Kerslake, of Christchurch, who came up with the idea after hearing about a similar concoction created from bull's semen.

'I thought, horses are all testosterone, they have hardly any cholesterol, so the idea is you have as much zizz as a stallion for a week afterwards. It's all safe, we get the semen in the same way breeders do, using an artificial vagina and storing it. You often hear from a female perspective that semen has an awful alkaline taste, so I thought we'd better make it more user-friendly. Think of it like a milkshake.'

Kerslake also offered an energy drink, 'Powerhorse', to wash the shots

– which were also served in a variety of flavours like cherry, liquorice and banoffee pie – down with. The drinks were served up by women brandishing riding whips.

One festival-goer commented, 'Just because someone does the donkey work for you, doesn't change the fact you are drinking horse sperm – it is like bestiality without the video camera!' Sea tulip, chocolate covered beetles, raw and cooked scorpions and weka, a type of wild bird, were also on the menu at the March event in the town of Hokitika.

5 WINKIE DETTORI

Frankie Dettori has a strange pre-sleeping ritual, revealed wife Catherine in a slightly indiscreet June 2008 interview.

'We have got the darkest curtains,' she told the *Daily Mail*'s Alan Fraser. 'It is like the blackout. He gets into bed. It is already black and he puts patches on his eyes.' Then, declared Catherine, 'He covers his winkie with his hand. It's a habit.' And once asleep, the Anglo-Italian 'dreams in English'.

6 BOOTSIEFUL! Australia

Many racing fans refuse to believe the story of Australian jockey Les Boots, the jump jockey who could never complete the course, which I outlined from the sketchy information I had in my last book of racing strangeness.

I confess to a healthy scepticism myself – but I recently heard from respected Aussie racing writer Phil Percival, who sent me a copy of an article he wrote, which included his report of a radio conversation between Boots and a popular presenter, so I can now treat you to a fuller, factually more accurate account of his remarkable career.

Read it and weep – with laughter!

Phil told me: 'The Grand National is run in July in Australia and the racing station 4BC used to play this tape of an interview between one of Australia's most loved race callers Bert Bryant and jumps jockey Les Boots on the morning of the race for many years. Bert was laughing so much he ended up in tears.'

It went like this:

'I rode for 18 years, but spent 12 of them in hospital. I broke just about every bone in my body. Bookmakers used to put up 100-1 about my mounts no matter how good the form read. Never once did I complete the course over the jumps. In fact I never got past the winning post the first time around.

'Once the South Australian Jockey Club was going to bar me from riding because I was putting too big a strain on the Workers Compensation Fund.

'My wife used to wrap my pyjamas in a brown paper bag and put them with my riding gear, which was embarrassing when other jockeys found out. She also barred me from taking the kids on the merry-go round after I fell off three times.

'The nurses at the Adelaide hospital used to buy the racing guides, and if I had a ride, they used to make up my usual bed. I once fell at the first jump, breaking my leg, then fell out of the ambulance on the way back to the casualty room, then while they they were carrying me across the lawn I fell off the stretcher.

'It got a bit much when the starter mounted his stand and just before releasing the field called out: "We'll call in to the hospital through the week Les and see how you're getting on"

'My worst fall was off a horse called Paria, I broke my neck and was in hospital for two years. The nurses ended up strapping me into bed every night because the night nurse never got any rest picking me up and putting me back into bed. My ambition was to ride in the English Grand National but my wife wouldn't let me go, as she thought I'd be the first jockey drowned in the water jump.

'My most frightening experience was on a misty, foggy day at Victoria Park. I fell off at the first and, being a bit winded, was laying on the track waiting for the ambulance to arrive when through the fog I heard this voice saying "I think we'll have to shoot him." I beat the ambulance back to the jockeys' room, where they sedated me and explained they were talking about the horse.'

I researched a little further into this remarkable man's career, and discovered that Boots (sometimes called 'Bootsie') was banned by stewards from race riding in 1949 on medical grounds, after he had sustained broken ribs, a broken ankle and concussion in a fall. His official record shows him to have contested 39 hurdles races, taking 37 falls.

Les was born in 1912, and ran away from home when he was 14 to become an apprentice. Increasing weight forced him off the Flat and over jumps, although he probably wouldn't have set the world alight on the Flat, either: 'Before I was out of my apprenticeship I was on first-name terms with every nurse and doctor in Adelaide,' he told one racing journalist.

But Boots was a popular man. One of his best pals was dual Melbourne-Cup winning jockey John Letts, who revealed that other jockeys would prepare themselves for a late day's work if Boots had a mount on the card – as he would invariably fall in the first race, whereupon the course ambulance would cart him off – thus delaying the rest of the races until the ambulance returned, and adding the best part of an hour to the afternoon.

Les died in 1987.

7 HORSE WHO FINISHED COURSE QUICKEST FINISHED SECOND Melbourne

Flemington hosts the world famous Melbourne Cup, which, great event though it has always been, excelled itself in 2008 when it was claimed that the runner-up in the race that stops a nation, as it is wont to style itself, finished the course in a quicker time than the winner.

No – I didn't, and don't, get it, either. Yet, when Bauer, trained by Luca Cumani, was a close second behind Viewed, his official time was, indeed, officially faster than that of the horse who beat him!

The newspaper *Melbourne Age*'s Tom Reilly revealed the literally incredible anomaly, asking in a headline: 'At which race does the fastest horse come second?' In Australia microchips are inserted into saddle cloths to reveal the precise timings every 200 metres.

And the *Age* revealed that Bauer completed the 2m race in 3m 20.40 seconds – while Viewed was credited with a time of 3m 20.41 seconds.

However, the result of a race is not decided by the time taken, but by the photo finish revealing which horse's head crosses the line first. And by that decision, Viewed was a nose clear where it counted.

'The difference came about because the timing devices are in the saddle,' lamented former Test cricketer Simon O'Donnell, one of 5yo Bauer's owners. 'Sadly, our guy is a bit smaller than Viewed.'

Bauer's official size was 15.3hh – Viewed's 16hh.

And Luca Cumani's daughter, Francesca, now a TV presenter in Australia, came up with a solution: 'If we come back next year we'll have to bring horses with long necks and big heads.'

8 KIWIS, CANARIES AND MONKEYS – NOT TO MENTION EMUS AND OCTOPUSES Gate Pa, New Zealand

Also known by the Maoris as Marawaiwai, they raced at Gate Pa in New Zealand from 1874. In 1880 they splashed out £700 to lay down a grass track, erect a saddling paddock and build a grandstand.

At a meeting here that year it was reported that 'the paucity of people under the influence of drink was quite a remarkable feature' and that 'punters paid out 2/6 and a canary or monkey would pick a number out of a hat' to give them a tip for the next race.

Cliff Sims, an Aussie trainer on the Gold Coast in the 1960s recalls 'a pet emu which earned a reputation picking local winners.' Puts the 2010 World Cup predictions of Paul the Psychic Octopus into perspective!

9 BY GEORGE, GEORGE, GEORGE, GEORGE! Leicester

On July 21, 2010, Leicester hosted a real racing oddity as the horse George Baker, trained by George Baker, ridden by another George Baker, and owned by, er, yet another George Baker, finished fifth.

Previously owned by Harry Findlay, whose ambition it had been to have George Bakers training and owning the horse, the three-year-old was put up for sale and trainer Baker said: 'I sold half a share to someone who promptly introduced himself as George Baker. You couldn't make it up!' I rather hope he didn't.

Baker, the Whitsbury-based dual purpose trainer born in 1965 was once confused with Baker, the 1982-born Lambourn-based tallest Flat jockey in the land at 6ft. They are not related but Baker the trainer was once asked by trainer James Given if he could ride a horse for him – and had to point out that he weighed several stone more than the rider Given really needed!

10 HAIRY MOMENT Adelaide

Peter Morgan turned up to ride at Australian course Victoria Park, near Adelaide, in 1972 only to be stood down by the South Australian Jockey Club – who ruled that his hair was too long.

Morgan, who eventually retired from the saddle aged 26 with some 200 winners to his credit, went on to make a name for himself as 'King of the Crocks', a trainer of 'broken-down' horses brought back to full fitness using a combination of swimming pool and treadmill.

11 WHIP ROUND The Curragh, Ireland

In Gaelic, the Curragh is known as An Currach – meaning 'The Racecourse', logically enough. There is written evidence of horse racing dating back to the third century when chariot races were held on the lands known today as the Curragh.

On May 22, 2010 one of the most bizarre incidents in the history of the course took place when the Stewards suspended jockey Ronan Whelan for three days for excessive use of the whip. This would have been fair enough, had it not been for the fact that the Jim Bolger apprentice had dropped his whip on leaving the stalls.

The Stewards later 'reviewed' their decision, dropped the suspension and apologised to the jockey. 'R P Whelan informed the further inquiry that he had lost his whip at an early stage of the race, a fact that he had not revealed prior to the first enquiry or to the acting stewards during the course of the first enquiry. Having considered the new evidence given the stewards were of the opinion that their original decision was in error and apologised.'

Quite.

12 SID JUMPS TO IT Australia

Putting up four pounds overweight on two-year-old Pyramid Peak at Gold Coast Turf Club, in June 1972, experienced jockey Sid Curran was going so well towards the front of the 14-runner field that he decided to make a move up the inside of the two leaders.

'The gap closed and Pyramid Peak clipped the heels of one of the leaders and stumbled, dislodging me'.

The crowd gasped as Curran was unseated – but then rubbed their eyes in disbelief at what happened next. 'I landed on my feet, ran alongside for a couple of strides and vaulted back into the saddle. I rode to the line, finishing eighth.'

Nicknamed Darkie because of his jet black hair, Curran rode around the Toowoomba and Brisbane circuit for 35 years – but never experienced another rodeo ride like that one.

13 BEST OF THE WORST OR WORST OF THE BEST? Gatwick, Sussex

Alfred Day came to The Hermitage, on the north side of the Chichester to Arundel road, in 1887 to train racehorses. While researching the history of the area, he found a reference on a 1630 map to 'Fontwell'. This was the name of the spring in front of his house, the only watering-hole on this major south coast route, and which the Romans had originally called 'Fons'. Passing monks are said to have added the 'well' part of the name. Day brought the name Fontwell back into use.

While not training any Derby winners, Alfred Day often managed to get inexpensive horses to win good races. He bought one horse for just over £20 and won a race worth £300 with it. He turned down an offer of £700 for it, but a week later the horse died. His best horse was Master Willie, who held the 'world record' for six furlongs for over 25 years. Day was able to buy more land in the area and by 1924, he had obtained a licence from the Jockey Club to create the racecourse at Fontwell.

Perhaps the strangest race a Day horse ever contested took place at nearby Gatwick, rather than Fontwell.

Day trained a horse called Shepperton with which he despaired of ever winning a race, and he declared it must be the worst horse in training in the land. Not so, thought rival trainer Sam Pickering, quite convinced his own stable inmate, Rowan Berry, was an even worse performer.

The challenge captured the public imagination – and was taken seriously enough for Day to book top jockey, the controversial American Tod Sloan, to partner Shepperton while reigning champion Sam Loates was brought in to ride Rowan Berry.

All of a sudden, rather than wanting to be crowned 'The Worst', both trainers wanted to prove their horse could actually win a race.

Since the match race had been announced, Rowan Berry was tubed to improve a respiratory complaint – which may have made the difference – as he prevailed by a mere neck in a pulsating, if sedate paced, desperately close finish in front of a large, enthralled crowd.

'Told you so' Day must have said.

And should you be sceptical that such a race actually took place, I discovered an eyewitness report of it: 'London – May 13, 1899 – At the second day's racing of the Gatwick Spring Meeting today, in a match race of six furlongs for the sum of £100, Mr A J Schwabe's five-year-old bay horse Rowan Berry, ridden by S Loates, beat Mr T Corn's three-year-old bay colt Shepperton, ridden by Sloan.

'Loates's mount won by a neck. The betting was 6 to 5 on Shepperton. The scene that followed this race was one to recall the victory of the Prince of Wales' Persimmon in the Derby of 1896. The air was for the moment thick with hats and the crowd yelled themselves hoarse. A more exciting contest has rarely been seen.

'Sloan made the running, but at the distance, Rowan Berry stuck his head in front and kept it there during the most exciting finish witnessed in a long time.'

14 SHURELY SHOME MISHTAKE! Mauritius

Officials at the Mauritius Turf Club may well have got their knickers in a twist when they were selecting jockeys to invite to take part in their international ladies' event at Champ de Mars racecourse in 2009.

The Club's official website reported: 'The lady riders Stephane Pasquier and Ahmed Ajtebi landed in Mauritius this morning in view of their participation in the International Jockeys' Weekend.'

It is not clear who was the most surprised when the mistake was pointed out – the (very male) jockeys to whom the story referred, Stephane Pasquier and Ahmed Ajtebi, or the officials who had lined them up for the women's races!

Pasquier made very sure that no-one was in any doubt as to his ability, let alone his sex, at the meeting on December 6, booting home four winners, none of them in a ladies' race.

★

Champ de Mars Racecourse is the race track in Port Louis, Mauritius, located close to the centre of the city at the Mauritius Turf Club, which was founded in 1812 making it the oldest horse-racing club in the Southern hemisphere.

15 FRANKLY SPEAKING Turf Paradise, USA

Frank Mirahamadi made his debut as a course commentator at Hollywood Park in the States on Christmas Eve, 1992 – but few in the crowd realised, because he called the commentary in the style of the resident announcer who was on holiday.

Also a comedian and impressionist, Los Angeles-born Mirahamadi continued to commentate at different courses in his unique fashion – peaking perhaps in May 2009 at Turf Paradise where he used over 20 different voices whilst calling the $50,000 Hasta La Vista Handicap, amongst them Robert de Niro, Marlon Brando and trainer D Wayne Lukas.

Search it out on Youtube to discover the 40-year-old's remarkable technique.

★

The filthiest race commentary ever was undoubtedly the late comedian Peter Cook's fictitious offering in the guise of his and Dudley Moore's 'Derek & Clive' vulgar alter egos. Far too rude to print here, the commentary features 'Vagina being pressed by The Pr*ck' and 'The Wa*ker coming with a late run' as 'The A*sehole tires'

There's more – much ****ing more!

16 GETTING SHIRTY Queensland

Aboriginal jockey Richard 'Darby' Munro, who numbered top races like the AJC Derby and Newcastle Cup on his winning CV, and in 1987 stood as Australian democrat candidate for the seat of Maranoa, Queensland in the General Election, told racing journalist Tony Arrold what happened during the Sixties when he arrived at Cunnamulla racecourse for a ride:

'The owner arrived having forgotten to pack his racing silks of white jacket with black spots, white cap,' reported Arrold. 'One look at young Munro and the owner solved the problem – he found a white shirt and began to cut out circles from the material. Then he threw the shirt over the shoulders of the tiny jockey. White jacket, black spots. The dark brown eyes of Darby lit up and his lips parted in the widest of grins.'

Darby won the race.

17 DR LIVINGSTON? I PRESUME YOU'RE JOKING Toronto, Canada

It took Dr William H Livingston five days to drive his $3,000 horse Ricks Natural Star, a seven-year-old gelding and possibly one of the world's worst turf horses, some 2,400 miles from his Artesia, New Mexico stables, to Woodbine, Toronto, to take part in one of the world's richest turf races, the $2million 1996 Breeders' Cup Turf.

The 66-year-old vet's pride and joy's previous three outings had all seen him finish stone last – most recently in a $3,500 claimer at Ruidoso Downs, New Mexico. He had won twice in New Mexico but that winning form was some time ago. Doc would not hear a bad word against the horse he had been determined to own ever since de-worming him as a two year old.

'Ricks' was his fourth horse – the first had died of a twisted intestine. Bad luck. The second – well, he ran on to a motorway and was killed by a truck. Even worse luck, I suppose. The third – tragic really, broke its neck.

Still, the good doc believed Ricks' form entitled him to take his chance in the big one, and importantly and amazingly, he had been nominated for the race as a foal – Doc claimed he was prepared to spend $50,000 entering him and getting him there.

He hadn't had a jockey in mind, though – until he stopped off en route to give the horse a spin at Remington Park, Oklahoma – where Sally Williams – 49 winners in, no, not that season, the last 15 years – partnered him and was promptly offered the ride.

Ricks had never actually run on grass before. He hadn't actually run the 1m4f distance of the race before. His prize money earnings in the last two years was $44.

Livingston hadn't any practical equipment with him on the trip – not even rudimentary things such as a water bucket, feed tub, saddle or brush – only a five-gallon bucket and an old halter.

It was as though a golfer with a child's set of clubs had contested the British Open or a tennis player with only table tennis bats had entered Wimbledon.

But once they were ensconced at Woodbine, Dr L (who was, he said, working on a project to produce fertilizer which didn't smell of manure) was keen to introduce himself and his horse to the media – offering them the chance to ride the horse themselves if they wished.

The *Racing Post*'s David Ashforth accepted the offer – he later told me his bareback ride was 'the funniest thing to happen' to him.

Naturally, the organizers of the meeting had not been too keen to have no-hopers contesting their valuable, prestigious event – but as other intended runners dropped out, there was no excuse to keep Ricks out of the race – not that the Doc believed they hadn't tried. 'They tried to talk me out of the whole thing to start with,' he said. 'And there was some trouble at the border. They may have encouraged them to be assholes there, but it may be that they just do that naturally.'

Ricks Natural Star duly took his chance in the race, despite Sally Williams declaring in the *Daily Racing Form* newspaper that he wasn't fit to run. Livingston brought in apprentice Lisa McFarland, but – 'he finished so far behind the other 13 runners' said Ashforth, 'that he wasn't officially even placed 14th.'

The official record of the race, won by Walter Swinburn on Michael Stoute's 13-1 chance Pilsudski, reads: 'Ricks Natural Star had speed for half, stopped suddenly, and was outdistanced.'

Incredibly, he had started at only 55-1 and at one stage early in the race was in second place. Undaunted, Livingston declared that he was hoping his horse would get into the Hong Kong Invitational – 'I only want to run him in $100,000-plus races,' he said. 'And I think that would be one hell of a trip.'

After the race, though, owner Larry Weber managed to purchase the horse from Livingston and retired Ricks Natural Star to Kentucky in an act of supreme kindness.

18 DON'T BELIEVE EVERYTHING YOU READ IN THE PAPERS Brighton

Most people interested in the sport have heard of the legendary fictitious Trodmore race meeting, totally invented by person or persons unknown in 1898 to enable them to pull off an audacious betting coup when gullible newspapers printed the racecard and then, next day, the 'results'. They collected their winnings and disappeared before alarm bells began to ring amongst fleeced bookies and embarrassed newspaper editors.

However, almost no-one knows of a similar hoax perpetrated on papers including the *Sussex Advertiser* and *Bell's Life*, which may well have acted as the spark for the Trodmore gang to ignite years later. This one was not to carry out a coup as the papers were persuaded to carry a completely invented report of a meeting supposedly held at a real racecourse, Brighton, on December 29, 1847.

The hoaxer, called Cornwall, conned the papers, even writing himself into the story – reporting that after his horse Chartist had won a steeplechase, 'Mr Cornwall, after the race, sold the winner for the foreign market at a high price.'

The clue to Cornwall's motives were in the name of his made-up winner – the Chartists were supporters of a rising political movement of the day, backed by Mr Cornwall.

I wonder whether he was related to anyone named Campbell or Mandelson?

19 I WANT TO BE ALONE – FOR EVER
Newmarket

Trainer Sir Mark Prescott is well known for his inventive 'scheming wheezes' which enable him to run his horses in races ideally suited to them, often running up quick victory sequences.

Thinking ahead in this way has also informed his private life and as he told *Observer* writer Will Buckley, he has also turned his mind to the end of his time on earth – 'I wanted to find myself a nice plot with some agreeable people around. I had to contact the Parks and Recreation authority. And there was a very nice fellow, he showed me the graveyard and there was Fred Archer, Mr Dawson, Mr Waugh and lots of nice people. I found a nice corner and said 'I want three plots down there' and he said, 'Would that be for Sir and Lady Prescott and your son and heir?'

'Certainly not,' replied the resolutely single Prescott, 'It's so I don't have to have any f***er next to me.'

Asked whether he believes in the after-life, Prescott declared, 'I'm not prepared to bet against it.'

20 IN THE TRENCHES Rouen, France

Incredibly enough, whilst the First World War was raging around them, some English officers and soldiers in France were more worried about organizing a race meeting.

Colin Davy, who described himself as a 'soldier-rider', who had raced over fences at home, had survived the Somme offensive but was given leave in England in 1917 because 'in a shell hole at Cambrai that good chestnut horse, Ginger, on whom I had won my first race, obliged me by breaking my elbow with his death kick.'

On his return, downplaying the fact that 'our squadron mess was sadly depleted, and there was only the shoeing smith beside myself left to represent the third troop', he asked his C Squadron commanding officer for permission to go to Merlimont, near Rouen.

'What do you want to go there for? You're not going to join the Tanks, are you?'

'No – but the Tank Corps are holding a race meeting. Arthur (the regimental second in command) is sending down two horses. He's asked me to ride for him.'

Davy was to partner a horse called Anytime over a mile on the Flat, and 'as we neared the winning post the crackle of whips broke out on both sides and three horses' heads on my right came up level with my knees. I clicked. Anytime quickened his stride. The winning post flashed past. The impossible had happened! We had won!' The horse returned 10-1 on the improvised tote. Davy finished second in a five-furlong sprint on his other mount, 'beaten a head by one of Geoffrey Brooke's.'

Returning to his regiment, Davy discovered that they had moved without him. He 'set off in pursuit' unaware that 'the move was prelude to the great advance; that at long last the cavalry were going to break through – that our next race meeting would take place on the frontier of Germany!'

21 PIS*ED OFF AND TAKEN ABACK
Moonee Valley, Australia

In 1984 trainer Bob Hoysted got literally pi**ed off when stewards would not permit his sprinter River Rough to urinate in the 'swabbing stall' prior to the running of the Moir Stakes at Moonee Valley, Australia. Hoysted declared that the horse had not passed water in his own stall and would be, er, inconvenienced by running with a full bladder – so withdrew him from the race.

There was a 'wild demonstration' by disgruntled punters at a 1960 meeting at Moonee Valley after an oddly well backed apparent no-hoper won the Tweedside Hurdle, run 'on a fast track in very hot conditions', in which six started and only four completed.

The biggest race at Moonee Valley is the annual W S Cox Plate, named after the course's founder, whose name eludes me. In 1976 when three-year-old filly Surround won the main event, there was an unusual one hour interruption during the afternoon – to allow for an eclipse of the sun.

In February 1999 racegoers were taken aback by six-year-old gelding High Stream, who went down to the starting stalls from the parade ring backwards. The horse was not for turning despite the best efforts of his jockey and handlers, and insisted on giving an indication that backing him each-way may not be a forward move. He eventually raced in the right direction – but slowly enough to finish out of the prize money.

22 I ENJOYED THAT SO MUCH, I'LL DO IT AGAIN WITHOUT THE HORSE! Gloucestershire

There aren't many races in which the winning jockey then goes back on track to run round the course under his own steam. But the (Hayes) Golden Button Challenge is not any old race.

Run by the River Severn, in January, for the fourth time in 2009 (first time it was held was in 2006, when local lady rider Yvonne Goss won on Perry) it was won by Paul Carberry – who was serving a suspension from 'real' racing – on Mandingo Chief, just holding off Piper, an unraced thoroughbred of 15 hands, partnered by 40-something mother of two Zoe Gibson (who would win in 2011 when Zara Phillips was the official race starter) while Lucy Holland took on the 24-fence, hedge and natural obstacle 3m+ event riding side-saddle – and duly took a premature tumble. Carberry won a prized Gold Ledbury Hunt Button as his prize.

An astonishing 52 runners set off, including Bryan Ferry's son Otis, on Cool Park, 32 of them making it to the finish. Said The Times racing writer Julian Muscat of the event: 'It is something between a scene from the Crimean War and a Grand National from an earlier century.'

Following the race the human version is run, missing out the obstacles, which attracted 70 runners, including several of the jockeys. No luck in this version for Carberry who finished well down the field.

Run by the banks of the River Severn, between the villages of Forthampton and Tirley in Gloucestershire, the race saw top jump jockeys Richard Dunwoody and Barry Geraghty also unseated – after the former champ started the race he and Geraghty followed the action from a quadbike which 'went right after going through a gate, ended up on two wheels, then none at all', according to Geraghty.

In 2011 an Irish-trained runner fell early in the race, ending up in the Severn. It swam half a mile downstream where it was rescued by outriders who had followed the horse's progress.

23 BARELY BELIEVABLE Greyville, South Africa

South Africa's Greyville is a track where, 'if a person wishes to witness debauchery and a set of semi-intoxicated, soft brained noodles, misnamed men, I would counsel that person to frequent the course'. Yes, there are plenty of tracks which might fit that description worldwide today – but that account was given by visiting English racing fan John William Coleman when he attended South Africa's Durban racecourse – in 1880.

Rather more recently, South Africa's President Zuma attended the twelve-race card for Durban's prestigious July day meeting in 2009 – like Royal Ascot, one of the highlights of both the sporting and social calendars in the country.

There had been controversy beforehand with the government's Disaster Management team insisting that the anticipated crowd of 50,000 was 'an accident waiting to happen and must be reduced' – we're not the only country with ' 'Elf 'n' Safety' issues, then!

As a result admission prices were almost doubled from 9R to 16R in an effort to keep the numbers down.

The President – the first to visit for more than 15 years – had an enjoyable day at the races and insisted on staying for the traditional, unlisted 13th race on the programme, believed to be a unique event, in which, reported a racegoer, 'some 50 men stripped off and performed the traditional final-furlong dash, cheered to the echo by most of the female racegoers.'

In 2008 – when some reports estimated the crowd at 100,000 – Prince Harry's Zimbabwe-born girlfriend Chelsy Davy had seen an estimated 100 men – and one woman (who 'came in for the biggest cheer of all when taking off her top and joining in' according to an eye witness account) take part in the naked sprint. The July meeting requires some stamina – the day usually lasts for the best part of twelve hours. In 2010 the first race was off at 11.35am, the last at 7.50pm.

24 'FAIR' ENOUGH? NOT REALLY Wales

If you believe the *Racing Post* website then the 4.40 race run at Bangor-On-Dee on March 9, 2005 was the 3m Llanfairpg Handicap Hurdle, run over 12 obstacles, and won by Sword Lady.

Well, that is accurate enough – to a point. The full name of the race was, in fact, the LLANFAIRPWLLGWYNGYLLGOGERYCHWYRNDROBWLLLLANTYSILIOGOG OGOCH Handicap Hurdle – much to the delight – and apprehension – of course commentator Malcolm Tomlinson.

Bangor clerk of the course Ed Gretton told me: 'I did feel like a bit of a sadist when putting that particular name into the Programme Book! I think he got through the full title on two occasions during the race and so it was lucky that it was a three- mile affair.

A serious contender for the 'longest racecourse name in the world' title, Polish course WROCLAWSKI TOR WYSCIGOW KONNYCH – PARTYNICE – one of three in the country – is based in Wroclaw. There has been racing in Wroclaw since 1833.

25 HE DIDN'T REALLY HAVE A LEG TO STAND ON Brighton

When a horse bolted on the way to the start at Brighton races in 1877, the animal knocked down a spectator, whose leg was broken as a result. The man subsequently wrote to Lord Lincoln's owner, George Chetwynd, demanding damages or he would go to court.

Chetwynd offered him a 25 guinea settlement, which was turned down. The case duly came to court where it transpired that the victim was a racecourse tout, who described himself as a 'horse watcher' which, given the circumstances, caused some hilarity in the court.

Chetwynd won the case – but had to pay his own, and the plaintiff's, costs. But you shouldn't feel too sorry for Chetwynd, whose much fancied 1,200gns purchase Little Harry, which flattered only to deceive on several occasions, was beaten in an 1878 race at Brighton – after which Chetwynd reportedly turned down a 200-guinea offer for the horse – and ordered his trainer to shoot it instead.

26 BEAUTY-FUL FUNERAL
Venue yet to be decided

If you come across a group of mourners listening to the strains of the 'Black Beauty' theme tune there is a fair chance you've stumbled across the funeral of Clare Balding.

Racing's leading lady nominated that piece of music as her funeral choice in an interview in The *Guardian Weekend* magazine in January 2011, during the course of which she also revealed that she hates being alone, 'even for ten minutes', that 'I deplore my thighs', the 'best kiss of her life' was 'the first time I kissed the side of a thoroughbred's nose – it's like the softest velvet' and that she would like to be able 'to twitch my nose like Tabitha in Bewitched and be in another place.'

27 WHALER OF A TIME
Wellington, New Zealand

I shudder to think what a current-day clerk of the course would make of the arrangements their New Zealand counterpart of 1842 had to go through to ensure that the day's racing on a beach track near Wellington went ahead.

The races, reports a contemporary account 'were run on the Petone beach, a day being selected on which low tide would leave uncovered a hard sandy surface.' Racegoers were arriving in carts, wagons and bullock drays as well as in a flotilla of boats, ready to occupy the grandstand, formed by planks placed on top of water butts.

Meanwhile the clerk of the course 'had a busy day arranging to have the native dogs tied up and the pigs kept at home, and imploring whalers to push their boats out far enough to give the horses a clear course.'

Racing started on New Zealand's Paraparaumu Beach, 50km north of Wellington, in the 1980s. They also have beach racing at Awakino, 100km north of New Plymouth, and at Castlepoint, to the east of Masterton.

28 HOT FAVOURITE Carrathool, Australia

The top of the range radio-cassette-turntable music centre which was the big prize for the day's main event at Carrathool races in New South Wales, Australia, during the 1970s, attracted admiring glances from the owners whose horses were contesting the prize.

When the time came to hand it over, there was consternation – it had melted. That's how hot it can get there during February or March when they race.

Carrathool is what they call a 'boughshed' track in those parts – the boughsheds comprise open steel mesh stretched across pole supports. Onto these are placed boughs from gum trees which are then hosed down by the local fire brigade before the first race.

When the local north wind blows across the course it creates a cool breeze for grateful spectators.

Another unusual problem for racegoers here is that when the horses start out they can kick up clouds of red dust which make it almost impossible to see the runners. Local committeeman Bill Ryan remembered one of the occasions when it wasn't blazingly hot for the meet: 'In 1956 a thunderstorm hit the course after the second – the dirt turned to treacle, and after two and a half inches of rain in an hour we couldn't move the cars from the car park. The races were abandoned and cars stuck for two days. The pub was a popular place for those two days.'

He also recalled the time a beaten odds-on favourite's jockey protested after the race that his opponent had gone inside a turn. A local tracker was deputed to go out onto the track and came back to confirm that there were indeed hoof-prints showing up on the inside of the course.

The favourite was given the race. Later, the jockey confessed that the hoofprints were from his own mount which had been the one to cut the course.

In 2009 the temperature hit 48°C and the racing could not take place becasue of the heat.

In March 2010 as the 99 permanent residents prepared for the arrival of several thousand racegoers, the heavens opened and it rained so hard the meeting had to be cancelled – twice – even the popular human races they hold here, the Jackaroo Dash and the Jillaroo Sprint.

Then the town's only hotel/pub burned down, and both the general store and garage closed.

The rains came again in March 2011, causing a second straight wash-out. The meeting may now become an endangered species.

29 INITIALLY, WHAT A STRANGE PRONOUNCEMENT FROM 'RALPH RAFE'
Whitsbury, Hampshire

Confusion initially reigned in January 2010 as Racing For Change introduced an initiative involving trainers' first names being printed in racecards – it went generally well except that Charlie McBride suddenly became 'Philip', while Jack Smith appeared as 'Ralph' – both were their actual first names but not those by which they are commonly known – and despite being universally known as 'Dandy', the sprint-meister appeared as 'David' Nicholls.

Some trainers, including Barry Hills, John Hills and Stan Moore, demanded the retention of their initials – the latter possibly to preserve his unique selling point of being the only trainer whose name is that of a London Underground station!

But most bizarre of all was the insistence of 39-year-old Oaks-winning trainer Ralph Beckett, that he shouldn't be identified as Ralph Beckett, but should remain as R. M. Beckett because, ahem, 'My Christian name is spelt one way and pronounced another, so that's the long and short of it. When you have a name like mine you don't need to encourage people to pronounce it incorrectly. It is nothing to do with the fact that I am R. M. Beckett Ltd. I simply get enough aggravation with people pronouncing my name wrongly and I don't need any more.'

However, on his own website, rbeckett.com, Beckett introduces 'The Team' thus 'Ralph started out having left school in 1989. He spent a year in Australia working for Bart Cummings and Colin Hayes.'

Presumably, internet readers are a brighter bunch and can tell how to pronounce his name when they see it written. Either that or Beckett is happy for them to mispronounce it. Nor does the website explain how to pronounce his name. So I asked Ralph why this was the case – and he told me:

'Your assumption (about the mispronounciation) is correct, but spelling it Rafe wouldn't go down well ... it is a family name! Good point about our website.'

Anyway, whether it was directly related to my contacting him or not, I don't know, but in early March 2011 Mr B announced that he had now changed his mind and would consent to his full name being used. The *Racing Post* announced it like this – 'R. M. Beckett is now Ralph*' '*rhymes with safe.'

However, there was another rebel still holding out – N. W. Alexander explaining 'Half the people I know call me Nicholas and the other half call me Nick, so I am neither Nicholas or Nick'. Mm, yes, I THINK I see what he means.

Southwell racecourse and Kauto Star were unavailable for comment.

30 FRANKIE, WE DON'T KNOW WHO YOU ARE!
Stansted Airport

He might be the most recognisable jockey in Britain, but Frankie Dettori was not allowed on a Ryanair flight at Stansted when he set off to Scotland to partner Redford in the William Hill Ayr Gold Cup in September 2010.

The Italian rider had not brought his passport with him for the domestic flight, but fell foul of the airline rules which, he said, meant that 'a driving licence was not sufficient to prove my identity – they wanted a passport, so I had to rush home, buy another ticket and then go back.' Doncha just love (a) rules which now apparently mean you have to take a passport for domestic travel in Britain and (b) Ryanair's customer service!

It was a worthwhile effort though as Frankie made it in time to drive the Dandy Nicholls-trained runner – which he had already told the trainer would win the race – to a 14-1 victory.

Dettori was completing a double, after winning the race the previous year on another 14-1 chance Jimmy Styles.

31 WHAT AN APPALLING TOSSER Market Rasen

The *Racing Post* couldn't have put it any more starkly when they described why the police were called to Market Rasen's Ladies' Night fixture on Saturday, August 14, 2010 to deal with some drunken male racegoers: 'One of the party began to masturbate in front of the Tattersalls stand during a race' reported Paul Eacott. It was also reported that one of the group, who had been wearing fancy dress, ran onto the track.

'We are appalled by this incident' commented Market Rasen managing director, Pip Kirkby. Former jump jockey Bryan Leyman, who was present, left before the last, feeling 'sick in the stomach'.

There was a postscript when the *Racing Post* 'Chatroom' carried a note from the almost certainly pseudonymous 'Begonia Perrywinkle (Miss)', commenting: 'Had I been at Market Rasen that damned fellow would not have been left with the wherewithal to perform such a disgusting act again!'

Back in 1859 at Market Rasen, they clearly intended to stage their big race – the Union Steeple Chase – however long it took them, to judge by the racecard for the March meeting there which stated: 'Should the weather prevent the races coming off on the day fixed, the stewards will have the power to postpone them from day to day, or week to week until they come off, and all entries to remain the same'.

Fun and games during a September 1861 meeting when as the jockeys passed the post for the second time, they pulled in, only to be told to go out again for a third circuit. The rider of Isle of Axholme had dismounted by this time and decided to take no further part, the other two went out for another circuit, Bentick coming first with Claret second.

Not everyone is a fan of racing at Market Rasen, as *Racing Ahead* writer Stuart Hogg suggested in a March 2010 article in that publication: 'I reside in Market Rasen. A weekend meeting always encourages a fleet of coaches. These disgorge their occupants into local hostelries sometimes three hours prior to the first race. The inevitable outcome of this for some is they end up vomiting in the Market Square before being literally carried to the course.'

There was a more poignant feel to the outcome of two races at the track on March 30, 2010 when jockey James Halliday rode his first ever double on Pokanoket and Issaquah – at the track where his older brother, Tom, was killed in a fall in 2005.

32 HARD AS NAILS? Twickenham

Promising jumper Rory O'More was contesting the Twickenham Maiden Hurdle on Boxing Day, 1893 when he was 'cannoned against' by another runner, Iconoclast, and 'knocked bang through an iron railing', reported the *Newcastle Journal* at the time.

Rory O'More was led back to the paddock 'with a great flap of skin hanging down his off quarter; and, there being no proper veterinary appliances at hand until about an hour afterwards, the flap was temporarily held in position by horse-shoe nails'!

Eventually, one Professor Pritchard arrived to 'sew up the rent' and then took the horse to his veterinary practice where he remained for six months as he recovered, during two of which his head and tail were tied up, But there was apparently some small solace: 'he drank, during his period of convalescence, more than half a gallon of the best Dublin stout per day.'

The horse recovered to race again, and started favourite for the 1896 Grand National, finishing sixth.

33 MINGING EXCUSE FOR A RACECOURSE! Western Australia

There doesn't seem to have been much truly strange or even unusual which has happened at Western Australian track Mingenew – but just look at that name – who could resist including it in a book like this! Not me.

Their meeting of the year is held each March when the Mingenew Cup is contested on a card which also sees a human barefoot race take place. The first recorded race meeting in Mingenew was held on 27th January 1896. The track is 383km north of Perth.

34 BULLY FOR THEM Australia

Camperdown Turf Club has been racing since 1886 when the first meeting was held in March of that year, with a distinctive iron grandstand which still stands today.

Camperdown Cup Day is held in February, together with the legendary 'Eat Bull Talk Bull' contest – Australia's biggest 'bull dust artist' (I think we know it as bull–something else!) competition where contestants are given three minutes to tell their biggest and funniest bull dust story to a big crowd of over 2,000 racegoers.

The 1997 Camperdown Cup was delayed by over 20 minutes as course officials tried to discover the owner of a car which had been parked close to the 2,100-metre mark where the starting stalls jut out into the car park – or would have done, had not the car in question been inconveniently parked. Eventually, a group of groundstaff literally lifted the car up and shifted it themselves.

Jockey Luke Williams, who had a mount in the race, eventually admitted that the vehicle was his!

35 MILITARY PRECISION Ireland

The South of Ireland Military Meeting in 1867 was organized by British regiments in the country during that troubled period of Ireland's history.

In an effort to lighten the mood, a spring jumps race meeting was organized by the 12th and 60th regiments which were to provide the runners on the day. The leading soldier there, Sir Claude Champion de Crespigny was looking forward to the meeting and had a fancied runner himself – his own Maid of the Mist.

Shortly before the day of the meeting, Sir Claude was out with fellow officers from the 12th regiment when they were approached by a man who proceeded to thank them for 'the capital day's sport' he had had watching the race meeting.

The officers were baffled as they knew the meeting wasn't being run until later in the week, but they decided to make enquiries. It soon emerged that some enterprising regimental grooms and servants, looking to set up a betting coup, had taken all the horses out to the course and run the entire meeting – correct weights, distances and all – in order to find out the likely outcome of the 'real' thing!

Sir Claude described this in his memoirs as 'a bit of enterprise which has probably never been eclipsed by those who lay themselves out to make money by backing horses. I don't know whether the bookmakers got wind of this extraordinary proceeding; if they didn't it is at least conceivable that they had rather a bad time when the actual steeple-chasing came off.'

Maid of the Mist won.

36 DEAD CERT LONG SHOT Panama

When Panamanian President Jose Antonio Remon Cantera set out for an afternoon at the races on January 2, 1955, he was probably not expecting to be returning from Panama City's Hipodromo Juan Franco track in a body bag, having been assassinated by machine-gun fire whilst he was there.

The crime was never officially solved although lawyer Ruben O. Miro was ante-post favourite, having initially confessed, only to be acquitted at his trial.

37 RACIST RACECOURSE? Stratford

I very much enjoyed an evening's racing at Stratford in May 2010, where we had gone to help celebrate a friend's most recent 'significant' birthday in a box at the track generously hired by her old man.

Lovely time had by all; sufficient winners backed to make a profit for a change; a few bob chucked in the direction of top man Bob Champion who was there as part of his 60 courses in 60 days cancer fund-raising effort; bizarre incident as fully kitted out 'jockey' ejected from the paddock before he could mount his horse – just as well, as he was a slightly inebriated groom-to-be on his stag night; lovely birthday cake; amazing sight of motorised wheelchair user, apparently keen to be viewed as the Lewis Hamilton of wheelchair drivers, swerving and swivelling his way through a packed crowd of departing racegoers at a mighty lick; and irritating wait for pre-booked cabs which never arrived. However, I left wondering just why there appeared to be in one of the remote areas of the course an abandoned former London tube train carriage. So I contacted the course to ask them, and 'Wendy' from the track told me:

'Indeed, there is a railway carriage at the far end above the track on the

Greenway, which was the old railway. This doubles up as a cafe and bike hire outlet.' There you are then, they hadn't gone off the rails, after all!

But in 2010 Stratford racecourse was forced to drop a promotion offering free admission to Irish racegoers – for fear of being branded racist. With its March 15, 2010 meeting taking place on the eve of the Cheltenham Festival, course officials at Stratford had thought they might swell their attendance by inviting Cheltenham-bound Irish racegoers to attend their Irish-themed day free of charge upon proffering proof of nationality.

That is, until course managing director Stephen Lambert revealed, 'I was told that we could have been done under the Race Relations Act 1976, and heaven knows what else, by not allowing other citizens, including those from England, into the races for free.'

After legal advice suggested the warnings were accurate, the idea was shelved.

'We really do live in crazy times,' reflected Mr Lambert, who presumably would have allowed himself in free.

A horse fell in, literally, a flash, at Stratford in 1992. With two to jump, odds-on favourite Plat Reay was clear. Carl Llewellyn rode him into the fence, there was a flash from a camera, and the horse fell. As the situation developed it seemed likely the jockey might snap – instead he opted to put everyone in the picture.

There was an international flavour to racing here in March 1995 when champion Japanese jump jockey Kazuya Nakatake won a selling hurdle on 25-1 shot Fred's Delight.

38 YES, THIS WAS RACIST COURSE OF ACTION
Johannesburg, South Africa

In 1964 when the policy of apartheid was all the rage in South Africa, courtesy of then Prime Minister Verwoerd, who wanted it applied to all aspects of life in the country – and the Johannesburg Turf Club was threatened with the loss of its licence to stage racing if 'it did not provide one enclosure exclusively for blacks, and another for people of colour.'

Up until this point racing had been a racism-free zone where all racegoers could stand and sit wherever they wished. A year later, trainers with stables in what were regarded as 'white' areas were informed by government officials that since blacks were living on the premises, their stables would have to be relocated.

In 1982 the JTC became the first racing club in South Africa to elect a black member, in the shape of Sowetan businessman Richard Maponya.

39 P.O.W. GETS PLASTERED Newbury

The Queen was refused admission to the royal box at Newbury on April 18, 2009, as the course had let it out for commercial use – reportedly for the first time.

Having been there the previous day 'the Queen was effectively evicted from her own quarters and had the ignominy of spending the day in a hospitality box,' reported Richard Alleyne of the *Daily Telegraph*.

Insurance broker John Finch from Denham, Bucks, had paid £10,000 to use the box and was unrepentant: 'I had arranged to rent it last July so there was no way I was going to pass it up. I'm a member at Newbury and had never been in the royal box before, so it was a lovely day out.'

The Queen did get revenge of a sort, as the lift to the suite in which she ended up was put out of bounds to racegoers when she was using it – as she was when Mick Channon was trying unsuccessfully to get down in time for the presentation after having a winner.

But in April 2010 relations between Her Maj and Newbury were back to their best as the course – and the monarch – witnessed the first occasion on which a female jockey had ridden a royal winner, as Hayley Turner won on Motivator colt Tactician.

There were strange goings-on here at a 2009 meeting when amateur jockey Victoria Cartmel was punished twice – for trying too hard, and not trying hard enough – in the same race. She was banned for both over-use of the whip, and for dropping her hands too soon. Understandably, she declared she would not ride again in the foreseeable future.

Newbury opened in 1905, and during the First World War the course became a prisoner-of-war camp, a munitions inspection depot, and a tank-testing and repair park.

The course was used as a US army depot during the Second World War from 1942, when it was covered with concrete and 35 miles of railway line. It took until 1947 to move all the military hardware out. Racing resumed in 1949, with jumping not returning until November 1951.

In March 1993 Native Americans were brought in to perform a rain dance at the parched track – but it didn't produce the desired downpour.

Channel 4 were screening the racing from Newbury in April 2010 when Hayley Turner won on 40-1 shot Brunston. As she made her way back through the crowd, there was panic amongst C4's racing team as Emma Spencer, who would have been expected to carry out the after-race interview with the winning jockey, declined to do so, leaving co-presenter Mike Cattermole to have to step in at the last second.

Reported the *Daily Telegraph*: 'Mrs Spencer, say racing sources, sees Miss Turner's affair with her husband, the jockey Jamie Spencer, 29, as the reason for the break-up of their marriage late last year.'

In July 2010 the course showed off a number of murals painted by a German prisoner of war straight onto the plaster walls of the stable block he was in during the Second World War. At one point the paintings were hidden from view, but it was decided to preserve them for posterity by removing them from the walls for display.

40 RACING MAD? Australia

Many non racing fans believe those who follow and bet on horses must be mad. The grandstand at Ararat racecourse in Victoria, Australia, was built with bricks left over from the construction of nearby Arandale Mental Hospital in 1867.

On December 7, 1970 jockey Kevin Sexton was coming to the finish line here three lengths clear when his mount Cloverleigh, who had been gambled on from 15-1 to 8-1, stumbled and threw him. The judge, who obviously could not have been involved in the gamble on the horse (!), ruled that Sexton's weight was still on the horse when he passed the line, the stewards agreed and he was awarded the race.

When the official photo finish picture was produced it suggested that Sexton had parted company with Cloverleigh just before the line and therefore should not have been awarded the race.

41 ONE DAY WHOLLY TRINITY
Cranbourne, Australia

'I thought I would let you know about a unique event that happens here at Cranbourne Turf Club.' wrote the Club's Vanessa Yates. 'Through my investigations, I know of no other course in Australia and quite possibly the world that runs what we call "Tricodes Day".

'Cranbourne Racing Complex in Victoria has three tracks, Turf on the outside, then harness, then a greyhound track in the middle. Each of the three codes of racing operates independently. However, on one day of the year we race all three codes on the same day. This equates to a total of 23 races, being eight thoroughbred, seven harness and eight greyhound races – each at 15-minute intervals, the first off at 11.50am.

'I've researched and cannot find any other racecourse to run three codes on the same day in this way, but I hesitate to call it "the only Tricodes Day in the world" without some sort of confirmation of this. I know that there is a complex in Tasmania that has all three tracks, but they only race two different codes on the one day, not three so perhaps we are the only one in the world?'

42 PREGNANT PAUSE New Zealand

Racegoers were surprised to see 25-year-old jockey Lynsey Satherley riding at Arawa Park in New Zealand on June 11, 2009 – as only 15 days earlier she had given birth to Sophie Angela. Nonetheless, Lynsey nursed home a winner, her 189th.

During the 1970s, Rotorua Racing played a leading role in promoting the cause of lady riders and supported a motion at the annual meeting of the galloping code's then governing body, the NZ Racing Conference, which ultimately allowed for the licensing of female apprentice riders.

The Rotorua Racing Club celebrated its Centenary in 1977 and then in 1998 completed 100 Years of Racing at its Arawa Park Racecourse, uniquely placed in the heart of Rotorua City.

43 SADDLED WITH A PROBLEM
Richmond, Australia

Richmond racecourse in Victoria, Australia, was the scene of a bizarre incident in 1899 when a Mrs Barlow's runner, Cherry, was 'made a strong favourite' for a handicap, 'and won pretty easily, to the joy of the punters'. However, as the jockey, Barbour, came back to weigh in, 'Thomas Barlow, Mrs Barlow's husband, dragged him from the horse's back and beat him, while a man named Jones ripped the saddle off Cherry and threw it into the crowd. It fell at the feet of a constable, who took it in to the scale. Barlow and Jones were arrested on a charge of insulting behaviour.'

It seems likely that the pair had not been expecting their favourite to oblige and bet against him accordingly.

The course closed in July 1931 after a colourful history during which it also hosted boxing title matches, hurling, motorsport and political rallies.

44 GOD'S OWN TRACK? Birmingham, USA

The first thoroughbred track in America's 'Deep South', Birmingham Turf Club opened in March 1987 despite objections from local religious leaders.

After a 175-day season, during which operators lost over $50m, the Turf Club went bankrupt. Bizarrely, the course apparently deliberately tried to keep out 'redneck' and other potential racegoers by imposing high admission and parking fees. The idea was reportedly to impress the religious lobby with the up-market nature of its clientele.

Andrew Beyer of the *Washington Post* wrote in August 1987: *'When the Birmingham Turf Club opened four months ago, people from all parts of the U.S. racing industry came to examine the $85 million racetrack and hailed it as evidence of the sport's health and possibilities for growth. Now, many of the same observers are scrutinizing Birmingham again – to figure out what went wrong.*

'The first thoroughbred track in the Deep South is a disaster, a monument to bad judgment and naive expectations. When the track opened, its officials were projecting an average daily attendance of 10,000 and an average handle of $1.3 million. Those figures were the basis for the lavish scale on

which the track was built – but they didn't even come close to reality.

'To date, Birmingham's average attendance has been 6,069 and the daily handle $409,825. Employees are demoralized; purses have been cut; horsemen have defected; management has made a desperate series of changes in the racing schedule. But the track is so deeply bathed in red ink that the current ownership may not be able to survive unless it gets some outside help with fresh money.'

The course reopened in May 1989 but failed again.

In August 2008, 'Tommy B' posted some notes on Bloodhorse.com's 'Racing Hub', in which he reflected on this track: *'I drive past the track entrance everyday – to and from work. It makes me sad every day. Horses have come and gone a couple of times – and now they have converted it to a dog track with simulcasting of horses. Even so, the religious groups still try to get it shut down on a regular basis. It was a beautiful place once.'*

45 WHAT A BUMMER Beverley

Racing UK viewers were not impressed when the last race shown on the channel from Beverley's evening meeting on May 30, 2007 was accompanied by the unedifying sight of the bared rear end of a probably inebriated racegoer, perched on a stool near the rails, aimed at the cameras, as the runners headed into the final four furlongs. Still worse was the fact that the bum pictures were still being shown the next day as replays of the meeting's races were broadcast.

One of just 14 courses to receive a Racehorse Owners' Association Gold Standard Award, Beverley was the first to be stripped of the prize when in April 2009 the track was demoted for refusing to supply free food for owners.

This is one of even fewer courses to have to delay racing because of a bullock on the track – as they did here in May 1989.

46 BET TURPIN? York

Legendary highwayman Dick Turpin, hanged in April 1739 at York racecourse, must have stirred in his grave as a horse bearing his name ran in the Juddmonte International at the same course in August

2010, causing the media to stand and deliver a host of coverage.

Derek Thompson even presented an item on Channel 4 Racing showing the site of Turpin's hanging and the cell in which he was incarcerated beforehand.

But it was the punters who were forced to hand over their money to the dastardly bookies as the Richard Hannon-trained three-year-old, Dick Turpin, was unable to finish in the money – unlike his namesake.

47 DREAM PUB Leicester

The victory of gambled-on Only Dreams, backed from 100-1 to 28-1 when winning at Leicester on March 7, 2008, really deserved the cheers it brought, as owner Howard Spooner's six-figure winnings from brewing up the plot were poured into purchasing the local pub in the village where the horse was trained by rookie handler Nick Lampard – Manton in Wiltshire.

After acquiring the hostelry, Spooner named it The Outside Chance – and then made it Lampard's stable sponsor.

The horse died in 2010, but is remembered on the pub's website. TV presenter Robert Cooper once observed, 'I often think of Leicester as the Longchamp of the Midlands'. Mm.

48 SHORT STORY Kelso, Scotland

Jockey Mark Bradburne recovered well from a serious back injury at Kelso in April 2010, but as he prepared to race again in September of that year he claimed that his treatment had resulted in his becoming two inches shorter.

Bradburne fractured a vertebra in the fall but revealed: 'I have lost quite a lot of height as a result. I used to be 5ft 9.5ins and I'm now 5ft 7.5ins. I have crushed the vertebra which means I am smaller, and I broke it before as well, so between the two injuries – and the spine has become much more curved – I've become a bit smaller.'

49 DILDO ROBBER IN DAYLIGHT RUBBERY
Leicester

The above headline was the one London's *Metro* chose to apply to the August 2007 story of robber Nicki Jex, 27, who held up a Leicester betting shop – with his girlfriend's vibrator.

A member of staff at the branch handed over more than £600 in cash when Jex pointed a carrier bag at her containing the Rampant Rabbit sex toy which he pretended was a gun, Leicester crown court was told. The incident was captured on a CCTV camera.

Sentencing him to five years behind bars, the judge, Philip Head, said: 'It's right to record that you did not have a firearm but you pretended you had and intended that those you confronted believed that you did, and it must have been truly terrifying for them at the time.'

Any betting shop robbery is horrendous for staff involved, but sometimes details of such incidents can be bizarre:

During 2010 a betting shop was raided by a robber clad in a Power Rangers outfit.

An axe-wielding robber was chased from a raid on a Betfred shop in Gillingham, Kent in March 2011, by a cleaner armed with just a 'Henry' vacuum cleaner. The thug stormed into the shop and grabbed a member of staff, but when the cleaner holding the Henry vacuum emerged, the raider turned on his heels and fled.

50 NOW, WHERE DID I PUT THAT NAG?
Taunton

On February 27, 1930 Bath Chap, owned by Mrs J Woodman, was withdrawn from his race at Taunton on the eminently reasonable grounds that 'the horse couldn't be found.' Stewards accepted the explanation.

Six years later at the track there was a tragedy – but with an historic slant – the Hon. Copplestone John de Gray Warwick Bamphylde, 22, became probably the longest named jockey ever to die as a result of a racecourse fall, doing so two days after falling from Row On in a handicap chase run on October 1, 1936.

Another fatality at Taunton occurred as a direct result of the fall of John

Tolly from his mount Kildybanks on March 31, 1938. He died from the injuries sustained, on July 27 that year – and it later emerged that whilst training the same horse to jump Tolly had been thrown three times and told friends he was convinced that every time the horse jumped he closed his eyes; nonetheless Tolly was – fatally – determined to persevere with him.

On December 27, 1972 a 20-1-shot, Lorac, ridden by a 7lb claiming amateur, ran out during the King Wenceslas Hurdle. The jockey injured his leg severely during the incident and could never ride again. He took up training instead, and the legend which Martin Pipe became was launched.

Strange goings on at Taunton during the auction for the winner of a seller on September 29, 1988 when a man began bidding at 1,100gns, pushed the price up to 2,800gns – then entered a bid of £1million – at which point the auctioneer called the local constabulary who led the man away protesting that he was a member of the SAS. The horse was sold for 1,880gns.

51 WELL, THE HORSE BOLTED! Kempton

Trainer James Fanshawe withdrew his horse Reveillez from a big race at Kempton in February 2007 after the animal injured his jaw on a door bolt in the racecourse stables.

52 GREAT SHAME Essex

'Let's hear it for England's first new racecourse since 1927 – Great Leighs!'

On April 20, 2008, just 23 months behind schedule, the cheers rang out for the brand, spanking new, but perhaps not entirely race-ready Great Leighs which, after a string of missed dates for its inaugural meeting, finally hosted a race card.

On January 16, 2009, having staged just 48 fixtures, the course closed, after the BHA refused to grant a permanent licence, and administrators were called in.

In February 2010, despite suggestions that they would soon be racing there again, it was reported that the course might well be sold for an alternative use if a suitable buyer could not be found. In July 2010 it was revealed that a £20m bid to buy the course by Northern Racing which would have had it up and racing again in 2011 had foundered.

But on May 16, 2011, four Newmarket trainers brought six horses to the track to test its readiness for racing. Martin Collins, the man behind Great Leighs' Polytrack surface, hinted there were possibly plans afoot to reactivate the course.

That wouldn't please trainer George Baker who called the track's original owners 'an egotistical embarrassment', and the place itself 'godforsaken'.

53 GREAT DAY OUT Victoria, Australia

Oh to have been at the Great Western Race Club in Victoria, Australia in 1860 for the meeting attended by the *Ararat Advertiser*, whose reporter recorded: 'Supporters of the favourite, Black Boy, had surged onto the track to prevent the second horse, Punch, from winning.

'This caused supporters of Punch to set up a great barney around the judge, and it was as much as the one sober policeman could do to stop the fighting.

'At about 5 o'clock, bystanders helped clear the course for the next race. Just as the last race was about to start, fighting broke out again and the day's racing terminated in a general free fight.'

54 FOOTNOTE Yorkshire

Curators at English Heritage's Brodsworth Hall in Yorkshire, where the Doncaster Cup won by Rataplan in 1855 is displayed, were delighted, but a little surprised, to be given two of Rataplan's feet. Mummified.

The hooves, which were once attached to the front legs of the top 19th-century stallion who won 42 of his 82 races including the Ascot Gold Vase, had been initially kept by his former groom, Edward Hornshaw, and handed down in his family.

Now his great granddaughter Jessie Hall had given up trying to work out what best to do with the pair of feet and instead decided to pass them on to the Hall where Rataplan's owner Charles Thellusson lived.

Receiving them in June 2008, Hall curator Caroline Carr-Whitworth admitted, 'It does seem slightly bizarre to keep mummified horse's hooves, but it was a way of remembering a much loved and prized racehorse.'

55 FFRENCH POLISH Doncaster

Royston Ffrench rode the winner of the final race at Doncaster on June 27, 2008 – but was not exactly able to assist his mount Sadeek to get home in front, as he passed the line dangling over the horse's neck, with his legs swinging about on one side and his body and head on the other.

Ffrench was applauded by racegoers and fellow riders alike as he brought the 5-1 shot in, after his saddle slipped some 50 yards from home during the race, leaving him hanging on for dear life.

56 FATAL ATTRACTION Cotswolds

It would appear that racegoers attending the sports at the Burford races in the Cotswolds in the 17th century were taking their lives in their hands. The local burial register records at what was probably the first meeting there in 1620, that on January 31, Robbert Tedden, 'a stranger stabde (sic) with a knife by one Potley at the races.'

On November 6, 1626, 'William Backster, Gent. Was slaine the next daie after race.'

William Howard, servant to Mr Rowland Lacy, 'received a wound at the race and died thereof' on April 10, 1654. And on June 8, 1679, William Clarke, servant to Lord Gray, was 'killed by a fall from his horse at the Race-meeting.'

In 1758 the Burford races were 'postponed' after an outbreak of smallpox. However, in July of that year 'the Race for His Majesty's Hundred Guineas' was run over Burford Downs – due to be contested by the excellently named Dormouse, White Legs, Juggler and Sourface, although 'Sourface, falling sick in the night did not make his appearance.'

During the race, though, reported *Jackson's Oxford Journal*, jockey Tom Marshal 'had the Misfortune to be dismounted in turning one of the Posts, whereby he broke his Thigh – when Marshall was taken up he appeared lifeless and his Thigh Bone was stuck through his Buck-Skin breeches by the Violence of the Fall; but he is now in a fair Way of Recovery'.

Marshal was in the care of 'eminent Surgeon of Witney', Mr Batt, but the media's optimism was premature – it was later reported in October that Marshal expired 'of a Mortification, occasioned by the Hurt he lately received upon Burford-Downs.'

57 BREAST OF BOTH WORLDS Japan

Jockeys were not permitted to leave the weighing room area until their rides were completed, but stewards at Taipa in Macau were faced with a dilemma when jockey Jenny Moller explained in December 1991 that she would have to leave in between rides – to go home to breast-feed her new baby.

'In the very exceptional circumstances, the stewards gave permission for Jenny to leave the course,' said Macau official Bill Charles.

58 WOOD YOU BELIEVE IT? Australia

Whilst researching for this book I received an email from a contact, 'Phil', in Australia, telling me about an incident he witnessed during a meeting at 'little country racecourse Talwood' which stages one meeting a year.

'The track, just outside town, is on a 'cocky's' (land owner) wheat paddock and can be pretty dusty. The ambulance man was a former shearer, so didn't mind a cold one on a hot day, and also liked a bet on the locals, so spent time between races in the jockeys' room looking for tips.

'This day he followed the fields around during the races and most times he had to apply the brakes to his ambulance to stop running over the nag he had placed his hard-earned on!

'Come the last race and he was told 'this is a bank teller's job'. It would win with a leg in the air. By this time he had a case of the shorts. He put the 'nip' on all his mates but couldn't come up with the readies, so ended up convincing a couple of local bookies that his dear old grandmother had passed away on Friday night and he would be coming into a large sum of money in the near future, so they let him in 'on the nod'.

'He had a few coldies to settle the nerves, then headed around to the start. Away they went, and his horse jumped straight to the front. He was leading clearly on the turn but was getting 'the wobbles'. It was pretty dusty back in the pack so our ambulance man pulled out wide and took after the leader,

winding his window down and extending his clenched fist whilst urging the horse to 'go on, you bloody beauty' before going past the winning post ahead of all the runners.'

Phil also told me of jockey Billy Barnes who, one day, backed another horse to win in a race he was also contesting. When the horse he had backed began to show signs of weakening, Billy pulled his whip – and whacked it on the backside in an effort to gee him back up. He got two years.

59 BUBBA BUBBLE BURST USA

'Due to unforseen circumstances, jockey Bubba Wilson is unable to ride in the next race and will be replaced by Herson Sanchez', racegoers at Tampa Bay Downs, USA – where female riding phenomenon Julie Krone enjoyed the first winner of her career on February 12, 1981 – were informed in April 1992 by the course announcer, who apparently forgot to explain that the reason for Bubba's absence was the arrival at the track of the local sheriff and his deputies to arrest him on a felony charge.

★

In January 1993 apprentice Ed Carvalho got off the mark at the track on Majestic Moran, his first winner after 41 losing rides. He was 43.

60 BROTHER BOTHER Buckinghamshire

Former jockey Paul Eddery took a claim for unfair dismissal to an employment tribunal in July 2010 after he lost his job as an assistant trainer. His claim was dismissed.

Paul had been assistant trainer to Buckinghamshire-based former champion jockey Pat Eddery – his brother.

61 WELL, AT LEAST HE STAYED FAITHFUL! South Carolina, USA

50-year-old Rodell Vereen was arrested in July 2009 after being caught on a surveillance camera having sex with a horse.

Barbara Kenley had spotted him in the horse's stall on CCTV and rushed to the stable near Myrtle Beach, South Carolina, keeping him at gunpoint until police arrived. She said she considered shooting him at one point but had been worried she would be jailed.

It emerged that Vereen had a previous guilty verdict for another charge of having sex with a horse – the same one!

62 PLUS ÇA CHANGE Kempton

Thirty-five 'heavily loaded' race trains departed from Waterloo for Kempton Park's Easter Monday card in April 1895.

Racing Illustrated's correspondent reported that not everything was hunky-dory at Waterloo, where 'the only booking office where the three-shilling second or third class tickets could be obtained was a wretched portable rabbit hutch on wheels containing two clerks. It really is too bad that the railway company – South-Western – should make it an unwritten bye-law that all passengers must, before they can obtain tickets, take part in a ferocious football scrimmage lasting about ten minutes, in the course of which their clothes are nearly torn off their backs, their feet trampled on, their ribs stove in, pockets perchance gone through – oh, for a man at the head of affairs at Waterloo who knows what racegoers want and who will see that they get it.'

63 PUNTERS LEFT BLUE Hereford

Set to partner Am I Blue at Hereford in September 2010, jump jockey Dean Coleman was unable to take the ride, because he had to visit the dentist. Or perhaps because his car had had a puncture en route to the track. Or maybe because he was too tired after taking his mother to hospital the previous night. Or possibly because he never fancied the ride in the first place. He also mentioned that he had 'been off for a bit because I had hurt my wrist.'

The 5lb claimer put forward all of these explanations at various times after he was replaced by the somewhat more experienced Richard Johnson shortly before the race, in which Am I Blue, trained by Delyth Thomas, and backed from 25-1 to 5-1, landed the gamble as she hacked up by 19 lengths – to ironic cheers from racegoers, slightly bemused at the improvement in form, the filly having been beaten by 88 and 75 lengths in previous outings.

Ms Thomas claimed that Am I Blue, her only horse in training under rules, had been suffering from spine problems and ulcers. Local stewards called no inquiry. 'It was not necessary to call a formal inquiry because there was nothing suspicious to investigate,' 'explained' stipendiary steward Simon Cowley.

The BHA did not agree and announced they would be looking into the race, to the relief of the Racing Post's David Ashforth who said that the lack of an inquiry had been 'a decision guaranteed to inflame punters.'

Professional gambler Dave Nevison weighed in with a comment: 'I really hope this was just a good old-fashioned touch landed by some clever cookies. Let's hope that no rules were broken along the way.'

64 KIL OR CURE! Victoria, Australia

The course at the Kilmore track in Victoria, Australia, was blocked at one point during the late 1930s – by a grandstand!

Members of the local Turf Club had decided that because the viewing from the grandstand was adversely affected by having to look straight into the sun, it should be moved to the other side of the course.

The wooden edifice was duly loaded on to a huge dray – only to become bogged down in the centre of the track – where it sat forlornly for the next six months until warmer weather arrived, enabling the move to be completed.

65 RACING'S FATAL ATTRACTION Cyprus

Horseracing was revived in Cyprus from the end of the 19th century. However, the tradition of the sport in the country, as evidenced by archaeological findings existing in the Cyprus Museum, is lost in the depths of the Hellenistic period, from which there are horseracing descriptions by Homer and other ancient authors.

Horseracing in those days was literally a 'sport of kings', who participated in it. When kings of ancient Salamis in Cyprus died, their horses were buried with them.

66 SHERWOOD SHAKING Melbourne, Australia

Sherwood Park is a now defunct Melbourne track at which, according to Aussie racing historian Andrew Lemon, on one occasion 'the judge's box collapsed just as the winner passed the post – but the judge called out his verdict as the stand disintegrated around him, and emerged safely from the wreckage.'

67 BEER BATTLE Bath/Cartmel

Keen to mark its bicentenary year, in 2011, Bath racecourse introduced a specially brewed beer subtly named 'The Wobbly Jockey', presenting bottles of the ale to connections of all races during the season.

But at almost the same time, Cartmel racecourse claimed to have become the first track to produce its own beer – 'Hurdler' – introduced for its May 2011 three day bank holiday meeting.

68 SLUGGING IT OUT AT SOUTHWELL Southwell

The biggest claim to fame for the Nottinghamshire course Southwell is that no-one really knows which way to pronounce it correctly. Rather like Kauto Star, really.

There are any number of people prepared to 'swear blind' that it should be South-well, but just as many opting for Suthell. I don't know. I don't really care, to be honest.

On February 12, 2010, Southwell set what the *Racing Post* claimed may be 'a modern day record for a racecourse in Great Britain' when staging its sixth consecutive days' racing.

Rarely has a racecourse been the scene of a fight between two jockeys – even more rarely between two female jockeys. On May 11, 2010 Sophie Doyle was banned for seven days for 'violent and improper conduct' after becoming involved in an altercation with Kirsty Milczarek in the changing room at Southwell. The pair had both ridden in the final race of the evening, with Doyle edging Milczarek out of fourth. Ms Milczarek suffered a black eye in the contretemps. Doyle later apologised to her former friend.

69 GALLOWS HUMOUR Afghanistan

British troops serving in the 40 Commando battlegroup in the dangerous town of Sangin in Afghanistan during 2010 frequently had to run the gauntlet of snipers, resulting in the deaths of 16 of their number up to August of that year.

Reporting on their bravery in *The Times*, under the headline 'They call it the Grand National: how Marines dodge bullets in sniper alley', writer Tom Coghlan revealed that they had dubbed their route around and over walls and through narrow alleyways and across fields, 'Grand Nationaling.'

70 HUGHES ARSEING ABOUT? Newmarket

Jockeys Richard Hughes and Frankie Dettori teamed up to leave a fellow rider feeling he'd had a bum deal one day at the races.

'Frankie and I managed to pull a lad's pants off passing the winning line at Newmarket,' confessed Hughes in September 2007. 'Gyles Parkin was riding in paper breeches and as we were passing the post, Frankie and I managed to get him. I think Frankie got more out of his horse after the line than he did in the final furlong. Gyles went back into the weighing room bare-ar*ed and slightly red-faced.'

71 BARKING MAD? Goodwood

Jockey-turned-trainer Walter Swinburn was asked in August 2008 about the funniest sight he'd seen on a racecourse – and nominated fellow rider Greville Starkey's antics on Donegal Prince during a running of the Goodwood Cup.

'They race the wrong way up the straight when they start, and Greville set off in front and did all the arm signals as we went round, turn left, turn right, that sort of thing. He was barking at the same time. All the jockeys were in hysterics, I don't know how anyone rode a finish.'

72 POSITIVE OUTLOOK Aintree

Jersey-born punter Richard Laurie landed a £200,000 win on Tony McCoy's first Grand National winner Don't Push It in 2010.

He staked £5,000 on the horse in February of that year when it was a 40-1 shot – purely because the *Racing & Football Outlook* newspaper had tipped it. 'I'd seen an advert for the RFO where they said they had picked Numbersixvalverde at 16-1 and Silver Birch at 100-1 in recent seasons, so I made a point of looking up the recommendation for this year.'

It may seem an odd system – but the middle-aged Falmouth resident had hit earlier National jackpots – £100 on Grittar in 1982 at 7-1; £200 on Party Politics at 18-1 in 1992, then in 1998 he stepped up a gear when he put £5,000 on the National winner – this time, Earth Summit, on the recommendation of the *Liverpool Echo*'s tipster Mike Torpey, winning £50,000.

But he deserted Torpey for the 'big one'. 'I told Mike that, nothing against his advice, this year I would be following someone else.'

Laurie showed his gratitude to RFO tipster Nick Watts by giving him a Nebuchadnezzar of Pol Roger champagne.

73 RECORD RUN Oaklawn, USA

On February 7, 1975, new Oaklawn racecourse commentator Terry Wallace took his bow behind the microphone to call the card.

Wallace then called the next 20,191 races to be run at the track, until he finally took a breather for the fifth race there on January 28, 2011.

'I am not retiring' he declared. 'But Oaklawn has been kind enough to bring in a sub for me once in a while this year.'

Perhaps Wallace's favourite commentary was for Zenyatta winning the 16th consecutive race of her career, at Oaklawn in April 2010 – 'It's a bird! It's a plane! It's Zenyatta!'

'My father always told me that if you show up each day it's hard for them to fire you,' said Wallace whose almost certainly record run of commentaries was threatened in the early 1990s when he was 'absolutely deathly ill. There was no shot I was going to be able to work, but a snow and ice storm hit and racing was cancelled.'

74 LOSING WINNER Epsom

When trainer Marcus Tregoning was working for Dick Hern, in 1989, he was convinced their Nashwan would win the Derby and after watching him go down to the start, 'gliding like a panther', 'I put every penny I had on him with a rails bookmaker'.

In the race Tregoning never doubted his bet was safe, so he went to collect his winnings – 'the sting in the tail was that the bookie had done a runner. I had to go and tell Dick I had no money.'

75 CHEESY FLORAL TRIBUTE Clairefontaine, France

French course Clairefontaine claims to be the 'world's most floral track', and backs up the claim via the president of the course, twinned with Stratford, who explains: 'There are 60,000 flowers scattered around the racecourse, and it takes six gardeners six weeks to plant them – and more are planned. We try to make the track smile, and enrich it with colour. All the plants are grown in our greenhouses and some have been alive for more than 60 years.'

The course opened in 1928 and also features a race for which the winning owner receives his or her weight in Camembert cheese.

In August 1989, Alfred Gibert was run away with here when his mount's reins broke. Spotting what had happened, Cash Asmussen forfeited any chance of winning the race by riding after Gibert and bringing his horse under control. Asmussen was later honoured for 'the year's most sporting gesture.'

76 HARE BRAINED Doncaster

In July 2010, after Paul Hanagan had ridden Patavium to win at Doncaster, trainer Edwin Tuer revealed just why he'd fancied the horse to go well after a recent gallop: 'A hare was sprinting along in front of him but he caught it up, stepped on it and killed it and flicked it up in the air – I've never seen anything like it.'

77 GILLTY? Penn National, USA

Racecourse officials refused to accept any entries for races from the US's numerically leading owner at the end of January 2010. Jockeys riding at Penn National had begun to boycott horses owned by Michael Gill

– whose horses won 369 races and $6.7m prize money during 2009 – after a string of 15 of his horses reportedly broke down badly with injuries, were pulled up, eased, or finished lame.

After jockeys refused to continue riding until Gill's horse Justin M was scratched, course officials asked the Pennsylvania Racing Commission to begin an investigation. Gill, who once had over 300 horses in training, claimed to have received death threats and told the *Daily Racing Form* that he was 'worn down' by the situation and was 'through with the business.' In March 2010 he was reportedly 'liquidating his stable'.

78 BROTHERS IN TANDEM Punchestown

It was not unheard of for racegoers to get to the sports under their own pedal power during the Second World War years when there were restrictions on car travel. However, in 1944 Irish jump jockey Martin Molony and his brother Tim turned up at Punchestown having travelled on a tandem bike from trainer Capt. Cyril Harty's stables at Chapelizod.

Martin promptly fell off of Pucka Man in the Prince of Wales Chase – breaking his collar-bone for the first and only time in his lengthy career. He was ferried off to hospital in the course ambulance – leaving Tim to pedal the tandem back on his own.

79 ONE FOR THE LADIES The French Riviera

March 1961 saw France's first official race for women riders take place 'at a fashionable Riviera Sunday meeting' according to the Irish Field who duly reported on the 13-runner event in which Mlle Janine Lefevre triumphed and duly 'received many congratulatory embraces in the spontaneous Gallic manner'.

The race was entitled, slightly contentiously perhaps, the Prix des Amazons, with all riders being required to submit a photograph, plus birth and medical certificates and, in the case of those under 16, written permission from their parents.

Such 'strictly amateur' races were now to become a regular part of the racing scene in la belle France reported the *Irish Field*, and here's the best bit

– 'married women must have the consent of their husbands before taking part in any race.'

Mais, d'accord!

80 THE STUD Wolverhampton

Trainers are notoriously conservative in their dress sense – apart from the occasional flamboyant maverick like Rod Simpson – but David Evans appeared at Wolverhampton in November 2009, sporting a stud in his left ear – claiming it was 'my wedding ring' after he tied the knot with Emma Folkes in Barbados. And, to be fair, there was no ring to be seen on his fingers.

81 CHAIN REACTION Hawera, New Zealand

Jockey Percy Johnson was booked to ride a fancied runner in the 1888 Opunake Cup at Hawera Racecourse in New Zealand – but the 16-year-old was shocked to discover that the horse had been allocated a weight of 9st 4lbs – and he weighed under 7 stone.

'What occurred in that race had not happened before, has not happened since and will never happen again,' recalled the rider an incredible 72 years later.

Faced with the problem of how to get Johnson's weight up, connections had to think fast: 'There were not many leadbags, and I could not make the weight,' remembered the now 88-year-old.

But Life Buoy's owner Albert Bayly knew what to do: 'he rushed out to his dray and procured a monstrous bullock chain' – which was carefully wrapped around young Percy's torso. The young rider, with the chain wrapped around the outside of his silks, duly took his place in the starting line-up – and proceeded to win the 1m 4f contest.

As if that wasn't enough glory for one day – Life Buoy, Johnson, and the chain, then contested another race – only to dead-heat and be called upon to take part in a run-off – which they lost by a mere head.

82 FALSE ALARM Windsor

Despite racecourse announcements, no-one at Windsor came forward in June 2009 to claim the full set of false teeth found in the course car park.

The course, where Sir Peter O'Sullevan finally broke his 15-year duck as an owner when Pretty Fair won in March 1954, broke new ground in 2010 when, thanks to what must have been an enormous sponsorship deal, the stable with the greatest number of best-turned-out awards to its credit during the season won itself a 'pizza party', courtesy of Domino's.

April 2010 saw French punters able to place bets on non-Group racing in Britain for the first time as a deal negotiated by France Galop and PMU provided pictures and betting access to pools for up to five races from the Windsor Monday evening meetings up to August.

Top political correspondent and racing enthusiast Robin Oakley revealed in July 2010 how he had once combined his two passions, when 'a Tory MP racehorse owner was so convinced he was going to win a race at Windsor that he hired a Rolls, had us driven down drinking unforgivably warm champagne from plastic cups, and promised us a three-star dinner at the Waterside Inn at Bray on the proceeds.'

Inevitably, it didn't all go to plan: 'The horse lost, the MP had a row in the unsaddling enclosure with the jockey – and we finished up eating takeaway pizza in the car park!'

83 IN THE PINK Chester

The jockeys all wore pink silks. Their horses carried pink number cloths. Many racegoers wore items of pink clothing. And they raced past a pink winning post.

Chester was staging what was claimed to be 'the world's first pink horserace' on July 9, 2010. And the reason that everyone involved in the race was literally in the pink is explained by the race title – the Breast Cancer Care Pink Mile. The race raised an estimated £25,000 for the charity, Breast Cancer Care.

In May 2009 struggling Premier League club Hull City's first-team squad was invited to Chester races by boss of the time Phil Brown so that they could all enjoy a morale-boosting day together. The players refused to attend, believing they should be concentrating on their next game at home to Stoke – which they lost 2-1.

Not everyone is a fan of this quirky, idiosyncratic track. Trainer David Elsworth said of it in May 2010, 'It's a wonderful venue. It's very popular with the locals, the atmosphere is fantastic and the ground super, but it's a glorified flapping track and I hate the place. You get more hard-luck stories here than anywhere else. When I do go I can't get into the car park. It's a farcical place.'

84 THAT'S WARI-ING
New South Wales, Australia

Stewards had their work cut out at Warialda in New South Wales in 1994 when, after a hard fought race, the runner-up protested, or objected, to the winner. Then the third objected to the winner. Then the third also objected to the runner-up.

Not to be outdone, the fourth objected to the winner – and the second. And the third. The fifth objected to the runner-up – and the third.

The harrassed stewards went into a huddle – then upheld the objection by the runner-up to the winner, but struck out the rest.

85 BONG APPETIT New South Wales, Australia

By the 1980s Australia's Bong Bong was the largest picnic race meeting in the world. At a time when race crowds were declining Bong Bong's were increasing, reaching almost 35,000 in 1985. However, poor behaviour on the part of some of this huge crowd resulted in the meetings being closed down. In 1992 the races were revived but under strict crowd control by limiting attendance to members and their guests only.

The Bong Bong Picnic Race Club was formed in 1886. The first Bong Bong Cup was held in the grounds of Throsby Park and was won by Don Antonio.

For many years now the meeting has been conducted at 'Wyeera', an aboriginal word meaning 'turning of the soil'.

A proud possession of the Club is the actual 1898 Bong Bong Cup which was won by Mr Thomas Rutledge's Record. The Cup is on display in the Club's Wyeera office. Gone from the track now is the notorious "drop" just past the winning post where unsuspecting jockeys sometimes became airborne! However, the famous hill in the centre of the course, the source of many tales about what can happen out of sight of the stewards, is still there.

86 FLAMINGOOD Hialeah, USA

The Hialeah Racetrack opened on January 15, 1925. In 1926, it was brutally damaged in a hurricane, and in 1930 was sold to Joseph Widener, who appointed architect Lester Geisler to embark upon what was to be the foremost modification of the racecourse. The newly revamped Hialeah Racetrack was opened to the public on January 14 1932, and featured extreme landscaping in the form of hundreds of royal palms and coconut trees towering above racegoers, swaying towards a lake contained by the track infield that was stained pink with flamingos imported from Cuba. The course soon became a designated sanctuary for the American Flamingo.

It was boasted of as one of the most beautiful racetracks in the world, becoming a playground for the rich and famous. Winston Churchill, Frank Sinatra, Bing Crosby and Joe di Maggio were amongst the glitterati who descended on the course. It even justified the construction of a station built by Seaboard Airline Railway to accommodate racegoers who travelled by special trains from Palm Beach.

A statue of great champion Citation, created in Florence, Italy, weighing 5,995 pounds and mounted on a base of marble, was unveiled in 1965. Seabiscuit made his racecourse debut at Hialeah in January 1935.

On 2 March 1979, Hialeah Park Racetrack was listed on the National Register of Historic Places. The track was closed to the public in 2001, but reopened in November 2009 – complete with the flamingos.

87 BOMBPROOF?

West country trainer Pat Rodford must have a fairy godmother of some kind – he was 'born the day they (the Germans) dropped the bomb in Yeovil in 1941' and when in 1982 he visited London to collect his licence from the Jockey Club 'I got out of the tube and an IRA bomb went off.'

And the arrival of his very talented hurdler Sparky May, runner-up in the 2011 Cheltenham Festival's David Nicholson Mares' Hurdle behind triple winner Quevega, was somewhat eventful, too.

In the spring of 2005 there was an overnight rainstorm. 'It was 2am and tipping down,' recalled Rodford, who went to check on the very pregnant Glassy Appeal. 'The mare was looking a bit agitated – and there was the foal, rolled down 20 yards the wrong side of the electric fence. I dragged it back up and as I went under – I was pretty wet – the fence gave me a hell of a shock'.

So, the foal was appropriately named Sparky May.

88 ICE ONE, FRAN Western Australia

Three weeks before the 1977 running of the prestigious Perth Cup, at the track of that name in Western Australia, the fancied Muros ran into a fence post whilst exercising and split a chest muscle.

Trainer Fran Gammon thought quickly and devised a unique chest sling in which she inserted ice and then hung around the horses's neck to sit on his chest to help reduce the swelling. Together with a programme of swimming, the treatement worked and Muros won, making his trainer the first female to train the winner of the Perth Cup – not too surprising, considering that women were only eligible for licensing by the Western Australian Turf Club in 1976.

As Muros was passing the post in front, down the field Khora Ribbon had fallen 600 metres out, breaking both of his forelegs in the process. As the horse lay writhing on the ground, jockey Gerry Donnelly, who had been dazed by the impact of his fall, crawled across to cradle the stricken animal's head, comforting him as best he could whilst waiting for the vet to arrive.

Donnelly was later presented with an award by the RSPCA and made a life member. However, Khora Ribbon's subsequent treatment was anything but dignified. Racing writer Dave Warner reported that 'in one of the most shocking incidents seen at a major racecourse, the horse was put down on the track then towed behind the semaphore board in the middle of the course and hacked apart by the knacker, all of this quite visible to the racegoers.'

89 CREAM OF COURSES Salisbury

Salisbury racecourse rarely attracts headlines but in the summer of 2009 scored quite the most extraordinary of public relations own goals when threatening to eject from the members' lawn a racegoer who had already spent £200 in the restaurant with his 75-year-old mother – because the pair were spotted eating ice-cream!

'We can't have people wandering around eating food. People pay extra for exclusivity in members. They don't expect to bump into someone carrying an ice cream,' declared general manager Jeremy Martin from his office somewhere on Planet Zog.

There were protests, and in a desperate effort to regain the PR initiative, at their next meeting Salisbury offered their first 99 racegoers free ice-cream with one Mr Jeremy Martin declaring: 'We are a listening racecourse and will be allowing ice-creams in members from now on. We won't be coning off special areas'.

What a flake! However, the course learned from the debacle and won the annual Racecourse Groundstaff Awards for 2010, the second time in three years they'd won it.

90 ICE CREAM CON Delaware, USA

Racing writer Red Smith wrote an article about Delaware Park racecourse in June 1957's Saturday Evening Post in which he reported that the course had been troubled by having to take care of a young boy on a daily basis during their summer meeting.

Every day for a week the lad – probably five or six years old – had turned up at the racing office, minus either parent. On each occasion he was 'stroked and petted and fed ice cream until the loud-speaker affected a family reunion.' Eventually the member of staff charged with taking care of the boy lost patience with the mother who arrived to take charge of her offspring: 'Lady, could you please keep an eye on your own boy?'

'Could you' she snapped, 'please stop giving him ice cream!'

91 THAT SANDY Newmarket

A short-lived training innovation emerged on the Newmarket scene in June 1896 when it was revealed that Messrs Duke and Wishard, local handlers, had installed 'sand-baths' for their strings.

Wishard had created a large area immediately in front of a stable wall, which was filled with sand, in which, in turn, horses would lie down and roll around while sand was thrown over them.

'What appears most remarkable about the whole process is that the sand does not seem to fill the eyes, nose, ears and mouth of the horse as one would suppose it would be sure to do,' reported an observer of the technique, calling it 'one of the most curious of all curious processes.'

92 G'DAY, GAY DAY Sydney, Australia

'The world's first gay race day' was claimed by Australian course Randwick in February 2010 as the track held its Pink Stiletto Race Day, a fund-raiser for the Sydney Gay and Lesbian Mardi Gras parade.

Highlight of the day was the 50m Pink Stiletto Queen race, run from the starting stalls, contested by six men in drag, although they had to run barefoot when they were banned from racing in stilettos or platforms.

The event was held in conjunction with the Australian Jockey Club and was supported by leading trainer, ahem, Gai Waterhouse, who commented, 'I'm delighted to be "coming out" at the Pink Stiletto day and joining the Bobby Goldsmith Foundation (HIV charity) in what will be the world's first gay race day.' Organisers said they raised over £17,500.

Back in 1974, Randwick had witnessed a streakers' race – although this one wasn't scheduled and anticipated – well, only by two people, that is. It took place whilst the 1974 Doncaster Stakes was being run: 'Streakers hit Royal Randwick,' wrote Roy Higgins, who handled the winner, Tontonan, in his autobiography, *The Professor*.

'The bizarre part about it was that the streakers did it while the race was being run. As soon as the field had set off, they came on to the track near the 100 metres mark and staged their own race down to the winning post, absolutely starkers. One erstwhile photographer [Ron Bickley] snapped the streakers in action (one of each sex) and, without being crude, you might say they were both very well endowed. The photographer inset the snap of the streakers into a corner of the picture of Tontonan beating Toltrice and copies are collectors' items. And the caption tells the story. It says: "The colt won by a good length". added Higgins.

Another, more recent, and female Randwick racecourse streaker's exploits are displayed at www.womenstreakers.com.

93 CURLEY'S CONSUMATE COUP

Controversial trainer Barney Curley, so often one jump ahead of the bookies, did it again in May 2010 when he arranged for 'hundreds' of multiple bets to be staked on three of his own, and one of trainer Chris Grant's horses.

Hoping to win up to an incredible £20million, the almost-priest turned gambler/jockey/confidant/trainer/philanthropist 'didn't even see the first race because I was in the queue to give blood at the hospital.'

Curley's recent illness was the casue of the blood test, but as he took the call telling him the first horse had won, he was beginning to smell the blood of his arch-enemies, the bookies.

The second horse won as well. The third, 1-3 favourite Sommersturm was beaten – but Grant's Jeu de Roseau romped home at Towcester.

Curley's winnings totalled £3.9m, he revealed. Not that he had collected all of that when this book went to post – some offshore bookies apparently refused to pay.

A reflective Curley told the *Racing Post*'s Nick Townsend: 'In 1975 I got more money out of a horse than anyone had in the 20th century – referring to his infamous £300,000 Yellow sam coup – it was always in my mind that I wanted to get more out of horses than anybody else in the 21st century.'

Looks like he achieved it too.

94 STICK THAT IN Beverley

Smokeyourpipe was a non-runner at Beverley on April 26, 2007. The vet's certificate pinpointed the reason – 'Coughing'.

95 SMALL EARTHQUAKE IN RIPON AND, ER, THAT'S ABOUT IT!

In the 'good old days' of journalism when the grizzled old hacks working on a newspaper needed a brief story on an inside page they'd often resort to running deliberately insignificant bits of news just to save time and fill the gap.

As a rookie reporter on the *Middlesex Weekly Post* I would often file non-stories beginning 'Rumours that ... were today denied'.

One such filler which assumed legendary status amongst journos involved a very small earthquake in a very insignificant South American country which appeared under the heading: 'Small Earthquake In Peru; No-one Injured'.

On Wednesday, January 5, 2011, the *Racing Post* carried the almost equally thrilling headline: 'Ripon escapes undamaged after minor earthquake.' Barely able to contain his excitement, Graham Green reported that Ripon racecourse was, well, 'unscathed', after the tremor caused the, er 'rattling' of crockery and the 'shaking' of doors.

Concerned lest such massive mayhem should have brought the racecourse grandstand crashing to the ground, Green interviewed course managing director James Hutchinson, who bravely fought his way to the phone, somehow keeping his footing as the earth swayed, to reveal to the concerned nation that there had been 'no damage at the racecourse' but that head groundsman Carl Tonks had 'felt as if something had knocked into his house.'

Phew, a narrow escape all round, then!

In 2008 Market Rasen had survived being the local epicentre of an earthquake registering 5.2 on the Richter scale – the strongest to hit England for 25 years.

Racing was postponed at Hipico de Santiago in late February/ March 2010 after a huge earthquake hit Chile, causing widespread death and damage.

Christchurch's (New Zealand) two major racetracks, Riccarton Park and Addington Raceway, where trotting is staged, escaped the devastating earthquakes of early September 2010 virtually unscathed.

There was superficial, but no structural, damage at both courses. However, in February, 2011 the area was hit by another, more damaging quake which did affect racing at local tracks.

Addington Raceway chief executive Shane Gloury said some structural damage occurred to the building with massive windows either breaking or coming away. Addington's back straight had a 30m long crack and an area of liquefaction, stipendiary steward Nigel McIntyre said.

The mammoth quake of March 2011 which wreaked havoc on Japan caused the immediate cancellation of all horse racing, with officials ruling it would not be appropriate to continue with the sport whilst people were coming to terms with the devastating event.

96 GETTING THE SACK AT KELSO Scotland

Kelso introduced a welcome present for winning trainers during 2007 which had some trainers drooling at the thought of collecting gold jewellery for saddling winners.

However, it soon emerged that the rumour that the course was handing out '24 carat prizes' was accurate, but misspelled – rather than 'carats', winning trainers were receiving 'carrots', sacks of them!

Trish Spours of Kelso told me in early 2011: 'I think we are quite unique (!!) when presenting each winning horse with a bag of carrots. It started out in the spring of 2006 when one of our sponsors decided that the horses should be given a treat for their win as they had really done all the work and it was awful to miss them out!

'He has since carried on and generously presented each winning horse on every day with the bag of carrots ...

'Another of our little quirks ... I think we are possibly the only racecourse to operate a Charity Tea Room! Each raceday a different charity provides teas for racegoers raising much-needed funds for their respective charities and at the same time providing somewhere different for our loyal supporters to have a quick bite during racing.'

97 SUE'S AD HER ASCOT WINNER Ascot

Short of someone to accompany her to Royal Ascot, Sue Phillips, from Weymouth, placed an ad in her local paper offering the right person an expenses paid limousine trip to the races, complete with champagne.

The 52-year-old marketing executive backed a winner when she selected 56-year-old Rod Grainger from the nine applicants. The pair enjoyed their time at Ascot on Ladies' Day in 2008 – and continued their relationship afterwards – 'I never expected things to continue, but I've found myself a lovely gentleman,' she told *The Sun*.

Anyone know whether they are still together? I bet they aren't!

98 VERY STABLE LADS Co Meath, Ireland

Stable lads working for Irish trainer Harry Dyas, from County Meath, had to be more stable than most.

For Dyas was prone to using them for target practice to test out his shooting skills.

The trainer's brother-in-law Campbell Russell, an owner-trainer and rider, explained in his 1930 book *Triumphs and Tragedies of the Turf* how Dyas 'would place an apple or egg on the head of a stable boy, and from forty yards distance blow it to pieces with a bullet from a rook rifle.'

Whether from loyalty or terror is not explained, but Russell claimed, 'There was not a boy in his employ who would hesitate to hold his target, so great was their confidence in him as a shot.'

Russell was a keen gambler who lined up a coup on a horse named The Doctor, running at Ballina. All went well and the money was in the bag until, 'a few yards from the winning post The Doctor suddenly stuck his toes into the ground and came to a halt. There he stood, rooted to the spot with the crowd yelling at him.

'Three more strides would have taken him past the post but nothing would induce him to make those strides. Like a bronze statue he stood there while one by one the other runners passed him.'

Russell believed the horse 'had been stricken by some sudden pain' as he never repeated the quirk.

99 BURGER ME – WE CAN'T RACE!
Laytown, Ireland

Laytown – in Gaelic Port na hinse ('The Port of Ninch') – is an Irish seaside track where a race was once delayed because a fast-food van was impeding the stewards' view of the action.

Claimed as 'the only officially approved beach racing in Europe' the September action can attract crowds of 5,000.

Tradition has it that it was the parish priest who first organised this meeting back in 1876 until in 1901 the fixture became a regular in the calendar as landowner Paddy Delaney gave the go-ahead. Not even two World Wars stopped the Laytown races.

In 1958 ten runners set off for the 1m4f Committee Plate. Oriental Cottage didn't make it to the start, though, heading off towards the waves instead.

As the horses started, Nook whipped round and headed off in the opposite direction.

Casenco led them along until going the wrong side of the course-marking flag, almost followed by Headwave, whose quick-acting jockey J Cox just pulled him the right side. Stalstarino, Opening Bars and Gay Navaree were the only others not to take the wrong course.

Headwave passed the post in front of Enfield Colleen, Stalstarino and Tartan's Choice – but the second and fourth had taken the wrong course so there were only two places confirmed with no third horse placed.

In 1993 racing was delayed not by weather or water, but because the judge's view of the finish was obstructed by a burger van.

The future of beach racing at Laytown in Ireland was in doubt after a spate of horse deaths at the evening fixture there in 1994. Reported the *Independent on Sunday*, 'Racing authorities are currently carrying out an investigation. The mayhem started in the opening race when Five Little Girls crashed to the ground, bringing down three others. She had to be put down and another broke her neck when she fell over the leader. A third died after a collision with one of the loose horses after the winning post. Ten jockeys were injured in total after horses fell in other races.'

JP McManus, Ireland's biggest owner, finally achieved his first winner at Laytown – The Hamptons, at the 2009 meeting.

The enclosures at Laytown consist of a three-acre field elevated above the beach, and the grandstand is hewn from steps cut into the sand dunes. Marquees are erected for use as weighing/jockeys' rooms and bars.

The course itself is on the three-mile stretch of sand or strand, which is closed on the morning of the races.

100 FIERY HISTORY Caulfield, Australia

There have been one or two problems associated with racing at Australian track Caulfield, the course which first hosted a Victorian Amateur Turf Club meeting in August 1876, three years before the first Caulfield Cup was staged there.

There was racing on the site, though, as early as 1859 – and two years later it was almost turned into a cemetery.

In 1885 the Cup attracted 41 runners – but in a horrendous incident, 16 of the horses fell in an accident which left one jockey dead and several badly injured. Thirteen years later seven of 31 fell and another jockey died. Fire destroyed the members' stand just before the 1922 race, although it went ahead with tents brought in for temporary use.

Amazingly, it happened again in February 1927, during Oakleigh Plate Day, when the stand in the guineas reserve went up after a lighted cigarette was carelessly discarded. A contemporary report pointed out that 'hundreds of people congregated on the two decks of the stand remained there until the race was over'. Despite the stand continuing to burn all afternoon, only four people were injured, and the race meeting was duly concluded. It was later rebuilt at a cost of £60,000.

101 BY GEORGE! Santa Anita, USA

Top US rider of the 1930s and 1940s George Woolf, who partnered Seabiscuit and many other equine greats of the era, was very selective with his rides. He was noted for disdaining run-of-the-mill races and meetings and concentrating on the big-money purses, seldom riding in midweek as a result – hence his 'Saturday's child' nickname.

In 1944 his 13 stakes wins were half as many as rivals Eddie Arcaro and Ted Atkinson, who both boasted 27 – but Woolf's mounts won $324,330 –

more than either of his two opponents.

Suffering from 'a diabetic condition', which resulted in him sleeping for longer than he was awake, Woolf's recipe for sparking himself up pre-race might raise eyebrows today. Explained the 1945 *Year Book* of the Jockeys' Guild:

'In the jockeys' room on a Saturday afternoon before a rich stake race, George usually takes a nap to be awakened by his valet prior to weighing in. Just a few moments before leaving for the paddock the jockeys' physical director hands George a glass of coca cola spiked by a few drops of ammonia, with Woolf wiping his mouth while murmuring, "let's go get this money and go home"'.

During the running of the fourth race at Santa Anita Park on January 3, 1946, George Woolf fell from his horse as he rounded the clubhouse turn. Suffering from concussion, he was taken to hospital where he died the following day. Both the jockeys in the race and the track stewards reported that they had not witnessed any incident that would have caused such a fall and it was generally believed his diabetic condition may have resulted in him suffering a dizzy spell or fainting. He was just 35 years old.

102 WATERED DOWN Chepstow

Chepstow organized a charity raceday in September 2008 for 'Water Aid' which 'uses practical solutions to provide clean water, safe sanitation and hygiene education to the world's poorest people.'

The meeting was abandoned due to waterlogging of the course.

103 GRAY DAYS Fontwell

Jockey Carroll Gray gave up riding in 1987 after he suffered a broken neck – the last of a series of serious injuries, including a broken thigh, twice breaking his right leg, suffering a punctured lung and having part of his liver removed.

Gray opted for what he described as the 'safer' job of training – which it was until in October 2008 he was leading his runner, Madame Helga, on to the course at Fontwell, when she knocked him over and trod on him, breaking his leg in two places.

104 TO RIDE, OR NOT TO RIDE?
Beulah Park, USA

Former Brooklyn factory worker-turned 22-year-old 'wannabe' jockey, Canadian-born exercise rider Theodore F (known as Ted) Atkinson had almost given up hope of a breakthrough and was sat on a paddock bench at Beulah Park racecourse reading a copy of Hamlet during racing hours on May 18, 1938, when he was approached by a stranger looking for a rider for his Musical Jack in the next race.

Atkinson dropped the book, raced to the changing rooms, and within half an hour had ridden his first winner, despite being self-aware enough to aver after the race that his mount 'gave me a look of utter disgust in the winner's circle'.

By 1944 Atkinson had grabbed his lucky break with both hands and in that year (and again in 1946) was the USA's top money-winning jockey with $899,101 to his credit, scoring 287 winners from 1,539 rides.

Nicknamed 'The Slasher' because of his unusual, high-arm whipping style, he hated the name and claimed that in fact by this method he hurt horses less than those using the conventional method of the day.

105 COUNTED OUT Bellewstown

Jockey Adrian Heskin dismounted from well fancied Warcraft, who was playing him up, and trotted the horse down to the start at Bellewstown in July 2009, but as he did so he was astonished to see the race begin without him as Starter Derek Cullen sent off the other eleven runners. At least punters got their money back when Warcraft was declared a non-runner.

'The incident arose as a result of the starting procedures not being followed by the Starter in that he did not count the horses at the start prior to the tape being released,' reported the Turf Club later.

Known in Gaelic as Slieve Baile na Gcailleach, which, as you may know, translates the course name to 'The Town of the Hags', Bellewstown is a dual-purpose course in County Meath, which has a history of racing stretching back as far as 1726. King George III was the first English monarch to sponsor a race at the track after being persuaded to do so by the Mayor of Drogheda in 1780. His Majesty's Plate was worth a massive, for the time, £100 and English monarchs continued to sponsor there until the 1980s.

106 WEIGH-HEY-ING ROOM York

York was the scene of one of the earliest reported examples of racecourse skulduggery when, in 1718, according to a contemporary report 'Crutches started a very hot favourite for the Plate, but Thomas Buck, finding his horse winning, in spite of all his efforts to stop him, with courage worthy of a better cause, threw himself off when leading at the distance post.'

Racing had begun in the area when the River Ouse froze over during the winter of 1607-8 and impromptu contests were organized. Racing began at Acomb Moor and the Ings before finding a permanent home on the Knavesmire from 1731 – the year in which they had to cut down the bodies of three recently hanged robbers to give racegoers a clear view of the action at the August meeting.

In 1788 the track hosted a two-runner race over one mile for 100 guineas. The grey horse owned by Durham MP George Baker was ridden by trainer Michael Mason, while opponent Mr Maynard's bay mare was partnered by his anonymous coachman.

The grey started at 1-2 favourite, but the mare prevailed – despite both riders weighing out and in at 30 stone!

Racegoers were surprised to see a bride in full regalia standing at a bookmaker's pitch at York in August 1994 – Mrs Mary Bogle had been expecting a honeymoon in foreign climes after marrying bookie Ronnie – but he told her he had to cover the meeting at York first. 'I told him the only way I would go with him was if I wore my wedding dress,' she said – and did just that.

Racing commentator Mike Cattermole revealed a little known aspect of racing here when in April 2009 he told *Racing Post* readers, 'I once saw a couple engaging very intimately, shall we say, behind the weighing room at York.'

107 PIS*ED IT Kempton

Many horses who win easily are welcomed back by happy punters telling everyone – 'he pis*ed it' – and on January 2009 Namu literally did just that in the 2.35 at Kempton. The six-year-old was about to enter the stalls when she stopped and relieved herself copiously, causing jockey Adam Kirby to declare he had never seen such a thing before.

Commentating, John Francome called it 'extraordinary' while trainer Teresa Spearing revealed the mare normally did such things in the privacy of her box.

108 TWO FALLS, NO SUBMISSION Ballinrobe, Ireland

In a very rare event during a race in 1960 at Ballinrobe, Ireland, one jockey fell twice – from different horses – in the same race.

Mr H Kerrigan rode Bridge Echo in the Hunters' Chase, only to fall at the start of the second circuit. Kerrigan rose from the ground and, as he did, Glenmore Girl fell nearby. Kerrigan caught Glenmore Girl, jumped up on her and set off after the two horses still on their feet.

They fell at the last but, undeterred, Kerrigan mounted Glenmore Girl again and finished the course.

In May 2010 the course unveiled a 1.3mE refurbishment with a track extension scheduled for 2012.

109 TONGE TIED South Africa

John Tonge was a top jockey riding in South Africa in the 1880s when the sport was taking hold there – riding in Johannesburg in 1888, he was expected to win the Farmer's Plate on Maritzburg, but as a contemporary report in the *Calendar* newspaper reported, the horse 'seemed to have the race in hand two distances (furlongs) from home, where he unaccountably stopped and took no further part in the race.'

That was bad enough, but the combination then turned out for the Digger's Plate later in the afternoon and won in 'a common canter' by four lengths. The locals were not happy, and nor were the Johannesburg Turf Club stewards who hauled Tonge in and found him guilty of stopping

Maritzburg in the first race, promptly warning the jockey off for life.

When Maritzburg next ran at the Port Elizabeth course he pulled the same trick under a different rider – but Tonge was not reinstated for 18 months. This time he lasted six months back before he was again warned off – this time for three years – after he warned a younger jockey not to win a certain race as Tonge had backed his own mount.

The youngster, William Whiting, pulled his horse so blatantly that he was 'severely mauled' by the crowd after the race. When the reason was ascertained the Jockey Club accused Tonge of 'one of the most daring and flagrant breaches of the rules of racing that ever disgraced the turf of South Africa.'

110 WALKOVER IN FIVE-RUNNER RACE Southwell

When four of the five jockeys contesting a 1m race at Southwell in January 2008 ignored a recall flag and completed the course, Chris Catlin, who was partnering 10-1 shot Rebellious Spirit, pulled his mount up.

As the other four were ineligible for the re-run, Catlin and Rebellious Spirit jogged round in splendid isolation to take the honours.

111 NEVO MIND Taunton

Professional punter Dave Nevison was mentally counting his winnings as James Davies and Topless approached the winning line at Taunton in January 2009, with the race as good as won – until, that is, 24-year-old Davies – son of jockey Hywel – fell off.

Nevison, whose £400 Tote Super 7 wager would have burst through the £200,000 barrier was – almost – philosophical. 'I don't want to start slagging off the jockey,' he said commendably, before adding – and slagging the jockey off in the process – 'But he could have just sat on it and it would have won'.

112 POLES APART South Pole

Three times champion jockey Richard Dunwoody went where few men – and no jockeys – have ever been before when, on January

18, 2008 – his 44th birthday – he reached the South Pole 49 days after setting out on the 650-mile expedition with US explorer Doug Stoup.

In 2009 he tackled an even more daunting challenge when he took part in Strictly Come Dancing, but finished unplaced.

113 MOUNTING INTEREST Newcastle

The heavily backed beaten seller favourite ridden at Newcastle by Lester Piggott was being unsaddled by a nervous Mark Usher before he became an Upper Lambourn trainer.

In his confusion in the presence of the legendary jockey, Usher 'managed to pull the bridle' off the horse as well, whereupon, he recalled, 'The colt, Hot Prince, immediately tried to mount the winning filly, causing great hilarity and interesting comments at the subsequent auction.'

114 LUCK OFF Wincanton

Racing UK presenter Nick Luck startled viewers when he used a word rhyming with his own surname during a broadcast. Handing over from Wincanton to Dubai in January 2009 he expostulated, 'f***ing Nad Al Sheba'.

115 LOSING THE WHIP House of Commons

Although MPs are traditionally terrified of having the whip withdrawn, in January 2008 Lib Dem MP Mike Hancock tabled a question in the House of Commons demanding that 'police should be looking into cases of excessive use of the whip by jockeys.'

116 CRAIGLEAS LEFT, RIGHT AND CENTRE South Australia

Commentaries don't come much stranger than the one for the eight-runner first race at South Australian track Mackay's meeting on Friday, January 15, 2010.

'There's Craigleas left, right and centre,' declared the flustered announcer at the track – and he wasn't joking. Of the eight runners in the 1050m Red Carpet Two Year Old Handicap, seven had names beginning with Craiglea.

And the other one, Willy Nic, finished last!

Eventually, Craiglea Royale won the race, in the process beating Craiglea Rawie, Craiglea Smokie, Craiglea Edge, Craiglea Gal, Craiglea Matilda and Craiglea Time.

117 DOWNS IN THE DUMPS Atokad Downs, USA

Lucky Bob won the 2010 race at Atokad Downs racecourse in Nebraska. That's right, the track ran just one race during the entire year.

'Declining attendance and a fading interest in horse racing have forced the track to cut back on the number of live races per season,' explained the local media.

Even though it was the one contest of the year, run at 4pm on August 24, the South Sioux City track still simulcasts races from around the nation 363 days a year.

118 HAMMING IT UP Deauville, France

John Hammond, who at the time was assistant trainer to Andre Fabre, had an interesting couple of experiences whilst he was at Deauville in August 1985.

One night, reported the *Irish Field*, Hammond emerged from his Normandy hotel 'to find his Mini completely wrapped up in lavatory paper.' The car had previously attracted the attentions of some 'ardent young ladies', who 'expressed their love for the young gentleman by writing their feelings in lipstick all over the car's windows.'

119 SOAP BOXES North Somerset

Top jumps trainer Philip Hobbs named the blocks of stone stable boxes at his north Somerset yard after popular TV soap operas – 'Brookside', 'Emmerdale' and Albert Square – plus 'South Park'.

120 OBJECTIONABLE WINNER Punchestown

After Tiny Tim won the 1892 Punchestown Farmers Challenge Cup by 12 lengths he was disqualified for taking the wrong course. Runner-up The Linnet was awarded the race – until the owner of the third horse home, Woodranger, objected that the horse's age had been given wrongly.

The Linnet was disqualified and the race awarded to Woodranger. The connections of Tiny Tim objected to Woodranger on the grounds that his owner was not a bona fide farmer as specified in the race conditions, while another objection that Woodranger had also taken the wrong course was submitted too. Both objections were overruled.

To this day Punchestown stage a Hunter Chase for the Bishopscourt Cup, opne only to hunters 'the bona fide and unconditional property of farmers farming land in the Kildare Hunt district.'

121 HOT ROD Folkestone

Flamboyant trainer and heavy metal fan Rod Simpson, who nominated 'Del Boy' to play him in any film of his life, revealed how he landed a massive coup on one of his horses running in a lowly race – 'Pierrot August in a seller at Folkestone,' he explained to *the Racing Post* in August 2010. 'Trainer and syndicate didn't go to the races, but the 20 in the syndicate each go to a town and have £200 each-way at 33-1 – and all wait until one minute before the off to place their bet. Proper touch.'

If all of those syndicate members had their bets accepted and settled they would have won over £150,000 in total.

122 QUICK WORK Chicago

Jockey William Buick, 22, rode 11-1 chance Debussy to win the valuable Arlington Million in Chicago on Saturday, August 21, 2010 for trainer John Gosden. Fifteen hours later he was at Deauville in France, riding his first winner in that country, 8-1 Dream Ahead in the Group One Darley Prix Morny.

123 MAC CLEANS UP London

Not only did John McCririck earn what he described as 'the best (money) I've ever been paid for four days' work' he also collected on the 'very big' bet he placed on himself at 3-1 to be the first contestant evicted from the Ultimate Big Brother house in August 2010.

'Everything went according to script. I was in it just for the money,' declared the racing and betting pundit after he had carried an 'Evict Me Please' sign around with him and deliberately set out to alienate the other 'celebrities' in the house with him.

But his coup only just came off as it was revealed that in the closest ever eviction vote, John was ousted with 50.6 per cent of the vote against 'rapper' Coolio, who polled 49.4 per cent.

124 MINI-MUM EFFORT Huntingdon

A world record was claimed as 11 jockeys and a jockeys' valet managed to cram themselves into a mini at Huntingdon racecourse on August 30, 2010.

The stunt was part of a fund-raising effort for Racing Welfare and saw Dougie Costello, Tom David, Sam Twiston-Davies, 5ft 11in Lee Edwards, Sam Hanson, Daryl Jacob, Warren Marston, Denis O'Regan, Brian Toomey, Adam Wedge and Clare Wills join valet Andrew Gandy.

Another fun event during the day was a John McCririck lookalike competition, won by five-year-old Hannah Berkshire!

125 LOCKING THE STABLE DOOR BEFORE THE HORSE BOLTS IN Manton

Stable lads may believe they have a tough life these days, but it is fair to say it could be worse – witness those employed by trainer Alec Taylor, Sr. back in 1880.

When Taylor had laid out a horse called Loved One to land a big prize at Ascot for wealthy owner the Duchess of Montrose – aka 'Carrie Red' or 'Mr Manton' – she informed him she would be placing a big bet on the horse and didn't want word getting out to all and sundry via stable sources, thus spoiling the available odds.

In his book *The Masters of Manton*, author Paul Mathieu explains Taylor's solution to this problem: 'Before racing, Taylor called all his travelling boys together in a saddling box on the course. Then he locked them in. After

Loved One had won, the lads were set free – with a guinea each from the Duchess in recompense.'

126 COINCIDENTALLY, WANGANUI WARRIOR WINS Wanganui, New Zealand

Wanganui Jockey Club is the oldest racecourse (founded in 1848) in New Zealand still racing on the original track. A book was put together for its 150th anniversary in 1998 written by Laraine Sole, in which she revealed what must have been one of the greatest coincidence winners ever.

In December 1868 racing officials were in two minds over whether to run the meeting as Maori warrior Titokowaru and his rebel army were reportedly set to attack Wanganui. Not only did the organisers permit the meeting to go ahead – but owner Richard Day had entered his Titokowaru in two races at the two-day meeting – and he duly won both the Welter Stakes and the next day's Hurdle race.

The day after the races the very same Richard Day, an army Captain, led his troops in an attack on Titokowaru's rebels – only to find that their leader had made himself scarce.

127 RUTH REINED IN Vienna

Austria's well known old Vienna Freudenau track went into possibly permanent retirement in 2008, but not before trainer Ruth Carr was able to nominate it as the scene of her greatest racing frustration.

Riding in a lady riders' event there, 'I drew the odds-on favourite, who proceeded to hang violently left-handed. The problem was there wasn't a running rail – just a line of small bushes with gaps in between. I had two hands on one rein but still thought I was going to end up in the car park – and only got beaten half a length. The stewards took a dim view and, as I didn't understand a word of the inquiry, I later discovered I'd received a worldwide 14-day ban for not trying!'

128 OH, B-LIMEY! Kentucky, USA

British racing fans wishing to visit Turfway Park in Kentucky will be encouraged to know that Limeys are welcome at the track.

Not that the name refers in this case to Brits, instead to a unique feature of the track, a challenge called Corona Hall, requiring the racegoer to take a lime – and toss it into one of a line of numbered buckets. Achieving this feat entitles the successful punter to a modest free bet on that numbered horse in the next race.

129 RUSHED DECISION? Tumut, Australia

There have been many reasons given for the abandonment and postponement of race meetings – but perhaps only the Tumut Races have fallen victim to a gold rush.

They began racing here, en route to Australia's Snowy Mountains, back in the 1850s – but in 1860 the meeting did not take place – whether because too many of those who might otherwise have attended were off prospecting for more of the recently discovered gold, or because the jockeys themselves decided there was easier prize money to be had in them thar hills, is not recorded.

Still, they presumably didn't find that much gold as the races were soon back on in future years and by 1873 a grandstand had been constructed. The most popular meeting nowadays is held on Boxing Day.

130 (VERY) LONG SHOT Australia

Racing in Wagga Wagga, Australia, goes back as far as 1849 when the St Patrick's Cup was run for. The trophy passed into the safe keeping of the Murrumbidgee Turf Club who organise the sport here.

In 1868 a unique event was run here – a ten-mile race which attracted a field of twelve, each carrying 70kgs or more, which was won in 23 minutes 35 seconds by the appropriately named Australian.

The race was never contested again.

131 NAP OF THE DAY Storeton

Storeton, a jumping track on the Wirral near Liverpool, was one of the (very) few British courses able to boast that a French Emperor rode there – Louis Napoleon III, exiled in England from 1846-48, did just that before returning to his native land to become Emperor.

132 VUVUFAILURE South Africa

Vuvuzelas were the sensation of the 2010 World Cup, leaving many sports fearing the long, plastic noise makers would be imported to their events.

Sunday Telegraph reporter William Langley decided to test the 'instrument's' effects on competitors in various sporting contests and, having received a frosty reception at a tennis tournament, he set off for Newbury racecourse 'just as the runners were cantering out for the 4.15'.

Apparently attracting little attention, despite being clad in a highly visible crumpled white jacket and trousers and clutching a bright red vuvuzela to his mouth, Langley was able to let rip with a 'mighty blast' of the confounded contraption. 'As Mujdeya, the 9-4 favourite, galloped past to win I could have sworn the beast gave me a dirty look,' reported Langley, the first man to blow a vuvuzela at a racecourse and survive.

133 OIL BE SEEING YOU Goodwood

'There's gold in them thar hills' was the cry which sparked the original 19th century US gold rush – but few racing fans could have expected to learn that 'there's oil in them thar downs' as it was revealed in July 2010 that Goodwood racecourse might well be sitting on huge oil reserves.

It was disclosed that a field close to the racecourse, at Singleton, near Chichester, whose location was being kept secret, could contain 9 million barrels of oil.

'It was the steal of the century. We bought it (the field) for £12m three years ago and analysts will tell you it is now an £80m asset' said Tony O'Reilly jr, son of former international rugby player Sir Tony O'Reilly, owner of the site whose production of the black stuff was being boosted, doubling production in two years.

134 FIRST FLIGHT Wingatui, New Zealand

Mr J P Murphy, the owner of Almoner, who was contesting a big race at New Zealand's Wingatui track in December 1920, was granted special permission by the Racing Club to fly from Timaru and land on the racecourse – does anyone know of an earlier example of flying in to the track?

He must have flown out again pretty rapidly as his horse was unplaced.

135 NOT SO MAGNIFICENT SEVEN
Beaumont, New Zealand.

Seven horses lined up to contest a flat race at Beaumont, New Zealand, in April 1914. Four were left at the start and took no part. Of the other three, Afton Loch finished ahead of My Glove and Gunflash, but the riders of the latter two were disqualified for failing to weigh in, leaving Afton Loch as the only officially placed runner.

136 SAIL, SWIM, WALK, RUN New Zealand

Ladybird, a fancy for a big race in New Zealand in 1868, was sailed to Manakua Harbour, where she swam ashore from the boat before walking to the racecourse at Ellerslie, where, showing no signs of being bugged by her exertions, she ran in and won the race, before returning whence, and in the same manner that she came.

137 DOGGONE WINNER Dunedin, New Zealand

New Zealander Mr A L Aubrey did a deal with the owner of racehorse Mount Boa, buying the horse in exchange for his sheepdog.

The deal paid off when Mount Boa romped to victory in the prestigious 1931 Dunedin Cup.

138 MAJOR TRAGEDY
Monmouth Park, USA

The first event at the inaugural meeting of the Monmouth Park racecourse in New Jersey on July 30, 1870, was a hurdles race, followed by the $800 Continental Stakes for three-year-olds, run in mile heats.

The crack three-year-old Lynchburg, owned by Major Bacon and Mr Holland, won the first heat but fell in the second, breaking a shoulder blade and having to be destroyed.

The horse had a nationwide reputation amongst racing fans and the

Monmouth Park Association announced it was donating $1,000 to a fund for the owners, to which racegoers quickly added a further $4,000, the whole amount being handed over to Major Holland with the request that he 'buy another worthy horse to replace the best on the track.'

139 DONNA'S STALKER Calder, USA

As if there wasn't enough difficulty involved in trying to establish herself as a female jockey in the first half of the 1970s, US rider Donna Walsh, who rode at Belmont, Hialeah, and for an extended period at Calder, faced a problem few male jockeys have ever experienced:

'I had a stalker on the racetrack – that was the scariest thing about being a jockey; that stalker followed me for over two years and actually broke into a house I was renting and threw a hatchet into a living room wall and defecated on a master bed. How is that for fun?'

140 HOW LAURA WON 'EM OVER Venezuela

Laura Kornmeyer Schoeller rode in the States from 1989-93 and also enjoyed some successful rides abroad.

In 1990 she was invited to Venezuela to ride to help promote the girl jockeys there. 'When I won my race I was escorted back by the outrider, I had a standing ovation, three tiers of people chanting my name! The place was packed. You couldn't see anything but people! When I saluted the crowd with my stick, they yelled more!'

However, it wasn't quite the same on her next visit abroad: *'When we returned from that trip, my agent told me not to unpack because I was just invited to Kingston, Jamaica to ride in a jockeys' challenge.*

'Talk about an experience for a girl. Where I was treated with respect in Venezuela, I was cursed in Jamaica. They thought I was making a mockery of their serious betting parlor, the racetrack. I had the two biggest bodyguards you would ever see. The fencing that went around the track and the saddling ring was gated with barbed wire at the top. Yes, they are serious bettors!!

'When we went to our trainers ready to mount, the Jamaicans cursed me, cursed me bad. Words that I can't repeat. I just smiled because I had two

bodyguards and wire fencing between me and them. It had just poured rain before the first race like I've never seen rain come down. The track was like soup up to the horses' knees, it seemed like. These riders were crazy. They all came out of the gate like banshees!

I figured I'd sit back because I don't want my horse to fall down the lane. At the quarter pole these poor horses were legless. I, on the other hand, had a fresh horse. I just had to weave in and out of these guys with a pretty hand ride to win the race! I didn't know what to expect when I got back to the winner's circle.

'When I got back, to my surprise, they were cheering me on, telling me "You da Julie Krone of da south, man! Come back any time!" I had about ten pounds of mud on me, Man what a ride that was!'

141 KRIS'S COLD SHOULDER
Churchill Downs, USA

Jockey Kris Prather was very successful at many US tracks including Churchill Downs, Aqueduct, Keeneland, Ellis Park, and Turfway – where she once rode seven winners from eight mounts.

In 2001 she was forced to retire, after which she became a successful novelist. 'In 2001 I was leading jockey in the nation, and by the way I was the only female ever to do that.'

She was riding at Churchill Downs' opening day, she told the racing website, www.femalejockeys.com: *'as you know, opening day basically dictates your meet, because if you do well everybody is gonna ride and if you don't you can do all you want, but nobody is gonna ride you that meet.'*

Kris injured her shoulder during a race, but as *'the agents were hanging around like vultures, I refused to get in the ambulance – and I actually rode for two weeks with the shoulder broken.*

'I didn't know it was broken, I knew it hurt really bad, but I had that jockey mentality and about a week after it happened I asked fellow rider Greta Kunzweiler to tape my arm up, because it kept falling out of the socket and she was like "what?" I just told her to tape it, it will work, but it did not work.

'I actually beat Pat Day in a photo finish whipping left-handed with my broken arm. In my mind I thought I just ripped a muscle or something so

I thought if I just kept whipping left-handed it wouldn't lock up so I did not know it was broken.

'I got flown down for a stakes race, and went to turn on the shower afterwards, and I finished second in that race, which I still remember, and I totally should have won and I am still aggravated about that, but I went to turn on the shower afterwards and my shoulder fell out of the socket and wouldn't work.

'I went to see a doctor and they flew me out for surgery the very next day, but while I was in surgery they made a medical mistake, there was a pain pump that was supposed to be inserted into my neck and they inserted it directly into the joint and it ate the entire bone away and that is why I can't ride anymore. I am on pain pills now and I have had nine surgeries on it, two full replacements and it was all because of a medical mistake. I have broken my ankle, my knee and my pelvis three times, I mean everything. I have always held up perfect and everything else was just splendid, but I am in chronic pain and it is because of that injury.'

142 NO ANGEL? USA

Female jockey P J Lydon has been riding in the States since 1989 and still recalls an incident which resulted in a charge of sexual harassment for a fellow jockey, the legendary Angel Cordero:

'Angel Cordero and I battled down the whole stretch.' Lydon told website www.femalejockeys.com. 'It was him, it was me, it was him, it was me. Him, me, him, and on the wire, it was me with a 15-1.

Angel smacked my behind and told me 'congrats'. The Stewards came down and said to Angel, "Did you touch that girl's behind right after the wire". He said, "Yes, I congratulated her. She rode a great race and I tried to intimidate her. I taught her a lot and she did good". They told Angel they are going to fine him $250 for sexual harassment. He told them, "Next time fine me $500, I'll grab two". I couldn't stop laughing. Angel hit everyone in the behind when they won. That was him. I love that guy and still do.'

143 BOXING CLEVER Canada

Inez Karlsson was born in Sweden in 1983 and became a very promising boxer, winning 14 of 20 fights in the lightweight division, earning a number two ranking.

However, a move to Canada slowed down her progress and she decided on a drastic career change – becoming a jockey. 'I used to be scared to death every time I jumped into the ring. The only difference between boxing and race riding is that you don't ask to get hurt!'

Karlsson soon gained her first victory, with her very first ride, Death Valley, at Arlington Park in September 2007 when she suffered a typical US debut victory celebration – 'I got shaving cream all over me, Vaseline in my hair and a lot of cold water.'

144 BLACK LOOK Mountaineer Park, USA

US jockey Angela Owens, now retired, certainly stood out from the crowd when she raced – 'I always had to have two black rubber bands on each wrist, a black rubber band on my helmet, black leggings and all-black boots – and black girths.'

Although many superstitious people regard horseshoes as being lucky, Ms Owens had mixed feelings after a race-riding incident at Mountaineer Park: 'We were going six furlongs and I was sitting behind the three front runners when all of a sudden a shoe shot up and caught me square in the jaw. I remember thinking who just hit me with a sledgehammer? I had to take my horse up and out a little because I was a tad loopy from the blow and thought I was going to black out.

'Guess that was what my filly wanted because once we got in the clear (or the middle of the racetrack – whatever, I was out of it), she took off and we ended up catching them at the wire and winning.

'Everyone thought the horse had bled till they saw my face, it was gross. I found out later that thanks to what could only have been an act of God, my jaw wasn't broken – it just needed ten stitches – anything for a win!'

After retiring, Owens joined the Louisville Metro Police Department as an officer.

145 SEEING THE LIGHT BEFORE EVERYONE ELSE? Baltinglass, Ireland

Baltinglass reportedly (by the *Irish Racing Calendar*) staged a meeting with a difference in December 1791, the difference being that it might have been the earliest 'floodlit' meeting on record, as 'the last heat was not over at six o'clock, when lights were erected at each corner of the course.'

146 LOST COURSE Israel

In January 2009 the *Racing Post* reported: 'Last July Israel lost its only racecourse, Pardes Hanna. It really was lost – it was there on Sunday night, but had gone on Monday morning! The track had fallen victim to lease negotiations that pushed the patience of the landowner a step too far – so he sent the tractors in.'

The best horse to have raced there, filly Vanilla Bally, unbeaten during 2007, was sent to England to race but failed to trouble the judge during her three races in 2009.

In 2004, Israel's parliament passed a law allowing construction of racetracks, despite a gambling ban.

Israeli jockeys participated in a horse race at the first racecourse in Israel near the northern town of Afula on Wednesday October 11, 2006. This was not hugely popular with everyone. A website, Chai Online, dedicated to 'Concern for Helping Animals in Israel' raged: *'Horseracing already exists in Israel in a very small way, but there are plans to expand the races to include as many as 2,000 horses and to launch gambling on the races. As experience in England and the U.S. has shown, when gambling is involved, the welfare of the horses is sacrificed. The racing industry is built on the exploitation of animals, and cruelty and abuse are commonplace.*

'Religious Knesset members in Israel are opposed to gambling of any kind because Judaism is against the practice, saying that it causes one person to receive money to the detriment of another. The lure of huge profits has blinded the majority, however, who are intent on making it legal. We urgently need to educate lawmakers, and also the public, about the existing problem of horse abuse in Israel and how it will be multiplied tenfold if gambling on racing is legalized. '

They weren't the only ones complaining. On July 30, 2006, Rabbi Shlomo Amar, the Sephardic Chief Rabbi of Israel, issued a ruling (psak halacha) against horseracing.

The ruling concluded: '*It seems self-evident that one ought to instruct every God-fearing person to hasten to gather his livestock and his horses at home [an allusion to Exodus 9:20] and not to participate in horse-races – neither in establishing them, nor by watching them: because of the pain to animals caused thereby, because it is "a dwelling place of scoffers," and because it is "playing with dice" [that is, gambling].*'

147 THAT'S LIFE Newbury

On August 14, 2010, Newbury attracted its modern-day record attendance of 30,000, helped by the Westlife concert after racing.

Not everyone welcomed either of those things, and trainer Barry Hills stomped off before the end of the card, huffing: 'This is a disgrace. These aren't racing people. They'll probably never come again.'

It wasn't quite clear whether he just doesn't like Westlife or was objecting to all concerts at race meetings! Speaking on behalf of the racecourse, managing director Stephen Higgins insisted: 'We are conscious we have to get the balance right.'

148 DORIS IN THE PINK Washington, USA

The daughter of a plumber with no racing connections, Doris Harwood was determined to become a trainer, so approached her boss Ken Alhadeff and offered to buy and train a horse for him for a dollar.

He accepted and she duly bought Brooks Pebble for him for $1 – and managed to finish second with the horse.

She then went on to bigger and better things – in 2009 she saddled over 250 runners, producing over 60 winners and prize money of over $1m.

Doris, who saddled Smarty Deb at the 2007 Breeders' Cup meeting and is based at Emerald Downs, near Washington, USA, calls her training set-up Team Pink – which, together with her other favourite colour, turquoise, is reflected in everything from bridles to saddlecloths to leg bandages, to blinkers, to her lipstick!

'You and your owners can see it all the way across the track' she explained.

149 GORDON BROWN'S BEST MATE DATE
Exeter

How many racecourses have ever hosted an official government Cabinet meeting? Not many, that's for sure, but Exeter did so on Friday, February 5, 2010, when then Prime Minister Gordon Brown brought his team to the track's Best Mate Room. After the meeting there was a question and answer session in the Denman room with local residents.

The course hosted the Cabinet meeting after an earlier planned meeting at the City's University was scuppered by snow.

Exeter used to be Devon and Exeter, and before that, it was known as Haldon, where meetings took place as early as 1738 with, legend has it, a local squire being a regular attendee – along with his jester, who would insult the locals and praise his master.

The course became a steeplechase track in 1898.

150 FAIR ENOUGH Louisiana, USA

In 1852, Union Race Course, which became the site of Fair Grounds, was laid out on Gentilly Road, thus making it the oldest site of racing in America still in operation.

On April 13, 1872 the inaugural day's racing of the Louisiana Jockey Club at Fair Grounds took place. Frogtown, owned by the legendary General George Custer, ran second in a pair of two-mile heats to T.G. Moore's filly Hollywood and Grand Duke Alexis of Russia attended the races.

In 1893, Pat Garrett – infamous as 'the man who killed Billy the Kid' – raced a stable of horses at Fair Grounds, Louisiana, as the track held its first 100-day meeting.

In 1896 a new starting device perfected by H.H. Brown was tried out. Elastic netting about two feet wide and suspended on uprights on both sides of the track formed a barrier across the track about level with the jockeys' eyes. When the horses were properly lined up, the starter would pull a lever which operated springs, causing the net to fly up.

In 1898, a jockey named Coombs was indefinitely suspended for carrying out pistol practice in the jockeys' room!

More 'wild west' connections at the track in 1902 as Frank James, brother of Jesse, was appointed betting commissioner for Samuel Hildreth, owner of the largest racing stable at the track.

When betting on horses was outlawed in Missouri, in 1907, the grandstand from Union Park racetrack in St. Louis was dismantled, shipped to Fair Grounds, and reassembled. On the morning of December 28, 1918, Fair Grounds' grandstand burned to the ground. Three days after the fire, workmen had a temporary facility ready for the 54-day meeting starting on January 1. Later in the year, a permanent grandstand, which is the re-assembly of the grandstand from defunct City Park racetrack, was erected.

A seven-alarm fire completely destroyed the grandstand on the night of December 17, 1993. With a round-the-clock effort for 19 days, Fair Grounds erected temporary facilities and conducted racing for its remaining 60 days.

Hurricane Katrina struck New Orleans on August 29, 2005, flooding most of Fair Grounds' property and tearing the roof off of the grandstand/clubhouse. Fair Grounds officials, working with state regulators, shortened the 2005-06 season to 37 days and transferred the meet to Louisiana Downs, marking the first winter without racing in New Orleans in 91 years. Fair Grounds was partially rebuilt in time to host the New Orleans Jazz and Heritage Festival in late April, 2006.

Racing Post writer Nick Godfrey, a racing globe-trotter, visited the course in March 2010 when superstar filly Rachel Alexandra was surprisingly beaten on her seasonal debut, and said of the crowd: 'the prevailing outlook is perhaps best summed up by the beer-swigging gent whose top bears the legend: "If my music is too loud, you're too old"'.

151 FAKEN' IT Fakenham

Fakenham hosted a modern-day rarity when Huntress Grace ran in TWO hurdle races there on the same day in May 1983.

She was pulled up in both, but five years later, on the same date – May 30 – Silver Snow did the same thing there, winning once and finishing third.

Paul McCartney was refused permission to land his helicopter at Fakenham racecourse by its chief executive. David Hunter had been contacted by the former Beatle's helicopter company asking for permission for Sir Paul to land there in Autumn 2007 – his late wife Linda's food factory is in the area.

But Hunter was having none of it: 'The company would not tell me who their client was, but putting two and two together, I said 'if it's Paul McCartney tell him he's not welcome at Fakenham because of his views on hunting.'

★

Fakenham racecourse gave Tony McCoy an interesting gift in March 2009, to mark his recent achievement of notching his 3,000th winner – an apple tree.

In February, 2010, the Norfolk course witnessed one of racing's most emotional moments when amateur jockey and army lieutenant Guy Disney, who lost much of his right leg in Afghanistan during the previous year, finished second in a charity race on his return to the saddle, riding Oshkosh. Asked whether he intended to ride in more 'serious' races, Disney deadpanned, 'I will have to take it one step at a time – or one hop at a time.'

The course was threatened with closure in the late 1960s – appearing on a list which included now-defunct tracks such as Bogside, Buckfastleigh, Lewes, Lincoln and Woore Hunt. 'At that time Fakenham staged only four fixtures and our facilities not only lacked stabling and a hostel for stable staff, but also there were no refreshment rooms of any sort, and the public cloakrooms were of the most primitive variety,' recalled former clerk of the course Pat Firth. 'Almost worse, one part of the track crossed a meadow owned by a neighbouring farmer, who was under no obligation to remove his cattle until the morning of a race meeting.'

152 FFOS FFAS LOS LAS? Wales

Britain's newest track, Ffos Las in Wales, opened for business in June, 2009 – not everyone had got the hang of its name. Dear old Tommo [Derek Thompson] called it both 'Ffas Los' and 'Los Ffas'. Sir Peter O'Sullevan 'officially' declared the track open at its third meeting, which took place on August 28, 2009 when Tony McCoy rode a treble.

In February 2010, former jump jockey Luke Harvey decided to use the course to put in some training for his up-coming London Marathon charity run – and duly completed six laps of the track, 150 miles from his Lambourn home, clocking up some seven and a half miles in so doing in the pouring rain. Completing the stint he returned to discover that he faced driving home – half naked. 'I'm soaked to the skin and my girlfriend, Emily Jones, forgot to pack any spare clothes, including my pants and socks.'

In February 2011, just as the course prepared for its first live Channel 4 coverage via the William Hill Welsh Champion Hurdle, *Racing Post* reader Gareth Hughes from Gwynedd, irritated by what he believed to be the regular abuse of the track's name, wrote to the paper, pointing out – 'now might be the opportune time to remind the team that Ffos rhymes with "pause", and Las is slightly elongated to "Laas". As a parting shot, he couldn't resist adding, 'they do not race horses at "Banger-on-Dee", but they do at "Ban-gore-on-Dee".

By the way if you do visit Ffos Las (it means Blue Ditch, apparently), don't ask the locals where the town of that name is – there isn't one, the name is taken from the farm which used to exist on the site.

153 DREAD HEAT? Barbados

The racetrack in Barbados is at Garrison Savannah which is less than two miles outside the capital Bridgetown. It has been the home of horseracing on the island since the colonial days of 1845. The officers of the British Regiment who were stationed in Barbados used what was then the parade ground to match their horses in races, and the wealthy merchants and planters later joined them.

Jockeys at the Garrison Savannah track in Barbados were the stars of an entertaining TV series broadcast on BBC4 in March 2010, in which dreadlocked jockey J Crawford was shown 'blessing' all the riders with a communal prayer for their safety, prior to the off of the first race.

154 OIL HAVE TO GET BACK TO YOU ON THAT ONE Gold Coast, Australia

I went racing at the Australian Gold Coast Turf Club meeting run on January 16, 2010 and spotted the following announcement in the raceday programme – of which I could make neither head nor tail.

'On Track Thoroughbreds kindly supply the 'Good Oil' free of charge to our patrons.

Please note the GCTC and On Track Thoroughbreds are separate entities. Any enquiries concerning the 'Good Oil' are to be directed to On Track Thoroughbreds.'

No, me neither! Eventually, I became so curious that I contacted the track again – and discovered that the Good Oil is, in fact, a tipping service! Those Aussies – doncha just love 'em – if only they spoke the same language as us.

155 DOUBLING UP IN NO-RUNNER RACE' Stafford Cross

Quick thinking trainer Richard Barber was legging his grandson up to ride Cappoquin at a May 2011 Stafford Cross point to point meeting race when he heard that no runners had been entered for the next race.

Barbour grabbed a official and entered Cappoquin with seconds to spare.

Cappoquin duly won under Jack Barber, was washed down, given a drink, then went off to walk over for the £500 prize money, and more importantly, another winner for title chasing jockey Will Biddick who went on to complete a treble which but for Barbour would have been a double.

156 RACING DOWN THE TOILET Newmarket

Sarah Jarvis, manager at the National Horseracing Museum gift shop in Newmarket, was flushed with success after her idea for toilet seats bearing racing colours was introduced in time for Christmas 2007, with a bog-standard design selling for £98 and custom-made ones for £135. Surely, seats bearing the images of certain racing 'characters' might prove even more popular!

Racing Post writer David Ashforth achieved a unique honour when Market Rasen named its new toilet suite in their Brocklesby Suite after him in

November 2007 – having been inspired to do so by Ashforth's tour of all 87 racecourses in Britain and Ireland after which he identified the Lincoln track's facilities as the 'best racecourse toilets'.

156 THE WIRE (1) Pimlico, USA

How often has a racecourse been built just so that a specific race could be run? During the course of a dinner party in Saratoga, New York, Maryland's Oden Bowie presented a proposal to prominent racing figures. In order to observe the evening, they decided to run a race in two years, for horses that were yearlings at the time. The victor would host a dinner party for the losers (subsequently to become known as the Dinner Party Stakes meet).

Governor Bowie vowed he would construct a model racetrack in Maryland if the race were to be held in Baltimore. And in 1868, the Maryland Jockey Club bought the land and constructed the racetrack Pimlico.

Pimlico Race Course formally opened on 25 October 1870, making it the second oldest racetrack in the USA to Saratoga. The spelling 'Pemblicoe' appeared on the original settlement agreement which was awarded to a group of English pioneers in 1669; the settlers originally came from London, and reminisced about a local hostelry, 'Olde Ben Pimlico's Tavern' or, one suspects, possibly 'Olde Ben's Pimlico Tavern'! Whichever, the name 'Pimlico' was adopted.

It is said that the term 'wire' was coined here – legend has it that at the 1870 meeting a cord was tied across the track, from which hung a bag wired to that cord, in which was the prize money for each race. The winning jockey would reach up to retrieve the cash after passing the wire in front.

Pimlico is home to the prestigious $1million Preakness Stakes, so named in 1873 in honor of the colt Preakness, which won the first running of the Dinner Party Stakes.

The track could fill a book of stories about it. Just ask Peter Hermann, of The Baltimore Sun, who reeled off just a few of them in a 2010 article:
'Preakness 2006, when Barbaro, fancied to win the Triple Crown, collapsed in the first furlong with a fractured leg, prompting a police-escorted caravan up Interstate 95 to a veterinary hospital in Pennsylvania.

Preakness 2002, when Baltimore police officers removed badges and nameplates and were caught on video hitting a spectator with a baton during a melee in the raucous infield, embarrassing the department when it was aired nationally on television.

Preakness 1999, when drunken 22-year-old Lee Chang Ferrell scaled an infield fence, stood in front of eight charging horses during the Maryland Breeders' Cup Handicap, and swung at the favourite, Artax. Ferrell told police he was trying to commit suicide when he slipped by security and got onto the track. He assumed a boxing stance and swung as horses thundered by him, missing Artax but hitting jockey Jorge Chavez, who had to veer out of the way, hitting another horse. Artax lost, and Pimlico had to refund the $1.4 million wagered on him. Ferrell was sent for psychiatric testing, and later declared he was "committed to sobriety". Artax suffered few ill effects, going on to win the Breeders' Cup Sprint and earning $1.6 million.

Preakness 1998, when a power failure and an electrical fire plunged the track into darkness, shut down betting windows and cost the already cash-strapped track $2.5 million in wagers, a third of the typical take.

The course also survived the Running of the Urinals a few years ago — in which inebriated young men and women ran across the top of portable toilets as others threw full beer cans and bottles and other stuff at them. It became an Internet sensation.'

157 THE WIRE (2) Worcester

The conditions for jump meetings at Worcester before the First World War contained this interesting exclusion clause – 'The races are not, without the consent of the Committee, open to any farmer who has wire on his land which, in their opinion, interferes with the Sport of Foxhunting. Nor, subject to the Committee's discretion will any farmer who has such wire on his land, be allowed to ride in any of the above races – or be invited to the lunch!'

In August 2010, Worcester revived the Land O'Plums Handicap Chase, first run in 1899 at Pershore – as part of a month-long Pershore plum festival, with the track offering 'plum sampling opportunities'.

158 TRIPLE CREEK Stony Creek, Australia

Ninety-three years after the course opened for business in 1894, Stony Creek entered Australian racing folklore when its Rod Carmichael Handicap on January 23, 1987, produced a triple dead-heat, with Fast Seal, Chesterfield and Mr Spectre flashing past the post inseparably as race-caller Peter Eustace gasped accurately: 'I can't split these.'

Amidst the confusion of the decision, then only the third of its type in Aussie racing history since cameras were introduced (the first was at Flemington on November 3, 1956), club chairman Alan Bell turned to local racing stalwart Colin Carmichael – whose family had sponsored the race, and asked : 'What do we do now?'

'I don't know what you have to do,' replied Carmichael. 'But I've got to find two more trophies.'

The Stony Creek Racing Club logo now reflects the triple dead-heat.

159 SIR MARK, THE HOODY! Brighton

Sir Mark Prescott, lover of cigars, coursing and bull-fighting, has probably never been accused of being a hoodie, but he came pretty close at Brighton in June 2010 when he helped his runner Sumerian to win a maiden race, the horse clad in a double-headed hood which had many racegoers literally doing a double take.

Prescott, who had once invented a stalls blanket based on a 'picador's accoutrement', came up with the unique hood in an effort to help the filly overcome her stalls phobia.

She went down to the start wearing two hoods; the top one, with Velcro straps on it, had a blind added in the stalls to calm her down, but was then whipped off as the stalls opened.

'I had to make a few calls to the BHA to get the point across and get permission, but the rule doesn't say I can't run in six hoods if I want to,' said Sir Mark after the race.

★

Prior to July 13, 2010 Brighton 'appointed a seagull scarer,' according to the *Racing Post*, after a flock of seagulls had been blamed for a winner at a recent meeting, Celestial Girl, veering across the track in the process. The seagull scarer obviously carried out his task impeccably as Celestial Girl duly obliged again – without veering.

160 BATH TIME Bath

Presumably many racegoers come to Bath to get high – literally. Located on Lansdown Hill, it is the highest racecourse in the land – 780 feet above sea level according to John Tyrrel's *Racecourses On The Flat*; or perhaps 800 feet above sea level – according to 1971's *British Racing and Racecourses*.

The course gave commentator Richard Hoiles the opportunity to make one of the corniest puns on record during a race here in July 2007 when he announced 'Little Knickers on thong today' as that oddly named runner panted home.

161 HAY, JO, MARRY ME! Haydock

In July 2010, racegoer Andy Mills utilised the air above the track at Haydock Park to make a unique proposal to his girlfriend, when he arranged for a small plane to fly overhead, carrying behind it the message: 'Will you marry me Joanne?'

Joanne said yes.

162 PUNCHING ABOVE ITS WEIGHT Slovakia

In June 1994 Paul Kallai, a 60-year-old former professional boxer in Germany, rode the winners of four of the most valuable races on the card at Bratislava, Slovakia – all trained by Tibor Farkas.

You might want to consider whether you'd like to visit the Petrzalka track when you read what website www.bratislavastags.com says about the racing experience there: 'With beers included and a guide to advise on the Slovak betting system, you can't go wrong.'

163 RACING IN ANTARCTICA! Antarctica

Scott Base has been New Zealand's permanent base in Antarctica since 1959. The Base provides services and accommodation for the many research parties and groups who visit Antarctica during the summer. The Base is located on Ross Island in the Ross Sea region of Antarctica, 3,932 km (2,114 nautical miles) from Christchurch, New Zealand and 1,500 km from the South Pole. The closest neighbour to Scott Base is the American base McMurdo Station, a 3km walk over the hill.

In May 2006, a horseracing evening was organised at Scott Base – there may have been no horses there, but those taking part dressed up as jockeys.

'Sarah', one of those working at the Base, reported on the evening in her 'Antarctic Conservation' blog:

'A group of us acted as jockeys, rolling die to determine which horse moved and how far. The jockeys all dressed up in what they deemed acceptable jockey outfits, mine was a fairly standard set of jodhpurs and matching cap. The most bizarre was a Viking wearing a propeller! The crowd also came dressed in their finery for the outing. Nicola looked striking in an orange skirt and red top, dripping with beads and a pink boa. Suave Ainslie wore a fine gull-grey suit, with a sunflower in his pocket, and a boater hat.

'A spectacular grandstand, including a corporate box, was erected along one side of the canteen, complete with bunting and race flags. Donna served 'hot chups' and battered sausages from a tray suspended from her neck. The bar and the totalisers did a roaring trade. The whole night was full of excitement and laughter, with all money raised going to the Child Cancer Fund.'

164 ROO MUST BE JOKING
Hanging Rock, Australia

The 500 racegoers who turned up for the Australia Day meeting at the tiny Hanging Rock course in January 2011 were anticipating a great day's sport – which is what they got, even though they ended up seeing no horseracing at all. But they did get to watch the fruitless efforts of course officials to keep the course clear of kangaroos.

A troop of 'roos invaded the track before the first race could get underway, but efforts to chase them away were foiled by what appeared almost to be a pre-planned tactic', as Racing Victoria steward Peter Ryan explained: 'Three separate waves of kangaroos came on to the course and left me with no choice but to terminate the seven-race card due to safety concerns.'

The course had previous run-ins with the local kangaroos and constructed a large fence to foil them, but the animals outflanked the defences, firstly appearing around the back of the track to sneak in – and then jumping a smaller fence. At one point to raucous cheers from the crowd a 'roo ran a finish down the home straight!

Few racecourses can boast as mystical and atmospheric a backdrop as the volcanic Mount Diogenes, also known as Hanging Rock, immortalised in the haunting 1967 book by Joan Lindsay, and 1975 movie, *Picnic at Hanging Rock*. There has been a racetrack here, close to the towns of Mount Macedon and Woodend in Victoria, since New Year's Day 1878.

In January 2009, the Australia Day (January 26) meeting, due to be attended by thousands, had to be switched – as it also had in 2007 – to nearby Kyneton after an on-going drought affected the supply of water to the course. During that year the official stewards' report for one race read: 'The start of this race was delayed due to several kangaroos being ushered off the course proper.' A hint as to what would happen two years later!

165 LUCKY MILLION DREAM FOR 50P FRED
Yorskhire

The punter who became Britain's first betting shop millionaire by winning £1million for a 50p stake from William Hill found eight winners – starting with Isn't That Lucky and finishing with A Dream Come True!

Fred Craggs, who lives just outside Thirsk, celebrated his 60th birthday on the day in February 2008 he discovered that he had landed the biggest ever betting shop accumulator bet, beating odds of 2,000,000-1. He selected eight horses and duly placed his 50p bet, which required all eight to win to entitle him to a payout.

They all won. But Fred had no idea that they had until he visited another shop nearby, and was told that the betting slip he thought was worthless had actually made him a millionaire.

In March 2011, Steve Whiteley, in his fifties, used his free bus pass to get to Exeter racecourse where he obtained free entry from a local promotion, then staked a whole £2 on the Tote Jackpot, found all six winners, and won

£1.45m, the biggest payout in the bet's history. Asked by reporters what he did for a living he told them, 'I am – sorry, was – a heating engineer.'

166 SAVAGE BLOW Newbury

It isn't that frequent an entry in the form book: 'Upsides when tried to savage winner close home, just failed.'

But that was the *Racing Post* comment on 33-1-shot Sir Gerry, ridden by George Baker, runner-up in the Dubai Duty Free Cup at Newbury in September 2010 behind 3-1 winner Delegator, partnered by Ted Durcan – who had actually won on Sir Gerry at Meydan in Dubai during the previous winter.

A relieved Durcan, whose leg was apparently Sir Gerry's target when he lunged at him, joked that he must have done something wrong to the horse when he rode him.

167 WELL DONE Punchestown

Owner Mrs W. P. Cullen was looking forward to her runner at the big Punchestown meeting in April 1892 – until she had a dream that the horse's rider, Willie Beasley, was killed during the race.

Mrs Cullen duly withdrew her horse from the race, but Beasley was made of sterner stuff and managed to get himself another ride – only to fall at the 'Herds Garden' Bank. He never fully recovered consciousness, and died a couple of weeks later.

The horse he rode was named All Is Well.

168 DUNWOODY'S WHIP ROUND Newmarket

Richard Dunwoody walked 1,000 miles in 1,000 hours in Newmarket during May and June 2009, raising money for racing charities in the process by emulating the feat first achieved in 1809 by one Captain Barclay.

In his 2009 book, *Method in my Madness*, Dunwoody recalled that Barclay's most difficult times had come whilst walking through the night and that his manservant had had to beat him with a walking stick to keep him awake.

Dunwoody described how 'to recreate this authentically', actress Rachel Grant, who starred in James Bond movie *Die Another Day* as Bond Girl 'Peaceful Fountains of Desire', 'gave me a gentle whipping with her riding crop. Another inestimable advantage for me.'

169 DUEL PURPOSE Kentucky, USA

What a shame that the United States' sole turf-only track, opened in 1990, decided not to stick with its given name of Dueling Grounds – in homage to legendary 19th-century pistol duels which took place thereabouts.

The name lasted until 1996 when it became the rather less dashing Kentucky Downs, boasting that it is 'America's only European-style Racecourse'.

170 MINE, ALL MINE! Australia

Brett Kitching, the General Manager of Ipswich Turf Club, gave me the lowdown on racing at Bundamba in Australia:

'We have a meeting which is in the top 20 of the year in Australia. This meeting is the Ipswich Cup, run mid-June each year since 1935 at Bundamba where we have raced since 1890.

The quirkiness of our track is twofold. Firstly we are beside a small Creek that we irrigate from. However, in our part of the world we have some major flooding rains. In 1893 and in 1974 these rains were enough to not only put the 40-acre course under water, but ten foot under water – this included the offices, stewards' room, jockeys' room, and main bar. Also, an old rubbish dump was uncovered on the track as the flood washed the track away.

Secondly, our suburb Bundamba is an Aboriginal word for place of coal and the nearby suburb is Blackstone – indicating obviously that the region was once full of coal near to the surface underground. Coalminers of English, Welsh and Scottish origin heavily mined the area in the late 19th century and for most of the 20th century through underground mines. Geological studies show up to five levels of mines beneath the racecourse itself. In the latter half of the 20th century a collapsed shaft resulted in a dip in the back straight which caused the horses to run out of view.'

171 WORMS HALT RACING Chepstow

Racing at Chepstow was abandoned in August 2010 because of an outbreak of microscopic, parasitic worms known as root gall or root knot nematodes, which cause soil instability. 'They sit dormant in imported substances such as divot repair mixture,' explained clerk of the course Keith Ottesen.

172 MAINTAINING STAND-ARDS New Zealand

Ascot Park racecourse in Invercargill, New Zealand is home to Southland Racing Club and hosts five meetings a year. Wairio Jockey Club also stages an annual meeting here. Invercargill is within easy travelling distance of some beautiful scenery in the Catlins, Fiordland and Stewart Island.

Southland Racing Club's new grandstand was unveiled with a fanfare in 1894 – only for great embarrassment to kick in once it became clear that the roof was too low as patrons towards the back were unable to see anything of the action. The stand had to be rebuilt – at the architect's expense. Can't imagine that sort of thing happening at the English Ascot, can you?!

Another New Zealand course had similar problems to the Ascots – it was Wanganui, where in March 1876 the bright, shiny new grandstand was unveiled with great pomp and ceremony – until, as Laraine Sole's official history of the course revealed, 'it turned out to be too close to the track and subsequently it was moved back and enlarged.'

173 HARRYING THE MAN WHO 'RUINED MY LIFE' Doncaster

Disgruntled mega-punter Harry Findlay, the former owner of top chaser Denman, was not best pleased when he was warned off for six months by the BHA for laying his own horse Gullible Gordon to lose – and he held on to the grudge despite that punishment subsequently being reduced on appeal to a £4,500 fine.

And racegoers watched, astonished, as he launched an amazing personal attack on BHA chief executive Nic Coward at Doncaster races in September 2010, confronting him for several minutes, with, reportedly, raised voice and wagging finger, and demanding his resignation, along with his chairman, Paul Roy, whom he reportedly called 'a bully and a thug', and accusing Coward of 'ruining my life.'

Findlay's haranguing of Coward provoked very little response, and he then fumed to the media: 'I don't care if I never own another racehorse in my life. All I want is my respect back. You can call me a big-mouth, call me a loud-mouth, call me fat, but don't call me a liar – I haven't lied for 27 years.'

The case against Findlay hinged on Findlay's assertion that he had special dispensation to lay horses, denied by Roy – 'The BHA never gave permission to Harry Findlay to lay horses in yards where he had horses in training.'

Findlay subsequently disposed of his British-based horses.

174 SMILES ALMOST TURNED TO FROWNS
Uttoxeter

When Eastwell Smiles got loose shortly before the start of a handicap hurdle at Uttoxeter in September 2010 the six-year-old galloped straight into a nearby brook – and was only saved by the quick thinking of 19-year-old Ruth Bailey, a member of the course's 'treading-in' team, who jumped in to hold the horse's head above the water.

The horse was eventually pulled out by vets, fire brigade and other racecourse staff.

Trainer Richard Phillips said of the horse, 'He's a bit of a fruitcake.' More of a sponge, I'd have thought!

175 A SHOE-IN? Fontwell

When four-year-old La Belle Au Bois won first time out at Fontwell in September 2010, owner Howard Spooner reckoned the 14-1 shot was a shoe-in, claiming that the horse had won wearing revolutionary new horseshoes.

'La Belle Au Bois was the first horse to race wearing 'lightening' plates, a lightweight shoe made from a secret mix of metals that I reckon gives her a three and a half-length advantage over a mile,' said the owner. The horse finished 4th, 18th and 6th in her next three runs, beaten by a total of 220 lengths.

176 LEGENDARY LOMITAS Germany

Possibly the best racehorse and stallion to emerge from Germany, Lomitas, born in 1988, a chestnut son of Niniski, was put down aged 22 at the end of August 2010 after a life whose twists and turns Dick Francis and John Francome together would have been hard put to invent.

Lomitas overcame a rare phobia of starting stalls on his way to stardom. He had been Germany's champion juvenile colt in 1990, starting favourite for the following season's German 2,000 Guineas.

But at Cologne he refused point-blank to enter the stalls, injuring other horses and humans, and throwing himself to the ground during the protracted effort by stalls handlers to load him up.

His obstinacy – believed to be connected to claustrophobia – resulted in a ban from racing and it took horse whisperer Monty Roberts to exorcise his demons, eventually enabling him to enter the stalls again.

Trained by Andreas Wohler, he went on to win three Group 1 races – the Grosser Preis der Berliner Bank, the Grosser Preis von Baden and the Europa-Preis – on the way to being rated the third best three-year-old in Europe of 1991, inferior only to Generous and Suave Dancer. He also finished runner-up in the Deutsches Derby.

More drama came at four when Fährhof Stud owner Walther Jacobs received threats that Lomitas would be killed or harmed if a demand for money was not met.

After winning the Gerling-Preis and Hansa-Preis that year the horse was believed to have been poisoned after disappointing as the hot favourite in a Dusseldorf Group 1.

Lomitas had to be secretly removed from Germany, in a clandestine operation, to the Newmarket yard of Susan Piggott where he was given a new identity and renamed Pirelli, exercising pre-dawn in an effort to avoid detection.

He was later transferred to California, where he raced on despite suffering hoof problems from the poisoning. Trained by Ron McAnally, Lomitas was placed in 1993 in the Graded Bowling Green and Shoemaker Handicaps.

Lomitas was retired in 1994 with ten wins from 19 starts and earnings of $918,656. He was returned to Germany for stallion duty.

Sheikh Mohammed acquired a share in Lomitas and the horse stood at Darley's Dalham Hall Stud in Newmarket for five seasons between 2002 and 2006.

Lomitas then returned to Fährhof in 2007.

His progeny included globe-trotter Silvano, winner of the Arlington Million and Audemars Piguet Queen Elizabeth II Cup, German 2,000 Guineas scorer Sumitas and Deutsches Derby hero Belenus.

His best offspring from his spell standing in Britain were the useful Championship Point and Veracity, and Prix de l'Opera winner Shalanaya.

177 STARTER GIVEN SOME STICK South Africa

In 1915 Johannesburg Turf Club starter E A Halliwell was rebuked by the stewards for the way in which he was starting races, which involved 'an unacceptable amount of shouting by him as well as the employment by his assistants of whips and sticks.'

178 GOONER GO THERE ONE DAY
Gooniwindi, Australia

If we and the Americans are nations divided by a single language, then what does that make us and the Aussies, I wonder!

I've been racing in Australia, at Randwick in Sydney, Flemington where they run the Melbourne Cup and at the Gold Coast Turf Club. Those are terrific tracks.

But just take a look at this description, by an Aussie correspondent of mine called Phil Percival, of a tiny racetrack which blossoms once a year in honour of the local medical service; and the career of a horse which sounds like a kind of Seabiscuit mixed with Red Rum and Desert Orchid (complete with original grammer, spelling and punctuation – or lack thereof!) who was active in the early 1970s and raced at a track which, provided I am not being 'put away', has one of the most bizarre names I've come across:

'Hello from aussie. I received your email here in the little town of Goondiwindi in a roundabout way.

Birdsville, a tiny town on the edge of the desert, has 1 race meeting a year in aid of the Flying Doctor service which flies to cattle stations thousands of square metres in size to look after the pioneers of the outback. The town has a handfull of people but the weekend of the races around 2 to 3 thousand people arrive in 4 wheel drives across the desert.buses and planes which land beside the famous pub. Its back in time several decades. Boxing tents with blokes like the lizard man taking on the ringers over 4 rounds ,then theres the rodeo tent where aussie roughriders try to stay on for 10 secs on broncos mustered a few days before from the wild brumby mobs of the territory.

Another little town of 4 houses stages a race meeting on easter saturday . even though the boys drive around the track before the first there is plenty of scrub and i have witnessed when they jumped (off) a mob of kangaroos led the field to the first turn. the roos jumped the outside fence in a stride and left the rest of the race to the horses.

3 mates bought a grey colt for $1300 dollars because he had a bung leg to try and win a mug race at goondiwindi. the horse became an idol of the australian turf winning all the big races and in todays money about 7 million in stakes. he took his owners to all the big racing carnivals in the nation and was idolised by the australian people not only racegoers. he was such a character bred to win a mug race ,but would never give in and would try so hard for you he would mostly win under huge weights. he would do anything to win for you but off the track was a real softie. loved people. would stand to attention whenever the crowd clapped and took photos holding up the parade.after the race he would come back lathered in sweat stand at the gate ,look up to his people in the stands and when they clapped him he would lift up one leg and bow. even if he got beaten he would try and shoulder the winner out of the no 1 stall.

he loved children. when he finished racing he came to gdi and despite being a 5-year-old stallion stood for 2 days while children patted and stuck their fingers in his ears and up his nose.

I have a photo of him standing in his stallion stall at stud with 2 little tiny girls sitting on his back playing with his mane. a western singer wrote a song about him and it made the hit parade. You had to live in that era to understand just how the australian public adored him.'

The grey horse was called Gunsynd (1967-83: won 29 races worth Aus$280,455, including Cox Plate; 3rd in Melbourne Park; only animal named in 2004 Queensland Icons' List.) and I'd love to have seen him race. Doesn't that just make you want to jump on a plane and get out there to go racing – and maybe enjoying the odd drink – with those characters!

179 DASHING DISPLAY Falkland Islands

The Governor's Cup is the major prize contested at the biennial race meeting near Goose Green, a small Falkland Islands settlement, which was won in February 2010 by Dashing Dancer in front of a crowd estimated at up to 300 people. Dashing Dancer was reportedly sired by Nijinsky.

Eye-witness to the 2010 meeting, Martin Fletcher of *The Times*, reported that 'jockeys as young as 15 and as old as 67' contested 'more than 50 races over two days. Many ride in jeans and use heavy old gaucho saddles with sheep fleeces underneath.' The horses are unshod, he wrote.

In 1991 Sir Michael Oswald, then managing the Queen's stud, visited the island and arranged with Sheikh Maktoum bin Rashid al Maktoum, the Emir of Dubai, to send the islanders three-year-old stallion Thyer, who once cost $1.8m, and who had been stabled with Jim Bolger in Ireland.

The horse was offered on condition that the islanders should pay for the horse's transportation – which cost them £8,000 and took a month.

In the 17 years to 2010 he had sired over 100 offspring on the island, at a covering 'fee' of around £175.

Of the first six races at Goose Green in 2010, Thyer's direct offspring won four – a grandson winning a fifth.

180 VIRTUALLY IDIOTIC Cyberspace

I sat chatting to a friend about betting shops celebrating their 50th anniversary in May, 2011 – 'I like 'em' he said. 'I enjoy betting in 'em. I particularly like that vertical betting you have in your shops'.

'Vertical betting?' I asked. 'What, betting standing up?'

'No' he said, 'Vertical betting – you know – them cartoon horses you have.'

Oh yes, Charlie, of course, it is virtually vertical betting.

In his book, *Gambling*, former England cricket captain Mike Atherton tells a story against himself, about asking a group of punters their views on virtual racing – Atherton wonders why they bet on it when 'It's just pure chance'. He's told 'So are the horses. Odds-on shots get turned over all the time in real racing, it's still a lottery.'

'How do you choose your horse?' asked Atherton.

'Just a lucky number or a name we like,' he is told by punter Deon, whose mate joins the group – 'The horses have form,' he says and everyone nods.

'The races have stadiums,' he says, and everyone nods.

'They even have jockeys who are ferried to the races in helicopters.'

'As I'm taking notes there's a silence,' writes the former England skipper, 'I look up and the whole crowd explode with laughter, pointing at me.'

A couple of years ago, a William Hill telephone punter called up and asked when the next race was due 'off'. He was told that it would be the next race at Steepledowns in five minutes' time. 'And what price is the favourite?' he asked, going on to stake £25,000 on the 7-4 shot, which duly obliged.

It was unclear whether he knew that Steepledowns was a virtual racecourse – but his bet was a real enough winner.

I was in a Ladbrokes shop recently and enjoyed watching people having a flutter on the racing from subtly named Lucksin Downs. And in 2008 a prankster put a notice up in a West Midlands betting shop, informing patrons that: 'We're organizing a trip to Steepledowns. Anybody interested please put your name down'. And yes, some names had been appended.

Bath punter Duncan MacPail claimed in an August 2010 letter to the *Racing Post* that he had 'been in a shop where the "weighed in" cry came from a virtual track!' And in the same month, *Post* columnist Steve Dennis insisted 'I was in my local betting shop last weekend when one "punter" had a bet on the virtual racing. He justified his decision to the woman he was with by saying that his selection "had been in really good form".'

Dennis then asked, perhaps rhetorically, 'why should that punter be regarded as anything other than an idiot?'

181 WARNED OFF ... AGAIN York

When Dirar won the 2010 Ebor at York not everyone involved in racing was delighted for Marcus Reeder, the co-owner of the Jamie Spencer-ridden winner.

For Reeder, one of three owners, was banned in 2006 for laying one of his own horses through Betfair – and again in 2008 when he was deemed to have been part of a conspiracy to profit from the laying of horses.

Reeder was banned for a year for the first offence, when he profited to the tune of £5,610, and second time round for eighteen months when he reportedly profited by £4,683.

Guardian racing writer Chris Cook wrote that Reeder had sought permission to re-register as an owner after his second offence, and it seems he was accepted as an owner by Horse Racing Ireland – 'it might be expected that he would be denied a third chance to shame the sport but, depressingly, he was recently given a favourable answer.'

However, Cook's stablemate Lydia Hislop reported that the BHA intended to object to his application to rejoin British ownership ranks. Said Reeder, asked to comment on the situation: 'It would be silly to spoil a good day.'

Quite.

182 COULDN'T GIVE IT AWAY Wexford

Bookmaker Franco Hughes made the offer of a lifetime to punters at Ireland's Wexford point-to-point race meeting in late November 2009 – bets for nothing.

And was he knocked over in the rush?

Not exactly – 'Sunday was one dreadful day what with the cold and rain and total lack of interest from punters – I actually shouted out 'free bets' and, do you know what, not one person took me up – not one person even turned their head!'

The Sea Washed Place is the translation of Wexford's Gaelic name, Loch Garman.

183 'KINI YOU BELIEVE IT? Warwick

I'm not exactly sure whether the dress code of the course permitted it, and it was an unseasonably cold February 2010 day at Warwick when *Racing Post* reporter David Carr observed 'one intrepid punter who paraded through the betting ring dressed solely in a lime green mankini midway through the afternoon.'

History of a different kind was made here on March 10, 1919 when Wild Aster became the first and only horse to win three races at the age of 18.

184 ANTY POST? India

Racing was first staged in Calcutta, India, in 1769 – and, to combat the heat, meetings began as early as 8am. An advertisement for one January meeting from that era advised 'The Stewards present their compliments to the subscribers and advise them that breakfast with music will be provided in tents on the Course AFTER (my capitals) the racing.'

In 1880 – a few years after the grandstand received a major facelift, when it was discovered that the main beams had been eaten through by white ants – racing was switched permanently to the afternoon.

In 1890 the winner of a race was disqualified for carrying 4lb OVER weight, and in 1924 the three runners contesting a 1m 4f flat race were unfazed to be confronted by a set of hurdles left in place from the previous race. They all managed to negotiate the obstacle and a claim that the race should be voided as a result of the incident was dismissed.

In 1970 a huge riot broke out at the track when a hot favourite was beaten by an outsider. There was looting and arson, but an effort to steal the Tote takings was defied. Despite enormous damage the course was reopened a fortnight later.

185 DES-PERATE SITUATION Windsor

Riding at Windsor in 1976, pint-sized jockey Des Cullen, who stood 4ft 10ins tall, found himself facing a potential disaster that even he as an injury-prone rider had not anticipated.

As he and his equine partner challenged during the race, Cullen remembered: 'Instead of going straight on, the horse went left and straight through the rail as if it wasn't there, into the lake – and into the Thames. I couldn't swim, and could have drowned – but fortunately a guy on the track pulled me out.'

Cullen eventually retired in 1980 having suffered ten bouts of concussion amongst his injuries.

186 TAO MUCH?

Jockey and martial arts enthusiast Alan Munro is almost certainly the only member of the British racing community to have answered a question about his religion by stating, 'I'm not a Buddhist. I'm a Taoist' as he did in June 2008.

187 SCALED DOWN? Wincanton

A plaque was unveiled at Wincanton in January 2007 celebrating the fact that Andrew Thornton was the last jockey to weigh out on the course's mechanical scales before they were replaced by a new electronic version. The electronic ones then suffered a malfunction, and the mechanical scales were again pressed into use.

I wondered whether this might cause a plaque amendment and asked the course's commercial manager Pam Wills, who explained: 'The plaque in the weighing room won't be amended as Andrew Thornton was the last jockey to weigh out before the new scales were introduced. Even though there was a technical blip this is still the case.'

Weigh to go!

188 PUNTER ELTON?

Not really associated with racing and betting – although he did appear at the opening of Meydan racecourse – Elton John's album Songs From The West Coast contains a track called 'Emperor's New Clothes' which begins with the lyrics, 'Bet on our lives, and we bet on the horses.'

So maybe Mr Dwight does have a secret love of the sport – although his lyricist Bernie Taupin may just have been putting words into his mouth.

189

DIRTY DEED? Randwick, Sydney

Aussie racing magazine *Racetrack* told the story in 1995 of 'great rider of his time, and later an outstanding track assessor at Randwick, Mick Hayes' who had been expected to partner a well fancied runner, but instead, when the board went up indicating runners and riders, jockey A. Nugent was named as the horse's jockey.

Disappointed that Hayes was missing the mount, punters looked to place their cash elsewhere and the horse's price drifted rapidly out. However, with minutes to go before the off, a sudden rush of bets forced the price back down. Nugent rode well and duly won the race.

On their return to the winner's enclosure punters recognized Hayes as the jockey after all – and alerted course officials who duly quizzed him, only to be told that Hayes had changed his name by deed poll to A. Nugent – and he produced the relevant documents to prove it.

190

UNSUNG SINGH Mumbai, India

Hot favourite Mazan began to drift from 2-5 to 2-1 to the alarm of backers of the favourite at Mumbai in February 2010.

And when apprentice jockey Raju Singh kept the horse in the middle of the ten runners in the maiden sprint, before tamely subsiding to ninth without apparently making any significant effort to improve his position, he was never going to return to a hero's welcome.

In fact, he returned to a punch in the face from disgruntled owner Ashok Ranpise, a well known punter, while racegoers were in an angry mood.

A riot was brewing until the stewards intervened quickly to announce that they were withdrawing Singh's licence then and there – and also declared the race null and void.

Mazan's trainer S.S. Shah weighed in with a complaint that Singh had ignored instructions – but when the stewards tried to question the young rider he 'started crying' according to chairman Vivek Jain, who added, 'We have decided to file a case at the Tardeo police station.'

Singh was arrested, with subsequent reports suggesting he had attempted suicide, while an Indian racing blog later reported that he was 'dismissed from the sport, and has never been heard of since, dead or alive.'

191 MILES BETTER Redhill

Jockey Robert Miles, 26 at the time, was found guilty of assaulting a police officer during an incident in April 2007. He appeared at Redhill Magistrates Court in September of that year and was handed a 12-month community order and had to pay £100 compensation with £87 costs.

However, he was spared having to wear an electronic surveillance tag after claiming that he would then be unable to get his riding boots on which would, said his solicitor, 'deprive him of his occupation.'

192 TIGER FEAT Gowran Park, Ireland

In April 1999 the Aidan O'Brien-trained three-year-old Tchaikovsky was 4-7 favourite to win a race at Gowran Park.

He was cruising to victory only to swerve inexplicably and dramatically to the surprise of rider Mick Kinane during the final few yards.

Tchaikovsky still won by three lengths but spectators were baffled by the blip – until O'Brien revealed the reason – 'He was only shying away from the tiger'.

The trainer was not hallucinating. The race was sponsored by Esso, whose logo was a tiger – 'and some marketing genius had decided to put a giant, inflatable tiger the size of Montmartre just behind the finishing post' explained racing writer Brian O'Connor, who was there on the day. 'Not unreasonably, Tchaikovsky took one look at the thing and voted to take a swerve.'

Mind you, who knows what demons the tiger sparked in Tchaikovsky's mind – he never won again in four attempts.

193 APAULING INTERVIEW Kempton

Following on from AP McCoy's ground-breaking victory for racing by landing the 2010 BBC Sports Personality of the Year award, the sport began to take a slightly higher profile in parts of the media where it had rarely featured.

After the 2010 King George VI Chase at Kempton was twice postponed, leaving Kauto Star facing a wait for the rearranged date later in January to take his chance to set a new record of five consecutive wins in the race, Radio 5 Live decided they should interview Paul Nicholls.

Presenter Rachel Burden is a very knowledgeable rugby enthusiast but when she asked Kauto's trainer what he thought of all-weather tracks, given the fact that Kempton had twice had to postpone the meeting, it was a relief to hear Paul decide to be gentle with her and just give her a quick lesson on the surface used for jump racing.

She also asked whether the effect of AP's triumph would have worn off by the time the race was eventually run and wouldn't the delay in the King George affect Kauto's Cheltenham build-up.

With the running of the 2010 King George Chase at Kempton in doubt, sponsors William Hill had opened a book on whether it would take place on Boxing Day.

A telephone customer rang Hills' office and asked, 'I hear Kempton's even money to go ahead – you're the sponsors, so what are the chances?' The meeting, of course, was eventually postponed.

194 SYSTEM WORKING, SEND MORE MONEY! Cheltenham

Two punters came up with a cunning plan between them to guarantee a profit.

With the 1962 Cheltenham Festival about to kick off they decided to back each favourite to win a tenner and stop at a winner. There were to be eighteen races.

The punters, credit clients of Ladbrokes, began by staking (the pre-decimal equivalent of) £4.44 on Trelawney at 9-4 remembered Ron Pollard, who was the company's public relations man.

Trelawney lost, so they bet £28.88 on Scottish Memories at 1-2. It lost. Back then the Champion Hurdle took place on the second day.

'By the time of the race the pair had backed eight consecutive losers and had £257.52 on Another Flash at 11-10 to get back all their losses and post a profit of ten quid,' recalled Pollard.

No joy.

'By the first race on the Thursday they were laying out £1,703.48 to get back that elusive tenner.'

By the final race of the meeting they had to stake £5,000 on 9-4 chance Pegle in an effort to save the day and end up £10 ahead of the game.

They lost again. The system had ended up costing the pair £16,973.24.

195 KIN YOU BELIEVE IT? Bohemia

Aristocrat Count Oktavian Kinsky (born 1813) was largely responsible for introducing steeplechasing to his native Bohemia, the first such race taking place there in 1839, run over 1m4f, and four obstacles.

A confirmed eccentric and joker whose uncle once won a bet to ride naked for three hours by painting a uniform on his body, Kinsky welcomed visitors to his castle at Chlumec by supplying them with pillows full of frogs and once horrified a guest by leaving a toothbrush in his room only to later come in, pick it up and clean his buttocks with it. When the startled guest politely pointed out he'd believed the brush had been left for his use, Kinsky told him: 'This is my buttocks brush. I use it every morning. The toothbrush is in the drawer.'

An accomplished rider, Kinsky could, wrote an English journalist in 1872, 'vault on them when in the gallop' and 'stand on his head in the saddle'.

He died in 1896 and, on his deathbed, had his racehorses brought up the stairs of his castle to his bedroom so that he could bid them farewell.

196 ASHEN-FACED RACEGOERS Cheltenham

After England retained the Ashes with their victory in the Fourth Test against the Aussies in Melbourne at the end of 2010, officials at Cheltenham decided to test the patriotism of the defeated nation by offering free entry to Australians who produced their passports at the course's 2011 New Year's Day meeting – provided they were prepared to take the subsequent joshing!

197 ROYAL WHIP Austria

A riding whip belonging to Empress Elizabeth of Austria is kept in the headquarters of the Irish Turf Club.

The Empress, a keen horsewoman who learned to ride over hurdles without stirrups, was more than a platonic friend of leading Irish trainer Henry Linde, who twice won the Grand National – in 1880 with the not coincidentally named at all Empress – and was a dominant force at the major Punchestown meetings in the 1880s.

In 1898 the Empress was in Geneva to catch a steamboat on the lake when she was stabbed in the heart by an Italian anarchist wielding a stiletto knife. She reportedly managed to board the boat as though not badly hurt, but then collapsed and died.

★

Towcester racecourse owes its existence to the Empress, who in 1876 rented a property at Easton Neston so that she could hunt in the area. Whilst there she suggested that a race meeting should be held locally – and the first of them was duly run on Easter Monday that year.

198 THEY STARTED YOUNG Louisiana, USA

In the 1950s 'bush track' racing in Louisiana's Cajun country was a big social event, attracting large crowds and big betting. It had begun during the depression.

It was still going during the 1980s when top US jockey Kent Desormeaux's father, Harris, ran the Acadiana Downs track – 'The law didn't care about the bush tracks. There were no rules, no controls. It was exotic, a challenge, and a fantasy that I had to do, but it got old quick with the drinking, fighting and gambling.'

Jockeys wore no helmets or protective vests, and to keep their weight down they often rode in their underwear. The races were usually short sprints, often over 220 yards – or, even, just 12 yards! Their mounts were quarter horses. Floodlit racing took place – using car headlights.

In 1953 rider Glynn 'Tee Red' Bernis won on his debut. He weighed in at 32 pounds – well, he was five. He later explained his riding tactics in those days – 'You just held on and whipped.'

199 GETTING TO THE BOTTOM OF A HORSE
Cajun Downs, USA

Cajun jockey Ronnie Ebanks recalled a race in the late 1970s in which, aged 13, he rode a well backed horse at Cajun Downs in Abbeville in Louisiana for a senior official at the track.

'Right before the race, he told the groom to hold the horse,' Ebanks told Ed McNamara in the book *Cajun Racing*, 'and he took a pepper from the bottom of a bottle of vinegar. Then he bit off the edge of the pepper and stuck it up the horse's butt. When the gates opened, my horse flew and we won by two or three lengths.'

Amongst similar strokes pulled to win races at these tracks were smearing table salt all over a horse's rear end, which would start burning, and the rubbing on to horses' heads of a concoction called 'Jockey Club perfume', sold for 15 cents. It smelled so appalling no other horse would get close if the one in front had been daubed in it.

200 RANDY CHICKENED OUT Oaklawn Park, USA

US Hall of Fame jockey Randy Romero did a stint racing at the Cajun tracks. He was somewhat disconcerted to find that in one race his main opponent was not another jockey – but a chicken.

Some of the horses on the 'bush track' circuit were so 'ornery' that they would not tolerate a jockey on their back – so they would run riderless. The races were over very short trips so weight was not a factor and there was the option to run the horses riderless if connections felt that would give them a better chance.

In an effort to really get these horses to put their best foot forward, trainers would resort to unconventional methods, according to racing writer Ed McNamara, an expert on Cajun racing.

He reported that one trainer had come up with a wheeze to put rocks and stones into a beer can ('you wanted to put in only a few – not too many. Two would be good. If you put in more, it wouldn't rattle right,' said trainer Don Stemman) which was then attached to the horse's mane, the rattling noise startling the horse to run faster.

But Romero came up against a plan even more outrageous than that when a trainer tied a little bantam rooster to the mane. 'Man, my horse heard the chicken hollerin' and screamin' and flappin' his wings,' recalled the dumbfounded jockey. 'My horse was scared to death and wouldn't go past him.'

Yes, Randy and his horse literally chickened out.

Nicknamed the 'Ragin' Cajun', Romero suffered a near career-ending injury in 1983 at Oaklawn Park racetrack in Arkansas when he received major burns to two-thirds of his body from a freak fire that erupted while he was taking a sauna. He had rubbed himself down with alcohol and moved into the sauna in the jockeys' room. As he did he accidentally broke a live lightbulb that immediately ignited his entire body. After seven months of rehabilitation he returned to compete at the Fair Grounds Race Course in New Orleans where he won his third of four riding titles and set a track record with 181 wins.

201 WAS SECRETARIAT 'ANACHRONISTIC AND RACIST'? Hollywood Park, USA

Secretariat was one of the great American racehorses, his finest hour coming when he completed the first US Triple Crown for a quarter of a century by winning the 1973 Preakness Stakes, the Kentucky Derby and, by an astonishing 31 lengths, the Belmont Stakes. He died aged 19 and, so it is said, his heart was found to be two and a half times the average size.

Walt Disney produced the movie *Secretariat* in 2010 and, inevitably, took one or two liberties with the storylines involved, but the reaction from critics was remarkably diverse – in some cases extremely hostile, in others over-the-top enthusiasm.

'I much preferred *Secretariat* when it was called Seabiscuit,' scoffed John Patterson in the *Guardian*'s magazine *The Guide* in a review whose sub-heading declared the film 'anachronistic and racist'.

In the States, critic Andrew O'Hehir of *Salon* magazine declared '*Secretariat* is a work of creepy, half hilarious master-race propaganda almost worthy of Leni Riefenstahl.'

Another American review sniffed: 'If this movie were a horse, it would be shot – you know, for being lame.'

But the *Daily Mail*'s Chris Tookey disagreed – 'It is utterly harmless, supremely uplifting and one of the great horse-racing movies of all time.'

Film director Randall Wallace, not surprisingly, is a fan of the film, but may just have gone a little over the top when he declared: 'I believe that when Secretariat was running the last of his races, he was no longer running against other horses; he was running for the joy in becoming who he was meant to be'.

Er, pass the horse-feed bag!

202 TEUTALISATOR? Australia

German consul in Sydney for 30 years during the mid-19th century, Siegfried Franck had an interesting sideline – he had invented a totalisator machine which he was determined to introduce to Aussie racetracks.

His first effort, setting his equipment up at Randwick racecourse in 1879, resulted in his arrest by police – claiming that it was an 'infernal machine open to fraud'. The case did not go to court.

In January 1882 he tried again at the Geelong Cup Carnival meeting, in spite of police warnings. After three races, during which his machine did decent business, the police swooped – arresting a total of 20 racegoers, plus Franck, which prompted a hostile demonstration by some 600 protestors.

Charges were again dropped, but it was an idea ahead of its time, and it was not until August 19, 1931 that the first legal totalisator in Australia was used at Moonee Valley racecourse.

By the way – Franck deducted 10 per cent before calculating his dividends.

203 HUSHED UP

An owner with Clive Cox, Mike Hush knew what he wanted for Christmas 2010 and dropped a few hints in the right places that his racing library would be enhanced by a copy of former *Racing Post* columnist Sir Clement Freud's observations on punting and the turf, *Freud On Course*.

Spotting a book-shaped present from his wife Trish's mum amongst the gifts delivered by Santa on Christmas morning, he ripped off the gift wrapping and: 'I was somewhat speechless when I unwrapped a book on *Dream Psychology – Psychoanalysis for Beginners* by Sigmund Freud!'

204 IDEAL, HOLMES?

Sexy racing books are somewhat few and far between – particularly if you exclude raunchy novels a la Jilly Cooper.

So it was not surprising that a large-format volume, dubbed 'a photographic essay' by well known 'glamour' photographer Nigel Holmes, published in 2008, and featuring a number of well known jockeys like Hayley Turner, Kirsty Milczarek and Natalia Gemelova (all in perfectly respectable garb!) would raise a few eyebrows in the sport.

Ladies That Ride was created for a worthy cause, with a donation from the profits of the numbered, limited edition of 500 copies (yes, since you ask – number 109!) going to the Injured Jockeys Fund and the International League for the Protection of Horses.

The 112-page book was crammed with large black and white shots of 'lovely ladies who just hack out once a week, to the professional lady jockeys and trainers in racing.'

Few racing books feature nipple rings, body paint, navel jewellery, bondage, or a naked lady restrained by a bridle – but it is all done in the best possible taste, and along the way, there are a number of particularly risqué photos and captions, including:

'Crack the whip. Then hold on for the ride of your life', 'Well fitting jodhpurs will help your seat' and 'The early morning gallop means leaving one warm partner to go and mount another.'

As of May 2011, there were 'still just a few' copies to be had at the book's website, www.ladiesthatride.com – at a mere twenty quid each.

205 MONKEYING ABOUT Epsom

Lettice Miller was the first woman to own an Epsom Derby winner when Mid-day Sun, which she actually owned in partnership with her mother, won the 1937 race.

To celebrate, recalled a friend after Ms Miller passed away in December 2010 at the grand age of 103, she bought her children a rocking horse for the nursery 'with a monkey sitting on it in her racing colours.' Whether said animal was a toy or for real is not recorded!

After her historic victory Lettice rapidly tired of the attendant publicity – 'Journalists rather got on one's nerves,' she observed, criticising them for sticking up for her when she was not subsequently invited by the King to the traditional Derby dinner:

'It was the most tactful thing he could have done. I would have been the only woman in the room – it would have been very trying.'

Her win landed prize money of £8,941 – 'The tradition was that you had to make a very big contribution to the hospital and pay for the wine at the Derby lunch and an awful lot of other things. So after that there wasn't much left.'

206 UNEXPECTED RESULT Australia

Oddly named French horse Ob won the Lincolnshire Handicap in 1906 (run back then at Lincoln racecourse) – he would do so again the next year, becoming the first dual winner of the race – beating Dean Swift into second, with Roseate Dawn third.

The result was telegraphed through to an Australian newspaper – 'Lincoln, Ob, Dean Swift, Roseate Dawn' – but, just as abbreviated text messages or emails can be misconstrued today, the message landed on the desk of a journalist who excitedly wrote a story, which was duly printed in the paper:

'The death of Dean Swift of Lincoln, author of the famous hymn, 'The Roseate Hues of Early Dawn' was announced today.'

207 STARTER 'COCKED IT UP' Ludlow

Punters were certain that the starter had cocked it up when two horses at Ludlow were declared to have taken part in races on February 8, 1995 – even though one of them had been dismounted when the runners set off, and the other was over 100 yards behind the field when the tapes went up.

David Hancock ruled that Kitchi Koo was part of the field for a handicap hurdle, despite the fact that jockey Richard White was literally standing next to his mount as the others set off, and Bill Quill, who was owner-trainer Gary Baldwin's first ever runner, was so far behind the rest of the hunter chase field that the starter may well not even have realised he was taking part!

In both instances punters were left fuming – particularly the one who had £200 on Bill Quill – and lost their cash without a run, rather than receiving a refund, because of the controversial decisions.

208 LED ZEP DRUM UP SUPPORT FOR RACEHORSES

A rock music one-off rarity, from possibly the last ever Led Zeppelin concert, held in 2007, was used to help former racehorses.

Led Zep lead guitarist Jimmy Page, singer Robert Plant, bassist John Paul Jones and drummer Jason Bonham, son of the late John Bonham, the band's original drummer, all signed the drum skin and donated it to John Bonham's sister, Deborah, to be auctioned for the Racehorse Sanctuary at Belmoredean in West Sussex, of which she is a trustee – and which has two of her own ex-racehorses.

Deborah is a successful rock singer in her own right and she often enlists other rock stars, like former member of the Small Faces Kenny Jones, to help out with fund-raising events.

The auction at which the drum skin was featured in November 2010, along with other rock memorabilia from the likes of Fleetwood Mac, Paul Rodgers and The Doors, raised some £5,000 for the Sanctuary – details of which can be found at www.racehorsesanctuary.org.

209 HENRY PUFFED OUT? Newmarket

Henry Cecil has always enjoyed a puff – on a cigarette, having battled his enjoyment of tobacco with varying degrees of success over the years.

However, an amazing story carried by the *Sunday Mirror* involved the great man of racing with another type of puff. The July 2008 article was headlined 'Cannabis factory in Cecil pad' and went on: 'A house owned by champion racehorse trainer Henry Cecil has been used as a secret cannabis factory.'

A police search had apparently 'found evidence' that some 300 cannabis plants had been grown at the property 'on the racing legend's Newmarket estate – without his knowledge.'

The house had reportedly been let out to 'a family from the Far East. But in reality it's believed to be one of the notorious Vietnamese gangs who make millions from selling the drug.'

In February 2011 there was a similar scandal affecting a big racing name when, reported the *Cambridge News*, 'A cannabis factory has been discovered on land owned by Lord Derby, in a building used by tenants. Police were called to Hatchfield Farm in Fordham Road, Newmarket where they found more than 80 plants.' Police later confirmed, 'It appears a building has been used by tenants for a cannabis factory.'

210 LOST HIS SHIRT – AND MORE
Punchestown, Ireland

The bookie who endeavoured unsuccessfully to depart Punchestown racecourse in Ireland in the 1870s without settling his debts to clients who backed a winner soon wished he hadn't, er, overlooked the matter, according to a contemporary account:

'He was stripped to the skin, flogged unmercifully, daubed over with paint, and then kicked out on the course with nothing whatsoever upon him except one boot and a stocking.'

211 WELL DONE, CHAMP, NOW BLOW INTO THIS BAG Aintree

Leaving Aintree after finally breaking his Grand National duck on Don't Push It in 2010, Tony McCoy, driving his car with its personalised number plate, was reportedly pulled over and warned for using his mobile phone.

The officious traffic cop fined him £30 and, according to some reports, breathalysed the teetotal jockey.

212 OVER THE HILL Dublin

In order to get round the 1862 Dublin Diocesan Statute which prevented priests from attending the races, the racing-mad clergymen gathered together on a hill overlooking Punchestown – which is in the Archdiocese of Dublin and which not unnaturally became known as Priests' Hill.

They were depicted in the 1892 engraving by J. Sturgess celebrating the finish of the Conyngham Cup. The statute was relaxed in the 1970s and the hill vanished as part of a quarrying operation.

213 BEATEN BY A NECK

Droll racing writer David Ashforth, who retired from full-time journalism at the start of 2011, recalled one of his first assignments after joining T*he Sporting Life* in 1990.

He had to call trainer Gordon Richards and ask how his promising chaser Full Strength was doing: 'Not reet well, lad,' said Richards. 'He broke his neck at Ascot three days ago.'

214 SWAN SONG Swansea

Not everyone was delighted by the prospect of the 1836 Swansea and Neath races.

In fact, the Master of Neath Abbey Ironworks, a Quaker, was so incensed by the imminent meeting that he took out an advert in the local paper, *The Cambrian*, which he had placed right under the one for the races – 'In contemplating the approaching Races this year, I have been induced to take a retrospect of what in past years has been their obvious consequence – neglect of duty on the part of the workmen to their employers, to their families and to themselves. I hear of booths being erected where beers and spirits are supplied, and of the encouragement afforded on these occasions to excess in drinking, gambling and other scenes of vice and profligacy.'

215 NOEL GOES WEST

County Meath trainer Noel Meade is such a fan of western movies that it would be no surprise to see him turn up at the races with a six gun and a six-gallon hat!

His love of the wild west is reflected in the names of some of the inmates of his stables at the start of 2011 – Outlaw Pete; Leroy Parker (Butch Cassidy's real name was Robert LeRoy Parker); Pat Garrett (the man who shot Billy the Kid); Bat Masterson; Jim Bowie; Kid Curry (gunman credited with siring up to 85 offspring); Tom Horn (gunslinger for hire); Bob Younger; and Sam Bass (the latter two named after bad guy outlaws.)

However, it would be a brave man who called him a cowboy to his face!

216 DOGGED APPROACH TO TRAINING
County Kildare, Ireland

William Hanway, a County Kildare farmer who also trained horses, came up with a unique method of bringing his runners to the boil for their races. He would let his horses loose in a field, then set collie dogs after them to get them galloping flat out.

He claimed it was 'a performance both horses and dogs enjoy so much they they get plenty of it.'

It seems he wasn't far wrong – as his outsider John Kane upset the former Irish Grand National winner Billet Doux in winning the 1885 Conyngham Cup at Punchestown, while his horses achieved consistent success in the Farmers' Race at the same venue.

217 HORSEY CHRISTMAS TO YOU
California, USA

Unconventional US trainer Barry Abrams came up with a novel plan to get the best out of some of his more 'fractious' horses – he'd tried them out with music playing as they trained and they had seemed to enjoy listening to the song *Feliz Navidad* (Merry Christmas in Spanish, and a 1970 track by Jose Feliciano).

So, Abrams decided to run the horses at his local Del Mar track, in California, equipped with ear-muffs containing a musical chip playing just that song.

The stewards were unimpressed, and vetoed the plan – having already indicated their displeasure at the veteran handler's insistence of wearing shorts and t-shirt when saddling his runners for big races at the track – thus ruling him out of the traditional invitation to dine at the track's directors' room.

Israel-born Abrams, a gambling trainer, admitted: 'Over the last 30 years I've probably lost a million dollars betting,' in a 2008 interview with Rachel Pagones of the *Racing Post*, but added: 'I gained $20m in knowledge'.

218 TSUI EXCITED Sandown

Equine superstar, Derby and Arc winner (amongst his six Group Ones in total) Sea The Stars was so impressive in winning the 2009 Coral Eclipse Stakes at Sandown that owner Christopher Tsui promptly fainted after his horse passed the post in front.

'I was waiting for the horse to come back and it was maybe a bit too warm and I passed out,' said the Hong Kong-based owner.

219 FAIRY STORY – OR CUNNING PLAN COMING TOGETHER? Czech Republic

Was it a racing fairytale to match the fictional 1944 film story of *National Velvet*, in which a young Elizabeth Taylor played a 14-year-old who rode her horse The Pie to win the Grand National?

Once upon a time, Maria Magdalena Rossak (aka Rossakova) was an unknown 16 years and two months old jockey when in July 2010 she caused a sensation by bringing 7-1-shot Talgado with a stunning swoop from the rear to the front of the 16-runner field (15 of them ridden by male jockeys) in the Czech Derby. Held at Velka Chuchle, she won in a course record time and become the youngest female winner of a Derby – perhaps the youngest, full stop. The 1862 Derby at Epsom was won by John Parson, said to be 16, but no-one really knows his age.

As the teenage Slovak dismounted she could only gasp: 'I love him, I love him,' reported eye witness Rosalind Ridout, who bred the horse at her Rowan Farm Stud in Buckinghamshire. It was Maria's first ride in the country, swooned the media. She had never even sat on the horse until the day before.

There are one or two inconvenient facts, however, which slightly change the 'innocent abroad' aspect of the story. The horse was listed as being owned by the Lider Racing Stable – which conceals the identity of the real owner – Maria's father.

Maria had also, said other reports, ridden on the course just two races previously, when she demonstrated no obvious ability whatsoever as she steered her mount Novilly, also owned by good old Dad, into eleventh place of 11 runners.

And she was no green novice rider. With wins in amateur races to her credit, she learned her trade at a prestigious academy in Panama, which bears the name of legendary jockey Laffit Pincay Jr. By the time she left Panama she had 12 winners to her name – ten of them from 42 rides in 2010.

Record-breaking Czech rider Vaclav Janacek was 'jocked off' the horse in favour of little Miss Maria. On the way down to the start of the race Talgado appeared to be lame in his off-fore. Coincidences, or a well executed plan to keep the horse's odds up? Judge for yourself on YouTube at tinyurl.com/rossak.

Mind you, nothing seems to be straightforward where Talgado is concerned – as a two-year-old he reportedly won on his debut despite also crashing through the rails!

220 BOW WOW Toronto, Canada

Having won the 2010 Queen's Plate at Toronto's Woodbine track, Big Red Mike's Brazilian jockey, Eurico Rosa da Silva, was brought to meet the Queen, who was the guest of honour.

Her Majesty and the racecourse officials were at first astonished, then highly amused as da Silva clasped the Queen's gloved hand and, bending almost double, bowed so low that his head almost hit the ground.

It was the Queen's fourth visit to the race and da Silva revealed that she had been a driving force behind his victory:

'Always in the race in my mind I was thinking of her,' he said. 'I tried my hardest to meet her and now I did it.'

221 WATCH THIS – STRANGER THAN FICTION?
Kilbeggan, Ireland

Irish course Kilbeggan was the unexpected location for a bizarre betting coup on June 21, 2010. Organised by punter Douglas Taylor, and modeled on a Dick Francis novel plot, 200 'runners' were given a cheap watch, written instructions, and paid up to 30 euros each to put a 200-euro bet on D Four Dave, precisely five minutes before the 'off' of the Hurley Family Handicap Hurdle. In the 2009 book *Even Money*, by Dick and Felix Francis, a similar scheme is successfully enacted.

Taylor, from Cavan, admitted that his plan had been 'polished' after he read the book.

D Four Dave, trained by Conor O'Dwyer and ridden by Mark Walsh, was a 14-1 shot in the morning but started at 5-1 and won easily.

Had all 200 runners got their bets down in the designated betting shops in Dublin and Kildare, Taylor could have won over 200,000 euros.

But as many of them were 'foreign nationals', some had problems with the instructions they had been given – several were even trying to place the bets after the race had finished.

Taylor warned bookies: 'This was only ever meant to be a dry run. The big one has yet to come.' Taylor had been wed just a week earlier – maybe he needed the cash to pay for his honeymoon!

222 HATS OFF Longchamp, France

After winning the 2008 Arc de Triomphe on 13-8 favourite Zarkava, jockey Christophe Soumillion celebrated by flinging his helmet high into the crowd.

On the same card, the prestigious Prix de l'Abbaye sprint had to be run twice – once when one runner, Fleeting Spirit, was left in the stalls when her gate failed to open, only for several runners to compete the 5f course with Hungarian sprinter Overdose, aka the 'Budapest Bullet', 'winning'.

Then it was run again, four hours and 40 minutes later after Overdose and two others were withdrawn, and Marchand D'Or won this time.

223 HEAD CASES New Zealand

Kiwi track Tauherenikau's off-beat signature event is 'the three-headed classic' in which teams of three humans, kept together under a huge shirt with three head holes, charge up the racecourse in a running race.

224 HOW SCU 'STOPPED' ONE Cheltenham

Multiple champion jump jockey Peter Scudamore has revealed how he once deliberately stopped one of his mounts from winning. When the top US jockey Bill Shoemaker came to Europe for a 'farewell tour', Cheltenham racecourse staged a four-race series in which Scudamore competed against Shoemaker.

'Martin (Pipe) provided me with all my mounts and after the first three races the score was 3-0 in my favour, which was quite embarrassing,' explained Scu in a *Racing Post Weekender* feature in January 2011. 'So, in the finale I stopped mine from winning, with 'The Shoe' prevailing by a neck. It was all done in good fun and he was not only a great rider but a gentleman.'

★

I think Scu's memory may be letting him down – according to my records, he and 'Shoe' met in a THREE-race showdown on Sunday, June 11, 1989. Both rode at 10-7 (Shoe normally rode at 7-7!) and Scu won 2-1. There was no betting on the races.

225 THAT WASN'T VERY LADY-LIKE Overbury Stud

In the first week of June 2010, leading jump stallion Kayf Tara was going about his job with his usual relish as he eyed up his latest 'partner', three times Cheltenham Cleeve Hurdle winner Lady Rebecca. He vaguely recognised her – after all, even though he had covered this mare once before, uncharacteristically failing to get her pregnant, he does get to get intimate with scores of mares in his job.

Determined to get things right this time, Kayf Tara was about to climb on board, as ready and responsive as ever, when he backed off and stepped away from the mare. It was at exactly this point that she kicked out and landed a hoof hit straight on the tip of his action-ready manhood.

The resultant swelling was reportedly 'significant' and sidelined Kayf Tara for three weeks.

'It is a very unusual thing to have happened,' said Overbury Stud boss Sion Sweeting. 'We worked out that in our ten years here, over 3,500 mares have been covered and this was the first time one had connected with a stallion like this.'

Mares wear protective, cushioned boots just before they are covered, but in such circumstances even those boots are of limited use.

Kayf Tara was nursed back to health via a combination of creams, cold-hosing and, um, hand massage. He eventually returned to the fray three weeks later, with no long-term damage done.

226 PUNTERS' PARADISE
Turf Paradise, USA

The California Horse Racing Board launched an investigation in January 2011 after betting continued on the day's first race at Turf Paradise in Phoenix for five minutes after the race started.

However, excited punters who spotted the malfunction and rushed to get their bets on after the runners had finished the race were out of luck, as track officials ruled a 'communications failure' had occurred, and the 84 tickets purchased after the start of the race were refunded.

The statement added that $3,896 of bets placed at California racetracks and simulcast facilities were not merged with the Turf Paradise pools. Winning bets placed before post time were settled as normal.

227 CLARE GETS HER TEETH INTO LIAM – AND GILL

Five months before the Grand National was run in 2009, Middlesbrough man Danny Shea fancied outsider Mon Mome.

Shea, 66, feared he wouldn't live to see the race run as he was suffering from kidney cancer and demanded that his wife, Pat, 63, should put £250 on the horse. Dan didn't live until National day, but despite believing her husband to be 'generally pretty useless at picking winners' Pat obeyed his dying wish and backed the shock winner as requested, collecting well over £20,000.

After jockey Liam Treadwell romped to victory on Mon Mome, who returned odds of 100-1, he was teased by BBC presenter Clare Balding about his uneven, gappy teeth, producing a storm of protest from members of the public.

Treadwell was not that annoyed by her comments, and they worked to his advantage when a cosmetic dentist carried out extensive work – worth a reported £30,000 – on his now famous gnashers, free of charge.

But it was Ms Balding making her own stormy protest in the summer of 2010 when she was so incensed by *Sunday Times* writer A A Gill's description of her as a 'dyke on a bike' in a review of one of her radio documentaries, *Britain by Bike*, that she protested to the Press Complaints Commission which upheld her complaint and to the newspaper's editor, John Witherow.

Witherow dismissed the BBC presenter's complaint by replying: 'Some members of the gay community need to stop regarding themselves as having a special victim status and behave like any other sensible group that is accepted by society ... Not having a privileged status means, of course, one must accept occasionally being the butt of jokes.'

Liam Treadwell's opinion of this incident is unknown.

Gill is apparently no great fan of racing – if his June 2008 description in the *Sunday Times'* 'Culture' supplement of the Royal Ascot meeting is anything to go by – mind you, horseflesh didn't really get a look-in when he asked: *'Why would anyone want to go to this appalling event? It is a suppurating cornucopia of embarrassment, a humiliating parade of teetering naffery. The BBC's presenter is some huge bird who might be by Christopher Biggins out of a herbaceous border. Everybody has the grim, frigid, pinched expression of a congregation at a memorial service for a corpse nobody cared for. This Ascot is Big Brother for snobbery and putrefyingly dull social aspiration.'*

228 WELL BREAD RUNNERS Sussex

Mr W. Mitchell, the local baker, was a little shocked when he spotted three racehorses approaching his premises in Ditchling, Sussex, in April 1932.

He managed to catch and control the roaming runners, which he then stabled at the nearby Bull Inn.

The mystery was solved when he discovered that the three had been contesting a steeplechase at Plumpton and, after coming to grief at one of the fences, they charged through the course fence and set off along the railway track before cutting across country and ending up some seven miles away.

229 DICK WASN'T DICKING ABOUT Fontwell

Top jump jockey Dave Dick (1924-2001), who was the man to benefit on winner E.S.B. when Dick Francis' mount Devon Loch famously capsized on the run-in of the 1956 Grand National when well clear, had a reputation as something of a racing wit.

A typical example occurred at the start of another Grand National, always a fractious time for the jockeys involved. A man was spotted carrying a banner which read: 'Repent or your sins will find you out!' Dick gave the individual a long, hard look, turned to a fellow rider and said: 'If that's the case, I won't get to the first fence!'

But he wasn't joking when at Fontwell in 1961 he was disqualified after taking his mount, Bold Ruler, around a fence he erroneously believed to have been excluded because of the state of the going.

Unlike the stewards, not every racegoer and punter was convinced Dick had merely made an honest mistake – and one of them, a Mr Cole, was heard to declare just why he thought Dick had made this manouevre to his fellow occupants of the Amato pub in Epsom, frequented by many racing people who were friends of Dick, who lived locally.

When he heard of the public outburst, Dick sued Cole for slander – the latter eventually settling out of court for a reputed hefty sum.

230 YES TOR DAY Fontwell Park

I have to admit I included this story only so that I could use the headline! In February 1956, 16-year-old up and coming jockey, David 'Duke' Nicholson rode his first winner at Fontwell, and seventh anywhere, on Yes Tor.

231 AH, BISTOR Fontwell Park

Novice hurdler Bistor had a reputation for being temperamental and was ordered to race in a muzzle after taking a lump out of a jockey's breeches at Chepstow.

After contesting a race at Fontwell in November 1950 his muzzle was removed, only for the horse to break away from his handler and charge into the crowd.

Trainer Tom Gates went looking for a jockey he knew could calm Bistor, but another rider, Bill Marshall, came out to try to placate the horse – which promptly grabbed him and shook him 'like a dog shakes a rat' according to a racegoer.

A policeman intervened, thumping the horse with his truncheon to free the jockey, who was dragged clear by members of the crowd.

The horse pawed the ground in a rage but was caught and tied to a post.

Marshall was taken to hospital but survived, and Bistor was never permitted to race again.

232 OZZY ODDITY Plumpton

Stewart Nash's thorough history of Plumpton Racecourse catalogues an August 1969 performance at the track by infamous rock band Black Sabbath, whose lead singer was Ozzy Osbourne.

It also reveals that the six-track 'bootleg' recording of the concert is highly prized – but that fans should be aware that in actual fact the concert therein preserved for posterity was almost certainly recorded a year later – and in Germany.

Other rock sources claim that the Sabbath actually appeared at Plumpton a year later, in 1970 at the tenth National Jazz & Blues Festival held there –

'rubbish' declared respected music website Popsike – they were playing the Marquee Club in London on that date.

Yet another online report puts the gig at Plumpton's May 1970 Bank Holiday Festival.

233 UNSEATED BY DUKE

During the Queen's historic visit to Ireland in May 2011, her schedule involved a trip to the Irish National Stud where she watched apprentice Sophie Ralston, 18, on a racehorse simulator. Her husband, the Duke of Edinburgh, asked whether the pace of the machine could be upped. It was and, reported the *Daily Mail*, Sophie 'was promptly flung out of the saddle'.

Her Majesty asked Johnny Murtagh about such machines and he told her that in his day he used a hay bale instead.

234 EVERYONE KNOWS IT'S WINDY
Longchamp

One of the most famous landmarks in racing is Longchamp racecourse's 'moulin' or windmill, which gets remarked upon ad nauseam when the Arc de Triomphe is happening.

It was originally part of an abbey and the foundation stone was laid in 1256. The original mill was destroyed during the French Revolution and reconstructed in 1856 when the racecourse was built. The Group 1 Prix du Moulin, introduced in 1957, is run in its honour.

Brighton used to boast a windmill, too – but it collapsed in 1913 in no sort of revolution, was not rebuilt and has no race dedicated to it, as far as I am aware.

235 DAFFY WINNER Huntingdon

Dancing Daffodil, 5-2 favourite, finished fifth but rewarded punters who had backed her to win the 11- runner Cromwell Stand Conditional Jockeys' Handicap Hurdle at Huntingdon on January 14, 2011.

The Robin Dickin-trained mare was awarded the race, while in second was Giollacca, who finished sixth, and over a hundred lengths back, Sovereign Spirit was third, having finished eighth!

Of the eleven runners, eight took the wrong course – nine, if you count Sovereign Spirit, whose jockey turned back to take the correct course.

Eight jockeys were banned for up to two weeks. A similar incident had taken place at the same place on the same course in March 2009.

236 STARKEY RAVING MAD KEMPTON CAPERS Kempton

In January 2011 Amy Starkey made racing headlines yet again as she offered Kempton racegoers their money back for February's Racing Post Chase day – if the meeting turned out not to be exciting enough!

And how was that to be measured? Well, Amy commissioned 'biometric research' (no, me neither) which involved taking heart-rate, blood flow and perspiration measurements (yes, okay Amy) and apparently proved that horseracing generates more excitement and adrenaline rush than any other sport – and then she pledged that if a randomly chosen ten volunteer racegoers monitored by, um, Mindlab International researchers throughout *Racing Post* day did not demonstrate sufficient levels of excitement, everyone would get their admission fee back.

They didn't.

The *Post* confirmed on the day after the race, run on February 26, that 'several hundred racegoers' had signed up to get their money back if not enough thrills were forthcoming.

But, reported Jon Lees, University of Sussex scientists who monitored the requisite ten spectators 'found that the participants' heart-rates rose to an average peak of 109 beats per minute, with the top heart rate recorded as 129bpm.

Racing's youngest racecourse managing director, former William Hill betting shop manager Amy Starkey, appointed in August 2008 when she was 27, rapidly made a name for herself at Kempton, where she arranged for the Royal Philharmonic Orchestra to play the William Tell Overture at the course, not before or after a meeting, but actually playing alongside the track, accompanying a race at an evening meeting in July 2009.

It was a huge PR triumph, attracting massive coverage for the meeting and Starkey.

Not everyone thought the idea a success, however.

'It was ****ing stupid,' opined champion jockey Ryan Moore – and he won the race on Action Impact, while the *Weekender* called it 'a novel idea, but also a ludicrous one.'

In September 2009 Starkey promoted Kempton's Ladies' Day with a controversial ad campaign featuring naked ladies on horseback – and doubled the crowd to 4,000. 'Racing mustn't be afraid to be brave as it tries to promote itself', she said.

The hyperactive Starkey, who had Olympic ambitions as a young gymnast until she broke her arm whilst training in Russia, had also been responsible for the announcement that Kempton was placing a jet ski next to the course's infield lake after an incident during January 2009 in which a horse, Blue Warrior, broke free and ran into the water, having to be rescued. Again, the PR was enormous.

'The most suitable craft will be identified and it should be in place by the end of February. In the event of a similar incident – as well as a new rail being a deterrent to a horse entering the water – the jet ski will make it easier for the staff to assist an animal.' Quite how it would do that was not explained.

When I asked her how successful the jet ski idea had proved when we sat next to each other at the December 2009 Horserace Writers' and Photographers' Association annual lunch she beamed broadly, looked up from her i-phone, on which she was trying to locate a suitable musical track with which to accompany Kauto Star's forthcoming attempt to win a record fourth King George VI Chase at Kempton, (*Ruby* and *On Top of the World* were on the shortlist) and revealed: 'We never actually installed it'.

Kempton opened as a racecourse in July 1878 after businessman S. H. Hyde leased 210 acres of land containing Kempton Manor and Park. In May 1910 King Edward VII's horse Witch of the Air won at Kempton. When the news was conveyed to his Majesty, he expressed his pleasure – with what turned out to be his dying words.

In March 2010, Hayley Turner, a frequent winner at the course, undertook the most unusual ride of her career thus far when, clad in silks, she was carried round the track by Radio 1 DJ Scott Mills, dressed as a pantomime horse, in aid of charity Sport Relief.

Amy captured more headlines in June 2010 when she staged a man versus horse race over 100 metres – with former World Championships 400m gold medal winner Jamie Baulch, 37, being convincingly beaten by seven-year-old Peopleton Brook.

The race stirred memories of America's 1936 Olympic sprint winner Jesse Owens who managed to beat equine rivals over the same distance – albeit he claimed he made sure he raced highly strung horses who would be spooked when a starting pistol was fired.

In another musical moment, Amy brought in opera singer Natasha Marsh to serenade runners in the racecourse stables.

237 SNOW WAY TO CARRY ON! Australia

'The Adaminaby Jockey Club in rural New South Wales in the Snowy Mountains of Australia met last night (April 8, 2009) at which time your email was tabled. I am a Vice-President of this Club and have been requested to touch base with you regarding the information you require for consideration of inclusion in your forthcoming book,' wrote Ross McKinney, calling himself 'The Man From Snowy River Country'.

'Very briefly, we are unique in the fact that our whole complex is heritage listed in view of its historical cultural significance. It is also unique due to the fact that the film Phar Lap (based on the great Australian racehorse of that name) was shot here.

Memorable because when you visit this "very country" picnic race meeting, you never forget the atmosphere or indeed the people you meet.

'Quirky in as much as last year the races ceased half way through the venue due to snow blizzards in mid-summer! The beer sales were down but the whisky sales shot through the roof – all served from the wooden plank grass floor bar!

'Each year is themed, with the 2008 theme being "Flower Power"– and some *people couldn't see the races for "the smoke"! (or cared much) – and when a visiting racing steward mentioned that he would call the police if the crowd didn't stop smoking the grass – the reply was "Please don't call the police, we don't have enough for them!"'*

238 SHE WAS NOT AMUSED Reading

Queen Victoria was enjoying a rare visit to the races at Windsor in 1866. She was watching a steeplechase whilst seated in her carriage close to one of the fences.

As the horses approached the jump, jockey Ben Land drove his mount at the obstacle and urged it over the fence, said a contemporary report, 'in his loudest voice, with some of the choicest expressions of which he was so great a master.'

Shocked to hear such language, Her Majesty ordered her flunkies to drive her back to her Castle immediately.

239 SPOONERISM Friars Wash

Racegoers at the 1930 point-to-point meeting at Friars Wash in Hertfordshire were impressed when jockey Captain Spooner turned up to ride Lady Victoria in the third race in a light aircraft.

Despite the 'appalling' weather, the good Captain's craft landed in an adjoining field from whence he strode to the track and partnered the horse to victory before taking off – literally – straight afterwards to get to Sonning where he had a mount in the fourth race – only to finish second of 14 on Some Birthday.

In a 1951 Friars Wash meeting two horses, Pilatus II and Robin, got rid of their riders and somehow managed to exit the racecourse, causing traffic chaos as they set off down nearby Watling Street, where they were pursued for seven miles by a police car, during which time one of them collided with a coach, although he was not badly hurt.

Police finally managed to stop them in St Albans.

Meanwhile, in a later race, Hulo Bods had also run out of the course – eventually being caught in Redbourn High Street.

240 ROMANTIC WETHER? Wetherby

The Independent newspaper carried a list of Britain's '50 Best Romantic Places' in February 2008, featuring at number 49 – 'Wetherby Races'.

'Place a bet on the jump racing for your loved one and watch as the gee-gees increase your bank balance' advised the editorial, not really explaining why the same advice wouldn't apply to Cheltenham, Kempton, Newbury, etc, etc.

241 FERGIE'S EARIE NAMECHECK Worcester

Sir Alex Ferguson's horse, Cut The Lugsreilly, made his debut in a Worcester bumper in May 2009, after which the Manchester United boss explained why he had so named the horse:

'When I grew up in Glasgow there was a legend that a chap called Reilly was angry when a dog used to bark all the time in a pub. Reilly said that if the dog did not stop barking he would cut its ears off ... and he did!'

242 HORSE POWER? Japan

The Japanese government was reportedly looking to draw up legislation in January 2010, ensuring that a new generation of electric cars should be fitted with a standard warning noise to make up for their almost silent engine running level.

And, reported the *New Zealand Herald*, one of the favourites to be adopted was the sound of a running racehorse's hooves.

243 FANNIE-ING ABOUT ON DICK WARD DRIVE Australia

Fannie Bay Racecourse is unique compared to the traditional turf tracks seen around Australia. The Fannie Bay racetrack is an oil mixed sand track that is located just seven minutes' drive from Darwin.

★

The Darwin Turf Club was formed with a fanfare of trumpets in May 1955. The stage was all set then for the running of the first Darwin Cup at Fannie Bay on Saturday October 20, 1956.

The first Darwin Cup winner was Satan's Son, the only non-thoroughbred to win the Cup, covered the 1,200m in 126 seconds. The race now attracts around 20,000 racegoers to Fannie Bay, when it is the highlight of the eight day carnival.

★

Twenty-plus horses were killed here on Christmas Day 1974 when Cyclone Tracey struck and severely damaged the course.

★

The 1990 bicentennial Darwin Cup was the first A$100,000 race staged in the Northern Territory, an amazing turnaround for the Club, virtually decimated by Cyclone Tracey 15 years before.

★

It is believed that Fannie Bay, which stands on Dick Ward Drive, derives its name from opera singer Fannie Carondini, who performed in Adelaide in 1868 just before the first surveyors came to Port Darwin to establish a settlement in 1869.

Which is a bit of a let down, really!

244 CARR CRASH Cartmel

Now a trainer, then a lady rider, Ruth Carr recalls a hot day at Cartmel – 'I was tailed off, and as I pulled up and hacked back the drunken crowd started pelting me with beer cans and doing donkey impressions.'

Owners who win a race here get a package of the local speciality, sticky toffee pudding.

245 MINIAM Canada

In 1994 Miriam McTague was so determined to make her debut as a jockey at the Woodbine, Ontario track in Canada that she somehow shed an astonishing 84lb to get down to her 7st riding weight – thus acquiring the nickname 'Mini'.

246 HERE IS THE SHIPPING NEWS – HE'S HOT AND WET Tampa Bay Downs, USA

Four-year-old gelding Shipping News was pulled up by jockey Carlos Motalvo after seven furlongs of an eleven-furlong maiden race run on turf in very warm conditions at Tampa Bay Downs in the States in early 2011, then collapsed from apparent heat exhaustion.

Track vets began to hose the horse down to cool him off. As he got back to his feet his bridle came off and he broke away from his handlers, crashing through the inner rail. He then wheeled round and crashed back through the rail again, before doing exactly the same for a third time. He then ran to the course's infield lake and jumped in, wading through the water up to his chest.

Stall handlers stripped off and waded out into the lake to help coax Shipping News back out. He was treated for leg lacerations and taken off by horse ambulance, apparently none the worse for his exertions – which delayed racing by almost half an hour.

247 FLEA PIT Australia

Wollongong is a provincial Aussie track referred to proudly in the early days of the 20th century as 'a pile of sand with a flea on every grain.'

248 PM'S UNCLE PIS*ED OFF Aintree

David Cameron's uncle by marriage, Sir William Dugdale, fasted to ride 100-1 outsider Cloncarrig in the 1952 Grand National. Making the weight was 'crucifixion. An absolute bloody nightmare,' the six-footer wrote in his autobiography, *Settling the Bill*. He consulted doctors: 'One on Harley Street who made me pee like mad, one in Wimpole Street who made me go to the loo like mad. I didn't eat much – one meal of boiled cabbage and a glass of water.'

Carrying 11st 13lbs, Cloncarrig fell at the fence before Becher's.

249 NOR PARTICULAR PLACE TO GO Norway

Norwegians who enjoy racing are able to attend Ovrevoll, some nine miles west of Oslo or, well, nowhere else. Check it out at: www.ovrevoll.no.

250 MEDICS MOWN DOWN Worcester

Everyone respects and admires the trusty St John Ambulance volunteers who do so much to make life safer and healthier for jockeys and other racing folk without fear or favour. But one jockey was taken straight off the St John Christmas list after his activities at Worcester.

'I was riding a hard-pulling, 18.2 hh yoke for Graham Thorne,' explained Colin Brown, who became a racing legend for his association with Desert Orchid. 'It went to run out, saw the River Severn, and ducked back, leaving me to take on the wing. I took out two St John Ambulance medics, who were stretchered off to hospital – while I rode in the next race!'

251 GIRL POWER Australia

Australian history was made on Tuesday, January 19, 2010 when female jockeys rode all seven winners on the card at Callaghan Park's Rockhampton meeting in Queensland.

Alisha Taylor led the way with a treble, while fellow apprentice Carly Mae-Pye won twice with Trinity Bannon and Shayla Evans taking the other two races.

★

Ballina, on the New South Wales north coast, is famous for its iconic landmark – a Big Prawn. Some, that is, say it is an iconic landmark. Others, perhaps not fans of the prawn, describe it as 'a crumbling eyesore from another time.'

Anyway, the area now boasts another claim to fame, courtesy of the racecourse, which is making a name for itself by taking on the task of championing women's involvement in racing.

Ballina runs the Iris Nielsen Memorial Ladies Invitation Cup each year, which was inaugurated to remember the jockey of that name, tragically killed in a fall at Lismore (another New South Wales track) in 1988.

The Ballina Club has also founded the National Lady Jockeys' Hall of Fame, and there are plans for the town to host a museum and resource centre 'to acknowledge the contribution made by women to racing.'

I'm sure Aussie racing paper *The Winning Post* is all in favour of this scheme, but I'm not entirely convinced that suggesting in 2010 that 'Perhaps a Big Female Jockey can replace the ageing prawn as a landmark for Ballina' will have gone down that well in that area.

252 MAKING WHOOPEE Canada

Whoop-Up Downs and Bully's Sport & Entertainment Centre is a horse track in Lethbridge, Alberta featuring harness, quarter horse and thoroughbred racing. Fort Whoop-Up, situated at the junction of the Belly (now Oldman) and St Mary rivers, near present-day Lethbridge, was established in 1869 by John J. Healy and Alfred B. Hamilton of Montana. Its primary purpose was to gain a quick profit through an illicit trade in whiskey for bison robes with the native people of the unpoliced southern prairies of western Canada.

Initially called Fort Hamilton, it soon became known as Fort Whoop-Up.

253 THROUGH IT ALL, THEY RACED ON Iraq

As Iraq prepared for war and the final deadline for the country to pull its forces out of Kuwait passed in January 1991, the Iraqi authorities permitted racing to take place at Baghdad's Amiriya racecourse. After the 2003 occupation, military equipment was parked there and reportedly 'many horses' died there.

But by 2005 they were racing there again, and USA Today's Mona Mahmoud reported on this most obscure of racecourses: 'Three days a week, the railbirds crowd the edge of the 1¼-mile track to watch the thoroughbreds and place bets. It's the only public horse-racing track in Iraq, and it has managed to survive 85 years of coups, dictatorships, wars and foreign occupations.'

The Equestrian Club of Bagdad was founded by the British when they occupied Iraq after the First World War. Back then, the club was in a more elegant structure near downtown Baghdad. Although Saddam Hussein's sons were racing fans, the former dictator ordered that a giant mosque be built on the old site. The mosque was never finished, but the track was relocated in 1995 near the edge of the city.

The track closed for several months at the outset of the US-led assault. Horses at the track were killed and stolen. The club's management reopened the track several months after the invasion and spent some $500,000 refurbishing the facilities. Up to 2,000 people attend the track on race days explained Mahmoud.

In August 2009, the *LA Times* also carried a dramatic account of racing there, by Ned Parker and Caesar Ahmed:

'The Baghdad Equestrian Club is proud of its illustrious past. These days, stray dogs crawl around its dusty brown track, and children in shorts run through the dirt. Men in coffee-stained robes and the occasional John Deere cap slam down beers, puff cigarettes and take the name of Allah in vain.

But beneath its seedy veneer, the racetrack is one of the city's miracles.

In Baghdad's worst years, car bombs exploded at the track's gate, mortar rounds went off inside and gunmen assassinated spectators as they left. Attendance dwindled from thousands to a few hundred; some owners sold their horses.

Somehow the club defied the tide of extremism and anarchy. Veterans of the dark days are proud to point out that the track kept going, even when seemingly everything else in the city was shuttered.

Now Iraqis are coming to the races again in large numbers and the club is turning a profit.'

In May 2010 eight runners went to post for the Baghdad Cup/Iraqi Derby over 1m 4f on dirt, with Hameed Ameer riding Raqi to victory for prize money equating to 2,646 euros.

254 THE LAST WORD Serbia

Serbia's oldest racecourse and horse farm is also alphabetically, I believe, the last racecourse in the world! Zobnatica was founded in 1779. A museum of horse breeding and horseracing, a hippodrome, mini Zoo, a lake and a hotel are located on its grounds.

According to tourism website Airlift, 'At the Zobnatica hippodrome, in the beautiful environment in the heart of the Pannonia plain one may watch races of best-known horses in the region. There is a Horse Museum in Zobnatica, one of its kind in Europe.'

Another site added more information – 'Horse gallop has been resounding here for hundreds of years, sometimes faster, sometimes quieter, but always pleasant to man's eye and soul. One can only guess how much champagne has been drunk out of thousands of winner's cups.'

Indeed.

255 TRAGEDY IS ALWAYS JUST A JUMP AWAY Stevenstone

Husband and wife Dennis and Jane Wickett both had rides in the members' race at the Stevenstone point-to-point meeting at Crimp in May 1984.

'We actually had a chat on the way round, but he was going better than me and kicked on,' remembered Jane. 'I saw him fall in front of me. But I pulled round him, jumped the fence and went on to win.'

Dennis never recovered from the effects of that fall. He remained unconscious for over two months and eventually died in February 2010.

Jane, unbeknown to her at the time, had been pregnant when she took part in the race.

256 YARRAVIN' A LAUGH! Australia

The Yarra Glen course in Australia stages some jump racing during which the cross-country course takes the runners, almost certainly uniquely, through vineyards.

'Yarra Valley Racing is located at Yarra Glen in the heart of one of the most recognizable tourism regions of Victoria,' explained the information sent to me by the course.

There followed the note 'N.B: Yarra Valley Racing is a No BYO alcohol venue.'

257 JUMP TO IT Avondale, New Zealand

When trainer G. Walker was injured and taken off to hospital shortly before his horse Gold Man was due to contest a jumps race at Avondale, New Zealand, in July 1948, he asked a lad to saddle the horse up in his absence.

The lad, who did not know the horse well, instead saddled up similar looking Peria Chief, who had never jumped an obstacle in his life before.

The race was off before the mistake was noticed – but, somehow, Peria Chief and his jockey jumped round unscathed – unlike, perhaps, the lad when his error was realized.

258 SELFISH? Ayr

In 2009 Ayr's clerk of the course Katherine Self, 36, quit – to join the coastguards.

259 FIRST TIME FOR EVERYTHING Abu Dhabi

Racing at Abu Dhabi on Sunday, December 13, 2009, was called off as the meeting was abandoned due to heavy rain for the first time since the inception of racing in the UAE in 1992.

The only UAE track to race solely on turf, the course was found to be unfit for racing and Clerk of the course Pat Buckley, a Grand National-winning jockey on Ayala in 1963, explained: 'It was very wet underfoot early on and then we had a torrential downpour. I have been in Abu Dhabi almost 20 years and I have never seen rain like it. The sand training track is flooded inside and the water in the car park is covering the wheels on my 4 x 4!'

260 BUBBLY STEF ON PARADE Goodwood

TV commentators were shocked to see that the person leading Mac Love round the parade ring prior to the Group One Sussex Stakes at Goodwood in July 2010 was none other than the nine-year-old daughter of trainer Stef Higgins, apparently making her the first of her ilk to conduct such arduous duties in a Group One race.

Lambourn-based 'Top Gear' fan Stef has her own Twitter page (stefracing) on which she describes herself thus: 'Racehorse trainer, F1 fanatic, love bubbles, hate getting up.'

261 BOTH BEHAVING BADLY?

Actor Martin Clunes, who has starred in TV shows 'Men Behaving Badly' and 'Doc Martin', has an ambition to be Frankie Dettori for a day!

The racehorse-owning star, whose 20-1 Waltzing Beau gave him his first win at Fontwell in January 2005, said: 'It would be great to see what it is like being Frankie. I think the sport is very, very lucky to have him. His celebrations are infectious and they permeate through to the crowd. There is a sense of festival about the man.'

262 WILD PUNTER

Chip Taylor wrote the massive hit song 'Wild Thing' which gave the Troggs a huge sixties smash. The New Yorker also penned chart-toppers 'Angel of the Morning' and 'Any Way That You Want Me' before, in the mid-1980s, he decided to swap music-making for punting on the ponies and became a professional gambler – until he found it was too easy to win!

'I studied the mathematics of gambling. It was a very lucrative time. But the better I got, the more depressed I became. I remember coming back from a Philadelphia race having won $20,000 on a single horse, and crying. I mean, money? Is that it? I wanted to get back into music.'

Which he did – becoming a successful 'alternative country' singer.

263 YOU BET I'VE PAID FOR THE HORSE
Salisbury

Few punters have ever backed a 250-1 winner, but Northampton-based owner Alan Campbell decided to risk £30 each-way with bookie Dick Reynolds on his only horse, Bermondsey Bob, at Salisbury in August 2008 – and was rewarded with victory in a 6f maiden – after a prolonged stewards' inquiry.

'My winnings have just about paid for the horse,' declared the proud, retired, eight grand-plus better off owner whose animal returned a starting price of 150-1.

264 WHEREFORE ART THOU ON FIRE, ROMEO! Haydock

Apprentice jockey Pietro Romeo took the advice of one of the valets at Haydock to use an oil to help him sweat more easily when he took advantage of the sauna facility there in July 2008.

'He gave me an oil – I didn't know whether I was supposed to rub it on my body or pour it on the rocks, but the valet said it was meant for pouring, so I put about 10mls in a cup'.

Romeo, 25, who was riding for trainer Milton Bradley at the time, suddenly found himself on fire – 'The oil was supposed to be diluted. As soon as I splashed it on the rocks, a big plume of flames came up and, as I'm very hairy across my body and under my armpits, set me on fire.'

There was criticism of the course when it took some while for an ambulance to arrive but Romeo said a day after the incident: 'It's not as bad as it might have been. I don't need a skin graft and the burns aren't third degree, but my nipple ends are red raw and it will take three weeks for the skin to the left and right of my chest to heal, and a year for it to return to its normal colour.'

Romeo wasn't the only jockey to have a miracle escape from serious injury at that time. Just weeks later NH rider Joe Tizzard suffered severe injuries after crawling under a baler at his brother-in-law's farm and was dragged into the machine, which virtually scalped him, and caused a large cut and haematoma on his neck and head, but the 28-year-old lived to tell the tale.

And a third lucky escape at the same time belonged to 67-year-old David Wilson, assistant trainer to Gary Moore, who had taken his horse Vanadium to Lancing beach to paddle him in an effort to reduce a haematoma he was suffering from.

Wilson and the horse managed to get out of their depth in the water and in his efforts to return to safety, the horse lifted his head unexpectedly and struck Wilson in the face, causing heavy bleeding and knocking him into the water.

Fortunately for Wilson, Gary Moore's son Joshua was around and he managed to rescue Wilson, catch the horse and get Wilson to hospital. He was treated for concussion and given 16 stitches – then Josh went off to ride a winner at Warwick later that afternoon.

★

Back in December 1990 jockey Alan Proud had also suffered a sauna incident – but despite second degree burns to his buttocks in the Southwell sauna nonetheless went out to ride two-year-old Aberfoyle for trainer Mark Johnston. Two years later he was inspected by Jockey Club medical officer Dr Michael Allen who 'went completely up the wall when he saw the damage and thought I was lucky not to need a skin graft. It had become badly infected – every time I changed my underpants half my bottom appeared to drop off.'

Proud took three weeks to recover from the incident in which 'I just bent down to pick up my towel – and suddenly my ar*e was being welded to the unguarded stove. It was excruciatingly painful.'

265 TATTOO TOO MUCH

Richard Kingscote has yet to come close to being champion jockey – but he is by some distance the reigning champion jockey in terms of the number of tattoos he can boast.

Horses figure amongst the plethora of tattoo designs gracing his back, chest and arms, along with mythical beasts and other designs – courtesy of tattoo artist 'Painless Chris'.

'At £70 an hour the tattoos are a bit of a luxury,' said the rider in 2008. 'A lot of people in racing don't seem to like them, but I like the way they look (how can he see his own back? – GS) and I'm happy that they'll be with me for the rest of my life.'

'Tatty', as he has been nicknamed by fellow jock Jimmy Fortune, said in June 2010: 'I have lots of room left and lots of ideas but it just costs plenty of money and time, so I've only had one done in the last year. There will be lots to come. I like them all of course but I have a dragon which starts under my arm and heads down my arm which my tattooist has done a great job on.'

★

Jockey Sam Hitchcott has an Everton FC tattoo on his leg.

266 WATCHING, BUT NOT LOOKING
Ayr

Lester Piggott and two fellow jockeys deliberately delayed the start of a race at Ayr, where they were riding in July 1983, so that they could watch the Magnet Cup at York, which was being televised at the scheduled off time of 3pm, but did not come under orders until some ten minutes later.

The disgruntled stewards called Piggott, Walter Swinburn and George McGrath in with the intention of fining them.

They asked Irishman McGrath for an explanation of their behaviour but he denied having anything to do with it, explaining that he had no interest in English races contested by English horses.

'But you were seen with these jockeys at the television,' he was told.

'Sure, I was watching the television, but I wasn't looking at it.'

'Faced with such impossible Irish logic the Ayr stewards were unable to hide their amusement and abandoned their original pans to fine the three jockeys' reported the *Irish Field* newspaper.

267 COURSE NAMED AFTER
GROUNDSMAN Carlisle

Cynics thought the TV cameras may have had something to do with the decision to name Carlisle's newly completed hurdles track the 'Wootten Course' in honour of chief groundsman Tony Wootten.

The long-serving 67-year-old's honour, which left him visibly moved, was awarded by Paul Fisher, chief operating officer of Jockey Club Racecourses who had met, and worked for, Wootten as part of the Channel 4 series Undercover Boss in which a high- profile businessman disguises his identity to go and work at the 'coal-face' for a few days.

Wootten, who was shown in the August 2010 programme expressing concerns that as he was due to retire imminently he may be thrown out of the on-course house where he and his family had lived for many years, was also relieved when Fisher told him that his son would be promoted into his job, which would enable him to stay in the house.

But as *Racing Post* correspondent 'Nick the Greek', also clearly of cynical bent, mused in the 'Chatroom' column: 'I can't help wondering whether the Jockey Club has other tied properties and what will happen to the tenants there.'

268 GIVE ME A RING – IN 2016!

Point-to-point owner and trainer Robert Tierney was warned off in July 2008 by the disciplinary panel of the British Horseracing Authority after being found guilty of running gelding Max 'n Limbo, who had raced under Rules, in place of unregistered hunter Quintin at a Charm Park meeting in April 2006.

Amazingly, he was already serving a six-year ban for a similar offence and was warned off for a further five, with three years running consecutively, effectively giving him a further two-year sentence which left him warned off until February 2016.

The deception was discovered when jockey Charles Grundy had weighed out to ride 'Quintin', only for a check on the horse's passport to suggest all was not as it should be.

The panel declared that Tierney 'possessed a persistent and willful disregard for the fundamental principles of the rules which underpin racing.'

Oddly, no specific motive for the offence was identified and there was no evidence of a betting coup.

269 AJTEBI NEVER GETS THE HUMP THESE DAYS Ascot

Ahmed Ajtebi became the first jockey from Dubai to win a race at Royal Ascot when he scored on 25/1-shot Regal Parade in the 2008 Buckingham Palace Stakes, after which the apprentice revealed that he had learned his trade by riding camels 'from the age of seven to 15. They are totally different to ride than horses, but a bit easier – you ride them like horses but you have a long stick. You don't need to hit them with the stick, but if you wave it at them they will keep straight.'

270 THAT RIDE WAS PANTS Australia

Desperate to save the race as rival runner Bangster went past him during the 1941 Australian Jockey Club Breeders' Plate, leading rider Darby Munro, partnering Hall Stand, resorted to questionable tactics – he quickly reached across and grabbed a handful of Bangster's rider Paddy Delaney's riding breeches in an effort to slow him down or put him off.

All he achieved was to hasten the disintegration of Delaney's venerable breeches – leaving the victorious jockey to celebrate in tattered breeches showing off his underwear.

271 PUNTERS TURNED OVER Australia

A race was declared void at Australian track Dederang because of an occurrence almost certainly unique in the annals of racing. The course was holding its first ever meeting in 1865 and the judge's viewing point, or 'tower', was actually a horse cart.

As the two leaders in the race charged towards the finish line, neck and neck, two youths approached the cart and turned it over, pitching the judge onto the turf – from where he was unable to rule which of the horses had passed the post in front.

272 PORN TO RUN Sandown

After Sandown introduced a free internet service for racegoers it was forced to threaten to withdraw the popular internet booths in February 2007 – after discovering that at least one racegoer had taken advantage of the service to access pornographic sites.

'In theory this shouldn't have been able to happen,' said Course MD Julian Thick, explaining that filters had been installed to block such access.

273 CASINO BOY IS LOSER Australia

Born in Casino, New South Wales, Chris Munce grew up to ride the winners of Australia's three major races – the Cox Plate, the Golden Slipper and, in 1998, the Melbourne Cup, on Jezabeel.

But in 2007 he became one of the few jockeys to be imprisoned when he was given a 30-month sentence in Hong Kong after being found guilty of selling tips. He was freed in October 2008.

274 SINKING OF BISMARCK BARRY

After 15 years-plus as part of Channel 4's 'The Morning Line', high-profile bookmaker Barry Dennis announced he was not only standing down from the programme but also from standing up at the racecourse in January, 2011.

The 70 year old, Dennis, who introduced the 'Barry's Bismarck' feature to 'The Morning Line', in which he nominated a well fancied horse not to win, was almost lost to bookmaking as soon as he'd decided to enter the trade. He made a book at school on the 1954 Derby – laying his pals 33-1 about the winner, Never Say Die, and having to work at a market stall to win it back. His worst day since then was Frankie Dettori's 'Magnificent Seven' day at Ascot in 1996 when he lost £26,500:

'Walked in, wife greeted me in normal cheery voice – "Hello darling – good day"?'

'Dettori rode all seven winners.'

'Fantastic,' she said. 'What an achievement.'

'I collapsed in my favourite chair, silently crying.'

Dennis claimed he'd become disillusioned by on-course bookmaking which, thanks to the influence of betting exchanges, had turned the bookies into 'robots', all changing prices at the same time and for the same reasons.

Typically the colourful character, noted for turning small-staking women punters away from his joint and handing out Christmas puddings to punters had been in the news only weeks earlier when the Spurs fan became involved in a contretemps with former Arsenal player Frank McClintock at the Emirates Stadium during a match.

275 WHEN THE QUEEN MUM WAS TYRED
Lewes

In the oral history book *Lewes Remembers*, about the days when there was a racecourse in the Sussex town, one of the contributors revealed, 'The Queen Mother used to have horses with (local trainer) Tom Masson, and Tom used to drive her up the gallops in the back of his old van. She used to sit on a tyre and laugh and joke with him.' Another fine tale in *Lewes Remembers* which records anonymous memories, concerned the death of top jump jockey Fred Rees.

'It was arranged that his ashes should be scattered over the grave of Shaun Spadah, the horse that he'd won the Grand National on in 1921, who's buried in the paddock at Lewes racecourse.

'My wife and I walked up to the stands and we all gathered at Shaun Spadah's grave, and his youngest daughter Pat was going to scatter the ashes. There was quite a wind blowing and unfortunately she scattered the ashes to the windward of us, so the whole of the party were covered in poor old Fred!'

276 JUMPY WATCHER

Jumps trainer Ilona Barnett is a nervous watcher. She admitted in 2011 that when her Ocheekobee runs she 'stuffs her fingers so far into her ears they cross', screws up her eyes, chants, walks on the spot and performs half tucks.' Asked why she continues to train, she said 'We do it for fun!'

By the way – Ilona was not the female point-to-point personality spotted walking the course at Lockinge near Lambourn in April 2011 – topless.

277 MURDEROUS MYSTERY Kentucky

Murdered racehorses are, fortunately, rare indeed. We all remember the tragic Shergar case. However, much less well known on this side of the Atlantic is the story of the terrible end of an equally talented equine legend.

He was the horse who would have been feted as the US Triple Crown winner – if only he hadn't come up against his nemisis – who beat him narrowly in each of the three great races – the Kentucky Derby, Preakness Stakes and Belmont Stakes.

Alydar had to give best in each one of them to Affirmed, who did indeed land the 1978 Triple Crown and take plaudits for the feat.

But when the two went to stud, it was Alydar whose offspring proved to be better and his stud fees boosted the fortunes of Calumet Farm, Kentucky, where he stood.

In November 1990 Alydar broke a leg. He was put down two days later and buried with only seven people present. Insurance payment of a reported $35m was made.

However, some time later federal financial investigators looked into the event and rumours began to circulate that Alydar's death had not been an accident and had actually been a financially motivated murder.

It was said that Calumet Farm had been in very deep financial trouble. The farm eventually was auctioned. The Calumet that exisits today is another farm entirely with no connection to the Calumet of Alydar's days.

Ann Hagedorn Auerbach's 1994 book, *Wild Ride* (Henry Holt and Company), tells the whole bizarre tale.

278 VALENTINE DEBUTANT LOVED LOSING
Puerto Rico

Brown filly Dona Chepa made her racecourse debut on Valentine's Day in 2001, but the Puerto Rican horse started as she meant to go on by losing that race.

Her form improved and she was runner-up during a May 2003 race – but when, as a nine- year-old, she was beaten at Camarero racecourse in Puerto Rico in September 2007 she became a world beater, as that was her 125th straight defeat – beating the record previously held by Aussie horse Oureone, set from 1976-83. The racecourse marked the occasion by presenting a plaque to trainer Efrain Nieves.

However, Dona Chepa was far from done with and extended her record to 0-134 in February 2008 before seemingly disappearing from view, to what we can only hope was a well deserved retirement.

279 REV'S RACISM AND BURIED DERBY RINGERS Gloucestershire

Local rumour has for many years insisted that 'beneath a clump of trees on the old racecourse at Aldsworth, Gloucestershire, ringed with a low stone wall named Sadler's Clump, was buried the remains of a four-year-old horse which won the Derby masquerading as a three-year-old.'

The horse is variously said to have been either three-year-old Running Rein, or four-year-old Maccabeus – the latter substituting for the former in the 1844 Derby; possibly 1833 winner Dangerous, whose trainer had local connections; or 1830 winner Little Wonder, also suspected of being older than three. Local historian Jessica Stawell, who wrote a booklet about racing in the area, believes 'the story may be true'.

Racing was held regularly at Aldsworth in the early 19th century, and from 1835 until around 1848 the course hosted the famous Bibury Club meeting – but the meetings came to an end following a concerted campaign against them by the local clergy, and in 1859 the apparent killjoy Rev John Bellingham was able to boast:

'Races were held, training stables supported, which attracted a vast crowd of visitors of the lowest and most abandoned description.

The public house was thronged on such occasions and pugilistic combats were encouraged and all kinds of games prevailed for the space of a whole week and caused considerable disorder and licentiousness among the parishioners.

After much persevering effort for above five years, the Incumbent (vicar) succeeded at length in entirely abolishing the races, banishing the stable, suppressing the public house, closing the shops on Sunday and putting an end to the Sunday games and sports and wrestling, boxing, cock-fighting and cricketing which had been usual on the village green.'

280 BINGOES – BUT COMES SURFING BACK Del Mar, California

Hugely popular crooner Bing Crosby (1903-77) was one of the founders of Del Mar racecourse in California in the 1930s – and to this day the track still plays his 'When The Surf Meets The Turf', the course theme, every time they race.

The late Crosby's racing colours reappeared on a racecourse in late 2009 when Chatterchic and Ziggy Zariz raced under them at Cowra in New South Wales, Australia.

The horses were owned by Norm Stern, whose father part-owned horses with the singer during the 1930s and 1940s, trained by Fred Hood.

'Bing Crosby raced many horses in Australia during the 1940s, mainly under the pseudonym Jackpot Smith. When he went back to America, the Hood family got possession of the colours,' said Stern.

In tribute to Crosby's hit record 'When the Blue of the Night meets the Gold of the Day', his colours were royal blue, yellow halves and red cap, but lapsed during the 1970s before Stern had them re-registered.

Famous racehorse Star Fiddler (1946-58) is buried in the infield at Del Mar, where in August 2009 the track caused some controversy by staging a 'Miss Cougar' contest on the same day as their Cougar II Handicap. In the States the term 'Cougar' refers to a lady of a certain age whose primary interest lies in bedding younger men!

It was won by one Rosie Goldstein who, to judge by the photos on the racecourse website is, indeed, a very attractive lady of indeterminate age. Sadly, I am no longer a younger man, though!

281 STYLISH NUGGET'S TIMELY END Australia

Not everyone believed the evidence of the clock when Stylish Century won the valuable two-year-old 'Classic', the 1988 Golden Nugget Stakes at the Gold Coast Turf Club in Queensland, Australia, in what was claimed to be the fastest time ever clocked by a juvenile over 1,200m, of 1m 8.37s.

One subtle message from a racegoer came in the form of a Mickey Mouse clock – sent to the racetrack in the mail. The horse, runner-up in the WS Cox Plate and AJC Derby, and VRC Derby winner, died at the age of 16 – from the effects of a spider bite.

282 STRANGENESS OLD AND YOUNG

Britain's **oldest** trainer, 89-year-old Reg Brown, who had been running horses for 50 years, achieved what is a rarity even for younger practitioners of the art when in November 2010 he saddled a winner which returned longer odds than his age.

Tiptronic won a juvenile hurdle at Hereford, returning starting price odds of 100-1 and having been backed by friends of the trainer at odds of 200-1 and 150-1. Tiptronic was undoubtedly the star of Brown's Welsh stable – he was also his only active horse!

A few days later Ireland's **youngest** trainer, 22-year-old Emmet Butterly, scored his first British winner when Brabazon was gambled on from a morning price of 50-1 to start at 11-4 favourite at Lingfield despite an 892-day absence. He was partnered by 16-year-old Freddie Mitchell who got the ride only because intended jockey Graham Watters missed his flight from Ireland.

It was Mitchell's first ever ride under rules – and later in the day his brother, Jack, won on South African Gold – also getting the ride only because the intended rider was absent.

283 STOUTE FELLOW Santa Anita, USA

I first met the Chelsea Girls at the Melbourne Cup in 2006. One of these lovely ladies, Di, was sitting next to me, enjoying a drink – or two. We struck up a conversation, discovering that we were both Londoners, and she told me, 'Julie and I like to have a couple of drinks when we come to the races, but we're stopping after the sixth race.'

'That was the seventh,' I told her.

'Oh well, might as well carry on through the card, then.'

So I was delighted to be reunited with the pair of them, whose nickname was acquired for obvious reasons (one of them wore an armband for weeks when Jose Mourinho left), when we arrived in Pasadena for the 2008 Breeders' Cup.

My wife Sheila and I were sitting at a table with several friends enjoying the warmth of the day and some pleasant local wine when the Chelsea Girls returned to the table in a state of high excitement, explaining that they had just, almost literally, bumped into Sir Michael Stoute – who had tipped them up his raider Conduit as having a decent chance of breaking his Breeders' Cup duck.

The horse was trading at around 6-1 and the Girls told anyone and everyone who would listen about the great man's comments, before rushing off to the betting windows.

Conduit won and the party reassembled around the table – one member of the group had passed on the 'information' to a third party who had bet a substantial amount on Conduit and rewarded his informant with a sizeable tip, none of which was seen to be passed the way of the CGs, who were bubbling away at the victory of Conduit and congratulating everyone on backing the winner. I had to ask the Girls how much they had won – surely enough to cover the cost of their trip?

'No,' they confessed, 'we put the horse in all our combination forecast bets but got nothing to go with it, and didn't actually back the horse to win.'

That didn't stop Di and Julie toasting Conduit's triumph with a rather tasty local sparkler and with genuine pleasure – almost as much as I got from joining them. And one of them, Di, got her reward for her equanimity in the face of adversity, when, shortly after, she bought into a horse which turned out to be rather good, winning a couple of decent races and being placed in a couple of Guineas before going on to high profile success in Hong Kong – Xtension was his name.

The CGs also regaled us with another purported Stoute anecdote – in which the trainer had to explain to an owner of his, convinced that the man to whom he was chatting was Royston Ffrench, who had ridden one of his horses to victory, and was still congratulating the baffled looking 'jockey', that in actual fact he was addressing a certain ... Lewis Hamilton!

284 FRANKIE JETTORI

Frankie Dettori rode at Newmarket on Saturday, October 30, 2010, then caught a plane that night to fly to Melbourne, where he finished down the field in the Melbourne Cup on Holberg on Tuesday, November 2.

Then it was next stop Churchill Downs in the States where he won the

Breeders' Cup Turf on Saturday, November 6, aboard Dangerous Midge, complete with flying dismount and the hurling into the crowd of the flowers from the winner's garland.

On Sunday, November 7, after three hours' sleep he was in his native Italy at Capannelle to ride his 100th Group or Grade 1 winner for Godolphin on Rio De La Plata, about whom he made a dubious claim – ' I would have got here to ride him even if I was dead, because I love the horse.'

285 HONEYBALLS UP Towcester

Having prepared unraced six-year-old Sophies Smile for several months to contest a Towcester bumper in February 2011, trainer Anthony Honeyball was nonplussed when a check on the horse's passport revealed her to be nine-year-old Marigolds Way from a different trainer's yard.

It transpired that a mix-up had occurred when Honeyball first collected the horse from a field containing two animals: 'One was due to come to us to run in bumpers, and the other was to remain in the field and was going to be collected later to be trained (by handler Ron Hodges) for point-to-point races.'

So some horses evidently don't look their age, then.

286 NOT SUCH A BRIGHT SPARK Australia

Active in the 1940s and 1950s on the Queensland circuit, Australian lightweight jockey Billy Clarke was not averse to bending the rules – he booted home over 1,000 winners in ten years but would have clocked up far more had he not also picked up three and a half years' worth of suspensions during that time.

But even Clarke had his own code of morals, claiming he was never suspended 'for a race in which I was as guilty as hell'.

And Clarke baulked at the cunning plan operated by a colleague who devised a battery-powered go-faster 'jigger' which he wore as a money belt – 'he fastened it around his waist, with wires running down his legs to his spurs – but he forgot to insulate them. When he mounted he switched on the jigger, his horse bucked and sent him flying. As he landed on the ground, with his feet flaying the air, he screamed to everybody and sundry: 'Turn the bloody thing off!'

287 HARD LUCK IS RIGHT, MATE! Wales

A William Hill customer from Pencoed in South Wales wrote to me in late 2010 with an idea for what he called 'a new charity.'

So far, so good. I read on. 'It would be called the British Punters' Hard Luck Fund – founded by myself.'

Mm. How might it work, I wondered?

'You would set aside a small – or large – percentage of profits towards the charity, which would be solely based around the horseracing industry.'

And what has made you dream up this, er, intriguing suggestion?

'As recently as the Aintree raceday on November 21, 2010, I had gut-wrenching luck. I know there are winners and losers in life, but this charity would be some sort of in-between bit of help, to ease the pain of a could-be-life-changing situation.'

Right, and then what?

'It may produce a magic return to the gambling and bookmaking world. I've heard disgruntled punters over the last 40 years – as surely yourself have.'

Well, that's true, myself have.

'In what I call a touchy financial climate now would be the chance to give something back – how many times have you heard somebody say "those bloody bookies don't give nothing away"?'

That's true, too, I've certainly heard that phrase from time to time!

'Well, what do you think of my idea? If somebody had genuine bad luck, maybe there could be a percentage to be had after all.'

Okay, Mr A.H., I'm afraid I think your bad luck just got worse.

288 EASY AS ABC, BABY Czechoslovakia

British jump jockey John Westlake pulled off an amazing victory in one of the world's toughest races, the Czechoslovakian Velka Pardubicka chase in 1892 – doing it the hard way. He and his mount Alphabet initially took the wrong course, but the quick-thinking rider immediately took his horse back to correct the mistake.

They made their way back into the race, eventually finishing third behind Wolf and Lady Anne, only for the two of them to be disqualified for taking the wrong course.

Then the excitement of the victory had a startling effect on Westlake's pregnant wife – after watching her husband win the race she went into labour, producing a two-month premature son.

289 SUICIDAL SCHEME
Maryland, USA

The ninth race at Bowie Race Course in Maryland, America on February 14, 1975, was a maiden claiming race, not one which many ever considered might go down in racing history.

But it was to result in the tragic suicide of one of the jockeys taking part, while a total of four riders would receive prison sentences in the aftermath of the race.

It was later revealed that six of the jockeys in the race were responsible for the purchase of 38 tickets naming the first three horses home – numbers 8 (Mr Ransom), 12 (Choice Rib) and 2 (Sealand) – who returned 5-1, 7-2 and 47-1 respectively.

None of those six jockeys finished in the first six of the 12-runner race. Whether they had taken any steps to ensure that the 'right' three of the remaining six would finish 1, 2, 3 is not clear.

A trifecta (first three in any order) featuring these odds would normally have been expected to pay a dividend of some $2,000, but it actually returned $927.30 because of the number of tickets sold for the correct three horses.

One clerk had sold 38 tickets – all, it transpired, to Ernest Davidson, the brother of Jesse, one of the jockeys in the race. They would have paid out over $35,000.

Suspicious ticket sale patterns were quickly identified after the race, and payment on the tickets was officially withheld.

The FBI were called and, in a panic, two of the jockeys involved, in what was proved to be a conspiracy, burned all of the tickets except for two which had been given to two women to cash.

However, the two tickets which had not been destroyed were eventually used as evidence in a subsequent trial which resulted in the conviction and imprisonment of four jockeys – two others (Carlos Jimenez and John Baboolal) not being charged after agreeing to cooperate with prosecutors.

Eric Walsh, 35, one of the jockeys who burned the tickets and the most successful of those involved, estimated to be earning $200,000 a year, made two unsuccessful attempts to kill himself – but did so on the third occasion – on May 1, 1976 – the day of the Kentucky Derby. Maintaining his innocence, he had told friends he could not face prison.

Jockeys Ben Feliciano sr, Luigi Gino and Jesse Davidson all spent some five months in Allenwood Federal Prison – the latter two suspended from racing in the state for five years. Feliciano had been involved in another bribery case and was not to race again until 1985.

Inevitably the whole affair became known as the St Valentine's Day Massacre.

290 JUST THE TICKET – FOR 25 YEARS
Tasmania

A female regular racegoer at Tasmania's Mowbray track was able to go racing free of charge for a quarter of a century – after her trip to a 1934 card there was almost her last.

It was the last day of the track's big Launceston Cup meeting and all was going smoothly until, at around 4pm, a stiff southerly wind suddenly blew up, and, according to a contemporary report, 'there was a mighty roar as a portion of the roof over the stand lifted, and several sheets of iron were blown over the back.'

One of these sheets just missed the racegoer who, for the fright she suffered, was awarded 'an admission ticket annually as some compensation for the narrow escape from injury.'

291 HOW CLARE KIDDED HER WAY TO A GRAND Wimbledon

Acerbic sportswriter, restaurant reviewer and broadcaster Matthew Norman attended a 1998 greyhound meeting at Wimbledon Stadium in the company of the BBC's racing presenter, Clare Balding.

During the course of the evening whilst discussing various subjects, Norman claims that he was 'cajoled' into striking a bet with Clare – '£4,000 to her £6,000 that she would, within the next decade, have a baby.'

Happy at the odds, which he believed to give him an edge, Norman was subsequently concerned when 'a Sunday tabloid revealed the sexual preference that made such a nativity less likely.' Ms Balding asked whether the bet was still on.

Norman, an experienced gambler, was aware that 'the secret of successful betting is having the edge in inside knowledge, so the bet was entirely legitimate, and stood.'

But he was somewhat relieved when Clare accepted £1,000 in settlement of the wager.

292 KYLE SHOULD BE SO LUCKY Cheltenham

TV presenter Jeremy Kyle is a keen racing fan, and was at Cheltenham when Imperial Commander won the 2010 Gold Cup – but his loudest cheers that afternoon were for his own Sonning Star, which won at Fakenham.

Leaving the course to return to his hotel he was unable to find a taxi, so 'I stuck my thumb out in the hope that I could procure a lift and save my dear wife the long walk back, when a car kindly stopped and took us there. The driver was AP McCoy, which just about summed up our amazing day.'

293 SAUNDERS' OBSESSION Czechoslovakia

The story of the aristocratic Spaniard the Duque de Alburquerque, a gentleman rider who became obsessed with the Grand National, is well known. He contested the race seven times with varying degrees of success and disaster – falling off, cracking vertebrae, breaking the odd leg, pulling up, completing the course whilst wearing a plaster cast to protect another injury, breaking seven ribs, a wrist, a thigh and ultimately forcing race officials to change qualification rules to stop him taking part for an eighth time in 1977.

Less known is the story of the maverick 'Englishman' George Saunders, a gentleman rider who became obsessed with the Grand National's Czech equivalent, the Velka Pardubicka. Saunders was described as 'the epitome of the raffish pre-war perspective for which the Pardubicka is now the final repository'.

It transpired that he was actually born in Munich, the son of White Russian émigrés who fled Russia after the Bolshevik Revolution. He was in England when the Second World War broke out and became a commando, then a member of the SAS, a teacher at Prince Charles's old school Gordonstoun, a Singaporean police superintendent and a financial controller to the Sultan of Brunei.

Saunders was also a useful rider and polo player who, aged a mere 62, decided to have a crack at the Pardubicka in 1982. Saunders brought his 10-year-old hunter Pahang over for the race. The horse had never before run in a steeplechase.

Saunders was confident of success: 'We have jumped many fences like the Taxis' – the name of the most formidable obstacle on the course.

Indeed, Pahang flew over the Taxis but at the very next fence, as a vital piece of the horse's reins broke, he fell at the Irish bank. Saunders ended up in hospital after breaking his heel in the fall.

The Duque de Alburquerque said, after his Brown Jack III fell in their first National – 'Poor animal, it was past it'. Saunders, upon learning that Pahang's fall had proved fatal, said: 'He was a marvellous horse who died doing what he loved.' He added, 'I am an old man and now have only one ambition – to win the Pardubicka.'

Back he came next year, to partner French Pop. The combination parted company at the sixth fence and Saunders was once again stretchered off to hospital. In 1988 a horse called Free Flow, ridden by William Sporborg, finished second in the race. Sporborg had turned down an offer from Saunders to lease the horse to ride in the event.

Saunders was far from deterred by such minor setbacks and in 1989 he turned up with Torfha – only to be stymied by a broken finger. Instead, Czech rider Petr Vozab deputized. They fell at the Taxis and the horse was killed.

When Saunders reached 70 he announced: 'I want to win this race before I am geriatric.'

Probably fortunately for all concerned he never found the right horse on which to have another go.

294 IS BIG MAC A REINCARNATION?

During the 19th century an Englishman born in Devon with the Italian-sounding name of Francis Cavaliero was a big deal in Austro-Hungarian racing – importing horses there from England, being secretary of the Austrian Jockey Club for 48 years, helping to manage the principal Hungarian stud at Kisber and acting as official starter at a number of racecourses. Cavaliero, who died in 1882, reportedly taught the Emperor Franz Joseph to speak English.

But what really makes him of interest to the modern-day racing enthusiast is that his photograph on Page 65 of John Pinfold's fine history *The Velka Pardubicka and the Grand National* shows Cavaliero to be a dead ringer for John McCririck, right down to the mutton-chop whiskers, ostentatious head-wear, and flamboyant clothes.

295 COURT OUT Sydney

Officials at the Australian racecourse Victoria Park on the outskirts of Sydney were so determined to stop anyone other than those paying to get into the course to see and hear what was going on, that in 1937 they erected an 11ft high fence round the track.

They certainly did not want broadcasters transmitting commentaries of their races – it would encourage betting to take place away from the course and affect their revenue streams.

The Commonwealth Brodcasting Corporation wanted to boost listening figures by carrying coverage of horseracing at Victoria Park. George Taylor's cottage was situated opposite the racecourse. He permitted CBC to build a 16ft high platform on his front lawn – from which the track could be seen and races commentated on.

Victoria Park had been in the news before, in 1909 when Englishman Colin Defries crashed at an altitude of 15ft whilst attempting the first powered air flight.

Now the course made headlines again, bringing a legal action to prevent CBC broadcasting from Taylor's front lawn. These days they'd probably be suing because their cards weren't being broadcast!

The case went to the Aussie High Court with the track arguing that its rights to commercially exploit its business were being violated.

Chief Justice Latham cogitated before ruling: 'I am unable to see that any right of the plaintiff has been violated. A "spectacle" cannot be "owned" in any ordinary sense of the word' The case was thrown out. It may have been cheaper for Victoria Park to double the size of its fence.

296 I WOULDN'T PLUMP FOR THAT Plumpton

It isn't exactly like being the man who decided not to hire the Beatles for his record label after they auditioned, but when a firm of racecourse managers was given the opportunity of taking on Plumpton in February 1896, an anonymous official declared in an internal memorandum to his bosses – 'I don't think Plumpton in any form or shape would ever be a credit to us as a firm, and I shouldn't like to speculate in it.'

Ironically, that firm was Pratt and Co, who, six years later, did an about-turn and did take on Plumpton – and continued in that position until 1997. In 1998 Plumpton was sold to Captain Adrian Pratt – who had no connection with his namesakes – and Peter Savill.

297 FELINE GOOD? Texas

Betting was legalised in Texas in the 1930s, and as a result there are today four racecourses in the State where punters can see and bet on live horseracing – Lone Star Park, Manor Downs, Retama Park and Sam Houston Race Park.

But if one Texan entrepreneur's bright idea had taken off racing might have been very different there, because after the laws against betting were repealed in 1933 one person applied for, and was granted, a licence to build a racetrack in Mesquite.

It would have been, though, reported *Time Magazine* on July 5, 1937 – a cat racing track! I have a feline it never caught on.

298 WISE DECISION Wincanton

Twenty eight years after making his debut at a point-to-point meeting, Anthony Knott finally landed his first winner.

The 44-year-old dairy farmer with 300 cows to tend was driven by his desire to win a race – and when he did have one at his mercy – the *Racing Post* Hands and Heels Novices' Handicap Hurdle at Wincanton in November 2008 – he nearly blew it when, with half a furlong still to run, he began to celebrate so extravagantly that he risked falling off!

Riding his own horse, 7-1 chance Wise Men Say, he stood up in the saddle and started to wave on the run-in. 'I'm unaccustomed to victory and there was a massive roar from the crowd – it was just instinct to stand up and give them a wave. Then I could hear another horse coming up behind me and I thought "Oh God, it's not finished yet" so I sat back down and got on with it.'

After 28 years of losers his win captured public – if not professional – interest. In the *Racing Post* David Ashforth complimented him for 'bringing bouncing, upright, unrestrained, enthusiastic determination to the battle', adding: 'all that was missing was ability.'

For three days he was public property as domestic media and Irish, Spanish, Italian and American TV along with BBC Radio 4, BBC World News and Setanta covered the event.

Three days later he came 'back to earth with a bump when the cows' diet feeder broke down.' (Watch the race for yourself on YouTube.com)

299 THAT'S WHAT YOU CALL HOLDING A GRUDGE!

Jockey Brian Fletcher won the Grand National three times – on Red Alligator in 1968, and twice on Red Rum, in 1973 and '74. Rummy's trainer, Ginger McCain, won the race four times – three with Red Rum and again with Amberleigh House.

In 1976 Fletcher rode Red Rum at Newcastle, treating him 'sympathetically' in the closing stages of the race.

McCain was not best pleased. He jocked Fletcher off the horse – and never spoke to him again. In 2011, by which time the silence between them had lasted 35 years, Fletcher was unrepentant. 'I couldn't win the race, so what was the point, for the sake of a few shillings, of knocking the spots off a horse who had won us two Nationals and the Scottish National?'

McCain's view of the race, for which Red Rum was even-money favourite of five runners, was a little different:

'Lacking a little of his customary sparkle, he made several mistakes during the race, and once on the run for home, looked to have no chance of winning.

'I felt that he would, if ridden out, certainly be in second place. Brian Fletcher made no move at the last fence and was beaten by a short head into third place. Worse still, the jockey expressed views to the racing press without me or the owner being present. This was in my opinion totally out of order. It was an unhappy incident that could have been avoided. It was also, alas, a parting of the ways.'

300 RACING AT THE STRIP USA

US track Golden Gate Fields recently came up with an eye-catching advert for the track, featuring a scantily clad couple – inevitably both very good looking – playing strip poker.

With both down to their final piece of clothing the male player is helped to suss out the cards in his female opponent's hand by a jockey with a hand-mirror who appears in the room unseen by the lady and then disappears into a cupboard as the sign-off tag 'We want you to win' appears on screen.

Just how knowing what your opponent has in a two-person game of strip poker would help you win is not explained! And, no, no inappropriate flesh is bared!

California Horse Racing has also used an inventive ad to encourage racegoers as a sleepy householder answers a ring at his doorbell to find a very 'hot' babe there who leaps squealing into his arms, as his wife stands behind them not looking best pleased:

'Unfortunately, some things don't stay in Vegas' declares the voice-over. 'For more fun and less trouble, come to the track'.

301 MERVELLOUS Australia

One of the most successful Aboriginal Australian jockeys was postboy-turned-top rider Merv Maynard.

He began his career in 1948 and made rapid progress through the ranks, in 1952 winning the inaugural running of the valuable Queen's Cup at Randwick in Sydney on Salamanca.

But Maynard was very disappointed that the Queen-to-be in whose honour the race was named was not present, due to the official mourning period following the death of her father.

Maynard would repeatedly stress his frustration at missing out on meeting the monarch as his lengthy career hit the heights over years at home and abroad. His wife Judy became a successful trainer and they often teamed up for big-race winners.

Judy received a phone call in 1992 purporting to be from the Australian Premier's office telling her they had been contacted by the Queen saying that during her forthcoming trip to Australia she would like to meet the jockey Merv Maynard when she attended Randwick for the 40th anniversary running of the Queen's Plate.

The Maynards took some persuading that this was not a leg-pull, but it was true and on the big day Merv spent 40 minutes with Queen Elizabeth and Prince Philip.

And the 60-year-old even tipped them the winner of the race. He retired from the saddle in 1994.

★

It's difficult to establish who was the first Aboriginal jockey (back in the day Aboriginals tended to try to disguise their origins in an effort to avoid prejudice) but, in his book *Aboriginal Stars of the Turf,* John Maynard (who, before he was a year old, had visited every racecourse in New South Wales – he is jockey Merv Maynard's son) makes a case for Peter St. Albans who, aged 13, rode Briseis to win the 1876 Melbourne Cup. Injury forced St. Albans' retirement aged just 19, and he became a trainer. He died aged 35 and was buried with 'one of the largest (funerals) seen locally' – yet 'there is no marked account or record of his burial' at the Geelong cemetery where he lies.

302 GOLD RUSH COVER-UP Australia

It seemed like the track chairman Andrew Eggleston had come up with a brilliant idea which would attract publicity and boost attendance at Gold Coast racecourse in Australia.

But the track's September 2010 announcement that it would be staging a Bikini Race in which up to 150 scantily-clad women would race out of the stalls for a A$5,000 purse soon backfired on them.

First to criticise was the local paper, the *Gold Coast Bulletin*, commenting that 'some believe this will take the city to a tacky low.'

The organisation Women In Racing wasn't convinced that it was a good idea – 'I feel using ladies jumping out of the barriers is akin to someone jumping out of a birthday cake,' said spokesperson Jennifer Bartels.

Gold Coast Turf Club's Grant Sheather just dug himself into a deeper hole when he defended the race: 'When people say Gold Coast you think of beach, you think of girls and you think of bikinis, it's a marketing ploy to build racing.'

Er, no, declared website Collective Shout – 'When we think of girls, we think of people. Furthermore this event is open to women over 18. I guess referring to adult females as women is too much to ask of a man who would have treated us like animals.'

The Bikini Stakes was subsequently banned by Racing Queensland, saying of the course: 'It is not authorised to use racing facilities for a proposed novelty race in its current format.'

303 SCALPED AT THE SALES New York

The auctioneer was happy to have sold off a Kingmambo-Imperial Beauty yearling filly for one million dollars at the August 2009 Fasig-Tipton Saratoga Yearling Sale in New York.

The purchaser was a bald man clad in a plaid shirt, sitting in the front row of seats, who signed the sale ticket but then walked off, snubbing reporters wanting to talk to him.

Anonymous bidders are not unknown at such sales but this man also refused to cooperate with Fasig-Tipton president Boyd Browning and then strode off, leaving behind him a stunned silence – and no money.

'I've never seen anything like this, declared the yearling seller, Holly Bandaroff of Denali Stud, as police were called in to interview a man in a sleeveless shirt who had been seen talking to the buyer.

'I'm told he was drunk, had no credit and has run away', added Bandaroff – and that was just about the situation.

The filly later went through the ring again, to be knocked down for $300,000.

304 WHITE HORSE MAKING A MARK
Ebbsfleet

Sculptor and racehorse owner Mark Wallinger's sculpture was in 2009 announced the winner of a competition to design an artwork to mark the building of Ebbsfleet International station in north Kent, and Ebbsfleet Valley, a new town between Dartford and Gravesend.

The 25,000 residents of the new town will not have to stoop to view his work. They will, though, have to adjust to opening the curtains each morning to be greeted by a sculpture that Wallinger claims will be a 'faithfully accurate representation' of a thoroughbred stallion.

Passengers aboard Eurostar and motorists on the A2 should be impressed by the scale of the horse that looms over them. 'Each hoof the size of a bungalow, each eye the length of a pillar box, each testicle the volume of a people carrier', explained Jack Malvern in The Times.

The Turner Prize-winning artist told The Times that his design was based on a racehorse of which he was co-owner. 'I own half of a leg of Riviera Red', he said.

February 10, 2009 was Wallinger's lucky day. Not only had his horse won him the commission but it also came in first on the racetrack (Lingfield) at odds of 11-2.

Mark Davy, whose company Futurecity is curating the project, said that the horse had to be 50 metres tall to comply with the Highways Agency. 'you have to be able to see it from a long way off. It would be too distracting for drivers if they came round a bend and suddenly saw a giant horse.'

The statue was originally estimated to cost over £2million and was expected not to be finished before the end of 2012. However, towards the end of 2010 the cost of the project had reportedly spiralled to £12m and the size of the horse to 160ft. How would you bet on whether and when it will ever stand proud over Eurostar travellers?

305 FALSE START WAS FALSE CALL France

Despite the field being ordered to stop racing on six or more occasions, a race at Cagnes-sur-Mer in January 2011 was allowed to finish and the horse which passed the post in front was eventually declared the official winner.

The race started in confusion as one of the jockeys fell off as the runners left the stalls and the course PA almost immediately began to tell the remaining runners to stop racing.

They didn't, and with punters booing throughout the seven and a half furlongs of the race, Deauville-based but British-born trainer Jenny Bidgood's 15-2-shot Lisselan Muse galloped home to win under William Saraiva as racegoers looked on in bemusement. John Spouse from the Bidgood stable admitted, 'I have never seen anything like that in my life.'

Stewards later declared that the result would stand and, according to the *Racing Post*, claimed that the starter had transmitted 'fall at the start' which came across as 'false start.' Can those phrases really sound as similar in French as they do in English?

306 SUSPICIOUS MINDS New York

It is difficult to imagine the *Racing Post* running the headline: 'Suspicions follow Rodriguez's success as trainer' but they do things differently in the States, and that was the strap-line over David Grening's *Daily Racing Form* article concerning 38-year-old Rudy Rodriguez, who ended his career as a journeyman jockey in February 2010 in order to train.

By late January 2011 Rodriguez had chalked up 71 winners from 264 starters on the New York Racing Association circuit.

'Indeed, with success – especially rapid, unforeseen success – came accusations that Rodriguez was cheating,' wrote Grening. 'After he won eight races from 11 starters at the Aqueduct spring meeting, officials from the

New York State Racing and Wagering Board and NYRA began showing up at Rodriguez's barn – investigators would be camped outside Rodriguez's barn monitoring and documenting the comings and goings of workers, veterinarians, and other visitors. In some instances, security would be assigned to sit outside the stalls of horses running on that day's program.'

'A lot of people think we are cheating,' Mexican-born Rodriguez was quoted as saying. 'I wish I knew what we were doing. We just try to put a lot of work into the horses and try to pay attention to what the horses look like, and how they are doing.'

307 ADDRESSING THE PROBLEM

Faced with the problem of naming the horse they had bought, owners of the Coventry-based bookies (Jack) Turner & (John) Kendrick did so after their company address – Seven The Quadrant.

The horse was useful, and finished fourth in the 1974 Cesarewitch. Not, though, as useful as Bernard Carroll's 2006 Grand National Winner, Numbersixvalverde, named after his Algarve holiday home.

308 MR ROCK 'N' ROLL

Trainer John Gosden was described by Rolling Stone Ronnie Wood as 'Mr Rock 'n' Roll – he knows all the words to Bob Dylan songs, he knows all the Stones' songs'.

Wood, a keen punter, owner and breeder, is also complimentary about jockeys – 'They are the toughest guys you'll ever meet' and is a particular fan of Seamie Heffernan who won the Irish Cesarewitch for him on Sandymount Earl.

309 BLAZING SADDLE

US horse Hiblaze, who was foaled in 1935, contested a world record 406 races during the 14 seasons he was active, winning 79 of them for prize money of $32,647.

Oddly enough, Hiblaze's modern-day namesake, foaled in April 1994, finished eighth of ten when contesting his first race at Nottingham in October 1997 – and never ran again.

310 STRICTLY FOR THE BIRDS (1) Australia

The first race meeting held at the newly formed township of Birdsville, situated on the Diamantina River in Queensland, eight miles north of the South Australian border, was held on the 20th, 21st, and 22nd of September 1882, and was attended by nearly 150 station owners, managers, stockmen, and other employees.

The weather was delightful, the entries for the various events good, and the finishes in most of the races close and exciting. Nearly £200 was raised by public subscription, which speaks well for the prosperous condition of the district.

The 'settling' took place in Mr Tucker's hotel, where the amounts were paid over to the respective winners, the usual toasts proposed and duly responded to, after which a meeting was held in Messrs. Burt and Co.'s large iron store, when a jockey club was formed, to be called the 'Border Jockey Club', 42 names being enrolled as members. Stewards were appointed, a working committee elected, and the next race meeting fixed for July 1883.

Back in the day, professional riders would carry a 7lb penalty and special races were held for horses bred within 250 miles of the course.

Since then the reputation of this unique meeting has spread worldwide. Birdsville is, to quote the locals, 'a long way from anywhere, but when you're there for the races, it's the centre of the world'.

The course is 192 miles from Bedourie; 388 from Boulia, 687 from Mt Isa and 1,094 from Alice Springs. In the early 1990s well-known Aussie racing writer Phil Percival visited the Birdsville races and reported that much of the appeal of the event didn't actually involve the races themselves:

'From a normal population of 100 the township swells to somewhere between 5,000 and 6,000 for race weekend. Birdsville at race time is full of bizarre sights: a group of exuberant young men giving the 'one-eyed' salute from the pub roof being invited down by the ever friendly police, a 'gentleman' leaning against a police vehicle with a protective arm round a naked blow-up doll, race day and a group of young 'ladies' conducting a wet t-shirt competition in the grandstand – without the benefit of water or t-shirts, a clutch of young men streaking down the straight after the Cup, with the winner giving a most unusual victory salute, you may receive a bit of a start on your first trip to the

toilet block at the back of the course, generally being greeted by a 'g'day mate' by gentlemen with jeans around the ankles sitting on the thunder boxes.'

Some Interesting Birdsville Facts:

- A bell was rung as horses left the enclosure and connections were fined ten shillings for horses not at the starting post within five minutes.
- Separate races were programmed for corn-fed and grass-fed horses.
- Races were once started by the drop of a hat.
- The Birdsville Cup distance has remained 1 mile or 1,600 metres since its first running in 1882. In 1949 and 1950 the 'Hospital Handicap' (1 mile) was run in lieu of the Cup. Meetings were held then to raise funds for the construction of the Birdsville Hospital.
- The annual race meeting is now held to raise funds for the Royal Flying Doctor Service.
- With the exception of a period during the Second World War the Birdsville Races have only ever been cancelled twice. Firstly, in 2007 when the outbreak of Equine Influenza in Queensland and New South Wales (in the week prior to the races) saw a complete ban on horse movement. As a result horses were unable to travel to Birdsville and the races were cancelled. Entertainment and festivities did continue throughout the weekend despite the lack of horses. Wet weather did for the September 2010 meeting, stranding several thousand racing fans already there for days.

Racing Post writer Nicholas Godfrey attended the meeting in 2005 and came back in awe of its 'well-earned reputation for monstrous doses of mayhem', describing it as 'Oktoberfest held in the Wild West' and 'the place where someone stuck a few running rails around a patch of desert next to a couple of tin shacks and called it a racecourse.'

311 STRICTLY FOR THE BIRDS (2)
Brighton

Graham Smith was employed by Brighton racecourse as a parade ring safety officer – but in July 2010 he suddenly found himself in a flap and his feathers were ruffled as his role was added to – he was handed responsibility for scaring seagulls off the track.

In June 2010 a gull had come close to hitting Choreography and his jockey Pat Dobbs, then in July a flock took off in front of the field, causing Celestial Girl, partnered by Chris Catlin, to swerve sharply across the other runners.

'It seemed sensible to have somebody who can send them (the seagulls) on their way if they land on the track before a race' explained clerk of the course Ed Arkell.

Smith soon developed a technique involving high-tech tactics such as shouting, flapping his arms and walking rapidly towards the birds.

Geese in 2008, and swans in March 2011, held up racing at Kempton until a man with a stick moverd them on.

312 RACE RIOT Reading

A riot broke out at Bulmershe Heath races near Reading in 1775. After the last race had been run one of the riders going to weigh-in was assaulted, whereupon a pitched battle broke out between 'gentlemen on horseback and the foot people'.

It was later dubbed 'The Battle of Bulmershe Heath' by a poet whose work was reported by the local rag the *Berkshire Chronicle* – 'The Heath resounded with the clatter, Of whips and sticks which heads did batter' – no, it did not get any better!

Two people were sent to Reading jail as a result.

Eleven years later at the course one of the most blatant examples of 'stopping' a horse happened when the favourite Miss Tiffany, who seemed to have the race in safe-keeping, was ridden into by a mounted man, and knocked down.

The mare was awarded the race by the stewards and it subsequently transpired that the miscreant was the owner of another horse in the race, which he had backed heavily.

313 LONG AND SHORT OF THINGS
Downpatrick

The Gaelic name is Dun Padraig – 'The Fort of Patrick'. Most know it as Downpatrick.

The 2m6f Ulster Cesarewitch was the longest Flat race run in Ireland in 1984 when it took place at Downpatrick that October. It was won by the Janet Morgan-trained Bavard's Song, ridden by Andy Nolan.

But it turned out that the race was even longer than supposed. Because they started it from the wrong place on the course – which made it a 3m race. So they held a stewards' inquiry. And allowed the result to stand. That's the long and the short of things.

This dual-purpose course is the oldest in Ireland as racing began in 1685. One of the 'founding fathers' of the thoroughbred breed, the Byerley Turk, ran there in 1690.

314 WHEN SCU WAS BUSHED
Fontwell

Peter Scudamore came unstuck – literally – riding Vistule at a Fontwell evening meeting in the mid-1980s.

At the first hurdle in the back straight second time round, the horse dived off the track and Scu couldn't do anything about it. The commentator said, 'Vistule has run off the track and Peter Scudamore has disappeared into the bushes...' The crowd erupted with laughter which seemed to go on for the rest of the race. It was loud enough for the commentator to hear it up in his box. It struck a chord with those who heard it, for he was reminded of it twenty years later when a stranger asked him, 'Are you still commentating at Fontwell? I was there the day you said Peter Scudamore had disappeared into the bushes!'

Thanks to Fontwell historian Jim Beavis for that story.

315 FRANKLY, TUTU MUCH Fontwell

JP McNamara would have been forgiven for pulling up his mount Colonel Frank when one of his stirrup leathers broke midway through a novice hurdle at Fontwell in 2003.

Instead, JP decided to do without stirrups and rode the final circuit with his legs dangling free and clutching his mount's mane.

Amazingly, he hit the front and held off the late challenge of odds-on favourite Desmond Tutu by a diminishing distance, as the result went to a photo-finish which the favourite was 1-10 to get. But the photo showed JP and Colonel Frank had just got the verdict.

316 PENNY DREADFUL
Churchill Downs, USA

On November 22, 1968 Penny Early became the first female licensed to ride in the States, but when she turned up for her first race at Churchill Downs, she had no-one to race against as the male jockeys scheduled to ride in the race boycotted the event and refused to take part. 'I'm disappointed and disgusted. I've no respect for the jockeys – as riders or as males'.

After being treated in this manner three times, Penny found she did have support in some quarters as the diminutive, 5'3" rider was signed up by the Kentucky Colonels basketball team as the first female pro in the game. She duly made her debut, clad in a mini-skirt, against the Los Angeles Stars on November 27, 1968 – wearing the number 3 on her kit to refer to the three boycotted races. She actually got on court to take part in one play before making her exit to huge applause. That was the end of her basketball career, but the point had been made.

- Churchill Downs in Louisville has been the home of the Kentucky Derby – always preceded by the mass singing of the track 'anthem', 'My Old Kentucky Home' – since 1875. Seven years later they held the first jump race here on a course made up of 'hurdles, stone walls and water jumps.'
- Churchill Downs' Derby Museum houses film of all the races since 1918.
- In 1910 the first aeroplane flight in Kentucky took place, from and around Churchill Downs.
- The course was declared a National Historic Landmark in 1986.
- The course's trademark spires were refurbished as part of a $121m 2005 renovation.

- In 2006 the course welcomed the Breeders' Cup for a record sixth time and the next year the Queen and Prince Philip turned up for the Derby here – 38 years after President and Mrs Richard Nixon had done so.
- The ashes and a bronze statue of ill-fated 2006 Derby winner Barbaro are located outside Gate *1 at the track.
- Novelist Heather Clay, a local girl, said of the course's Derby Day, in April 2010: 'It is both an annual slice of Americana on a par with the Super Bowl and the Indy 500 – the track's infield scene is perhaps just muddy enough to appeal to hard-core English football fans – and in the clubhouse and winner's enclosure, a genteel meeting ground for owners and appreciators of fine bloodstock from all over the globe.'
- The Derby winner is covered by a horse blanket containing 554 red roses. In 2011 it was Animal Kingdom, a shock 209-1 winner who had never run on dirt before; he was trainer Graham Motion's second string before his Toby's Corner was withdrawn injured, as was anti-post favourite Uncle Mo, freeing up jockey John Velazquez to partner the winner, whose intended rider Robby Alberado broke his nose three days earlier.

317 PENNEY DREADFUL Newcastle

Long-serving ITV commentator John Penney – who covered the first ever screening of the ITV7 bet on October 4, 1969 – nearly had his career cut short shortly afterwards when he was at Newcastle.

'My position was at the top of a 30ft scaffold specially erected for the day. The wind can be very strong on odd days at Gosforth Park and this was one of those semi-hurricane days.

'I was none too happy climbing up the ladder and when I reached the top I was unable to stand in the conditions. Consequently I did the first and only race on my stomach as the tower swayed back and forward.

'The cameraman said "Come on, John, I don't care for this, let's get down." Not long after we reached terra firma, the entire structure keeled over and collapsed.'

318 THE DEADLIEST TRACK?
Puerto Rico

The Associated Press ran a story about racing in Puerto Rico in May, 2008, which shocked many who read it.

'Canovanas, Puerto Rico – For thoroughbreds in this U.S. Caribbean territory, being fast enough to win, place or show is a matter of life and death. Losers often don't even make it off the racetrack grounds alive.

More than 400 horses, many in perfect health, are killed each year by injection at a clinic behind the Hipodromo Camarero racetrack, explained chief veterinarian Jose Garcia. The Associated Press examined clinic logbooks that confirmed Garcia's account.

The handwritten logs list the names of the horses, the trainers, the date of execution and the dosages of lethal drugs. Garcia allowed an AP reporter to view the logs but prohibited him from taking notes or photographing the pages.

Unlike on the U.S. mainland, where many former racehorses are retrained for riding or sent to refuges, the animals have few options in Puerto Rico. Owners say caring for and feeding a losing racehorse is too expensive.

'If it doesn't produce, after a while I give it away or I kill it,' said Arnoldo Maldonado, 60, a businessman who races about five horses a year. 'It bothers me, but it has to be done because there is no money to pay for them .... I'm not going to keep losing.'

The killings also bother veterinarians who carry them out. While many horses are unsuitable for adoption because of injuries or bad tempers, far more could be rescued than the current few dozen a year, Garcia said.

The veterinarians at the racetrack clinic have an informal system of contacting farms and breeders about a possible home for the animal when a healthy horse comes in to die. But so far there are no programs such as the U.S.-based Thoroughbred Retirement Foundation, which rescues horses coming off the track.

The racehorses put to death in Puerto Rico are not being killed because they have suffered a serious injury. Here, even when a second home is available, veterinarians say that some owners want losing horses executed anyway – some to save money, others for revenge.

'You'll get a few owners who get so upset, they just want the horse dead,' said veterinarian Shakyra Rosario.

There are Puerto Ricans such as trainer Berti Zequeira who make it their business to rescue the rejects. Lionel Muller, senior vice president at Hipodromo Camarero, Puerto Rico's only racetrack, said owners generally have the horses killed only as a last resort when they cannot find a suitable second home.

'Most of the horse owners really love the horses. You don't want to get rid of a horse that way,' he said.

319 COURSE THAT ISN'T – AT THE MOMENT
New Zealand

NEW ZEALAND is pretty good at listing its racetracks. The official website said that there are 52 racecourses (65 Racing and Jockey Clubs in total) although it lists 53, explaining, though, that one of these is currently inactive but endeavouring to be restored to the active list.

Gus Wigley of a Kiwi racing paper told me: 'The additional course you counted may have been the Rangiora racecourse. Official racedays are no longer held on the course after a jockey was seriously injured (Judy Lawson was left in a coma for 11 days) in a fall a couple of years ago. The club is fighting to have its racedays restored so it's in limbo at the moment – it's a racecourse, but it's not officially raced on at the moment.' As of May 2011, racing was still suspended.

320 SMALLEST AND HIGHEST?
India

On the website indiamarks.com I discovered a reference suggesting that there is current racing at Lebong, Darjeeling – an area at 7,000ft altitude: 'Lloyd's Botanical Garden displays a fine collection of Himalayan fauna for those with an interest, and for punters there is horseracing at Lebong, the smallest and highest racecourse in the world.'

On the 8th of May 1934 a serious incident took place at Lebong racecourse. Two revolutionaries, Rabindra Nath Bannerjee and Bhawani Bhattacharjee, made an attempt on the life of John Anderson, Governor of Bengal, as the jockeys and horses were being led into the paddock after the Governor's Cup race.

The attention of the security staff was centred on the paddock. No-one noticed the two 'freedom fighters' walk quietly up and open fire. Each one fired one shot each, but both missed and were overpowered. Sergeant Coombs fired back and hit Bhawani, wounding him, while Rabindra's automatic jammed after his first shot. The police arrested both. The governor escaped unhurt.

Bhawani was sentenced to death, Rabindra to life imprisonment, and five other associates were imprisoned.

321 GOT IT TAPED Sydney

The 5-2 favourite for the 1908 Epsom Handicap at Randwick in Sydney, Australia, Soultline finished a well beaten fourth, but had a reasonable, if unique, excuse – the tapes from the starting gate wrapped round his forelegs as the runners started, and they did not come loose until the field had gone three furlongs.

322 LISA'S ON TRACK New York

Tim Snyder was destined for a life involving racing – having been born at a racetrack.

Tim's dad, Warren, was a jockey in the States and in 1954, when he was riding at Scarborough Downs in Maine and had just ridden a winner, his pregnant wife headed for the winner's enclosure to greet him, only she tripped on the escalator and went into labour.

Tim was delivered in the track's first-aid room. He grew up to become an owner, trainer and rider. His wife, Lisa, was a stable hand at Finger Lakes racecourse in New York who tragically died of ovarian cancer in 2003 aged just 38, having comforted her mother by telling her: 'Don't worry, I'm coming back as a horse.'

In 2006 Snyder took on a filly who had a clubfoot and had been blind in one eye since birth, named her Lisa's Booby Trap after his late wife, and sent her out to race at Finger Lakes where she won her first race by 18 lengths – encouraging an offer of $150,000 for 49 per cent of her ownership. Snyder turned the offer down. Lisa's Booby Trap won her second race by over ten lengths, then her third by over eight – now the biggest offer was $500,000.

'She's not for sale at any price,' declared the owner who then ran her in her fourth race, this time at the more highly regarded Saratoga track – which she won by six lengths under top jockey Kent Desormeaux.

'I basically talk to her the same way I talked to my wife – I always relate her with Lisa, I know that sounds kind of crazy,' said Snyder in August 2010.

Snyder said he was confident that a proposed movie and book deals will materialize. He said the latest offer for Lisa's Booby Trap was in the $1 million range. A defeat first time out on grass at Saratoga in September 2010, when she started favourite but finished last, suggested that Snyder should have taken the million and that the tragic story may not have a happy ending.

I have only been able to trace one race for the horse since, when she finished third of five at Finger Lakes, on September 24, 2010, ducking to one side at the start, then bumping another horse. Incredibly of $126,977 bet on the race, $120,021 was on Lisa's, the 1-4 favourite.

'Perhaps the end of the story is at the end,' wrote racing writor Tim Wilkin, of timesunion.com afterwards.

323 HERE, KITTY York

The running of a 1791 sweepstake at York for hunters carrying 12st, which had never won a 'plate, match or sweepstake' and were ridden 'by a gentleman', ended up in court after the winning rider's entitlement to be considered a gentleman was objected to.

Elderly Kitty Rowntree, already over 70 and a local smallholder, was hired by owner Mr Thomas Burdon to ride Centaur – which he did so capably that he won the race.

However, afterwards the runner-up's rider, Mr Chichester, objected on the grounds that Rowntree was not a gentleman, and clerk of the course Robert Rhodes withheld the prize money of £123, despite having approved Rowntree's bona-fides pre-race.

Incensed, Burdon insisted on taking the case to court where it was heard by a jury who were told by witness James Rule that Rowntree 'may be' a gentleman but 'has not much that appearance', being 'old, with one eye, dirty leather breeches and an old wig not worth eightpence.'

Despite that the jury found for Burdon, who was duly handed his winnings.

324 MAN ALIVE Isle of Man

In 1813, horseracing on the Isle of Man was flourishing. On Easter Monday, at Peel, there were a number of races run. These were as follows, according to the day's racecard:

- For horses – a saddle, value three guineas, and a bridle, value one guinea.
- For horses that have never raced before - a saddle, value three guineas.
- A pony race for a bridle and whip.
- A sweepstakes for the beaten horses.
- A pair of breeches, raced for by men in sacks.
- Three yards of linen, run for by women.
- Six pounds of tobacco, grinned for. (GRINNED for? What a laugh that must have been! GS).
- A pig, run for.

The *Isle of Man Weekly Gazette* of April 22nd that year gave a fascinating account of these sports:

'In the second heat for the Maiden Plate, the horses had not run half a mile before one of the jockies (Paddy), who rode Lord Doelittle's horse, was thrown into a dangerous position by the saddle slipping. His feet having quitted the stirrups, he actually held the saddle with one hand.

He lost that heat; to console him a subscription purse was handed to him containing three and sixpence.

The sweep was run for (course, one mile, horses rode by gentlemen) by the following thoroughbred mares:- Mr. C – tt's Long Back, Mr. H – d's Physic, Rev. Mr. M – d's Mountaineer. They went off at score, and continued neck to neck chief part of the heat, which Mountaineer won by a length and a half.

Many hundreds were depending on this race, though the mares were all 'broken winded.' The course was attended by most of the nobility and fashionables of the Island, and the banks on each side of the course were filled with beauty and elegance. The ordinary at Grant's Liverpool Coffee House was sumptuous, and conviviality was the order of the day.'

325 DEAD AND ALIVE IN KENTUCKY USA

Author Patti Nickell wrote a book, published in 2009, called *Horse Lover's Guide To Kentucky*. Morbidly, the book reveals that 'the tradition of erecting monuments to deceased thoroughbreds began with the death of the great stallion, Lexington. (presumably named after that area of Kentucky and leading US sire 16 times between 1861-78 – GS). Horses are buried and memoralized (sic) in the Bluegrass in different ways. Few are buried in their entirety.'

Mm, so only bits of horses get buried, then – but which bits, I wonder?

And as for Lexington, buried there – 'don't expect to find it' warns the book, 'as Lexington's remains were exhumed shortly after his burial and donated to the Smithsonian Institution – at press time, there were plans under-foot (underground might be more accurate, wouldn't you say?) to bring those remains back to the Bluegrass.'

See, who said Kentucky, which boasts five racecourses – Churchill Downs, Ellis Park, Keeneland, Kentucky Downs and Turfway Park – is a dead and alive place?

However, in June 2009 Kentucky Governor Steve Beshear did warn that the Kentucky horse industry was 'dying'. His solution was to legalise slot machines at racetracks in order to boost revenue and prize money.

326 TALL TALE USA

Founded in 1994, the Hoosier Park, Indiana track had a real tall story for racegoers who turned up there in October 2003 to see what they were told was the world's tallest jockey.

And 7ft 7in NBA basketball star Manute Bol would have been just that – had his arthritic knees allowed him to get on his intended mount.

However, as he was doing it to raise funds to help his war-torn homeland, Sudan, racegoers still afforded him a great reception.

327 EGGING GIRLS ON Canada

Canadian jockey Shannon Beauregard rode her first winner in 2003 at Assinaboia Downs. She still recalls the 'celebrations' – 'At the end of the meet the guys grabbed me and duct taped me and tarred and feathered me with corn syrup and big bags of coloured feathers.'

Such events are still apparently commonplace at US and Canadian tracks, and Chicago-born rider Sally Chappell remembered a double dose following her first victory at Remington: 'I got mustard, ketchup, eggs and honey and all that kind of stuff. Ice water too. After I thought I was all in the clear, the girls came in and did the whole painting and shoe polish thing. Luckily I didn't have to ride another horse after my win. It took me many days to get cleaned up after that.'

Allison DeMajistre Juvonen had another slant on the experience:

'Brent Bartram was the only guy I knew at Hialeah because I hadn't been in Florida very long and we had both been at Delaware. After the race he knocked on the door of the girl's room and said he wanted to congratulate me. He shook my hand with one hand and smashed an egg over my head with another. That actually meant a lot to me since no one else even mentioned it was my first win.'

However, jockey Anne Sanguinetti who had recently scored her first winner at Bay Meadows observed: 'It isn't as bad as it used to be because I think they had some lawsuits. They can't paint you or use tar on you like they used to do.'

328 DI-ABOLICAL TREATMENT USA

One of the early trail-blazers for female riders, Diane Crump rode from 1969-85, becoming the first woman to ride in the Kentucky Derby in 1970, before training and then returning to the saddle. Diane remembered a particular incident-packed race:

'The first time I was asked to ride in Puerto Rico I was in a match race with the leading rider. We were head and head around the first turn and my horse pulled about three-quarters of a length ahead and the Puerto Rican was holding on to my saddlecloth and let my horse carry him for about a quarter of a mile.

Then he came back head and head and pulled my stirrup leather and knocked my foot out of the iron, then jerked on my rein as he got close to my horse's head. Through the stretch I cracked him with my stick but he wound up beating me by a length.

When we pulled up and came back to unsaddle, the women in the crowd were throwing tomatoes at him and cussing him out!'

329 CHARLIE'S DARLINGS Newton Abbot

Chief Executive at Hexham racecourse, Charles Enderby responded to a plea for strange stories by telling me of the time when the course's first streaker ran past him whilst he was in conversation with an 'elderly, grand, blue-rinsed' female racegoer.

'As I tried to distract her from this unsightly scene, I told her "My goodness, I'm sorry" to which she responded, 'So you should be, he was a very fit young man and I could have done with longer to look at him."

And Enderby also recalled the big gambler who turned up in a Rolls-Royce some twenty years ago, staking a £25,000 bet on the first race and losing, before doing precisely the same thing on the second, third and fourth races. Realising it was not to be his lucky day he stormed back to his 'Roller', only to discover his chauffeur 'at it' on the back seat with his girlfriend.

330 TOWERING TREV

Owner Trevor Hemmings, whose Ballabriggs won the 2011 Grand National, sold Blackpool Tower and the Winter Gardens to the resort's council for £40m in March 2010. The self-made multi-millionaire also owns Preston North End FC.

331 UNDER AGE GAMBOLING

Grand National-winning trainer Donald McCain Jr learned to ride on a pony called Gambol and, thanks to a little 'creative thinking' by his Dad, Ginger, was under-aged at 15 when he rode on the Flat for the first time.

332 SING WHEN YOU'RE WINNING

Turf Paradise track announcer Michael Chamberlain was feeling nostalgic on Sunday, April 3, 2011. As the horses came down the stretch in race five at the Phoenix track, Chamberlain cleared his throat and called home winner Que Sera Sera to the tune of the same name in honour of Doris Day's 89th (possibly, she has claimed different birth years in the past!) birthday. The song was Day's calling card, one she made popular in the 1956 Alfred Hitchcock movie *The Man Who Knew Too Much*.

'I'm a big fan of that older entertainment genre with names like Sinatra, Martin, Cole,' said Chamberlain, 40, who is in his second year as the Phoenix track's announcer. 'I noticed it was Doris Day's birthday when I was checking my email, and when I got to the track I saw a horse named Que Sera Sera in the fifth, and thought it would be perfect to sing the song if the horse won and yell out 'happy birthday' to the woman who sang it. I just wish I would have been enough of a hunch player to put a couple bucks on it.'

Que Sera Sera paid $10.80.

333 THINK THEY'RE ALLOWED TIBET? Tibet

It was apparently decreed as long ago as 1408 that 10-28 April each year should be set aside for prayer ceremonies, featuring horseracing, at Gyangtse in Tibet. It is reported this happens to this day.

334 SO LONG Bath

At an evening meeting at Bath, three hot air balloons came low over the course and delayed the racing. They were hovering so close that Tim Long, the clerk of the course, could read the phone number on the side of one of them, so he rang it and asked the balloonists to go away – maybe in somewhat more emphatic terms than that.

335 CHEESE BERGER Tasmania

Off the coast of Tasmania is King Island which has something in common with England's Chester races – cheese plays a big part in the racing scene! Chester famously awards the winner of the Chester Cup a Cheshire cheese – on King Island they boast a world famous dairy, run by cheesemaker Ueli Berger, who just happens to combine his work of preparing firm cheddars and creamy bries with preparing horses to race on the island.

He also has one or two unusual training ideas – like preparing one of his decent horses, Malediction, for big races, by 'driving' the gelding as a pacer. It worked as he went on to win on the flat. The track runs a 'fly-in raceday' in January when light planes fly in from throughout Australia to enjoy the sport.

'It's always a great day with fashions, live music, cheese sampling, trotting and gallop races on our fantastic one-mile track with its natural amphitheatre,' said local trainer Ian Johnson, who gave a preview of a future attraction – a human hurdle race. 'Runners will start from the barriers then dash down the straight carrying a champagne flute and jumping over five hurdles. The winner will be the one with the most liquid left in the glass.'

336 TAYLOR MADE FOR RACING

'She loved her horses and was the perfect owner. She almost preferred not to run them,' said John Gosden, reflecting on the time Elizabeth Taylor, who died in March 2011, had horses with him. 'If she could have run a petting zoo for horses that would have been perfect for her.'

She did, of course, win the Grand National, albeit in the 1944 movie *National Velvet* in which she played 12-year-old Velvet Brown who dressed up as a boy to win the race, only to be disqualified when the truth was uncovered.

337 TAXING TITLE Newbury

The March 2011 running of Newbury's 'Floor v David HL 1979 Handicap Hurdle' was an example of accountant David Cliff's unique naming of the races he sponsors after tax cases in which he has been involved.

338 CRAZY FEET Cheltenham

The Cheltenham Festival of 2011 was notable for the sale of designer shoes for ladies made in the style of real horse feet – the E1343.67 footwear knee- and ankle-length zip-up 'hoof shoes' were commissioned as a stunt by Betfair.

At the same Cheltenham Festival, the Irishman who turned up dressed in a foam map of Ireland was rewarded, reported a *Guardian* journalist, by 'several undeserved kicks in the Cork and Kerry mountains!'

339 ROWDY RACE GOERS

Coming to the last, Harry Marriott on Rowdy Yeats had the race sewn up and just had to jump it to win.

He didn't jump it, instead taking his horse to one side of the fence – and automatic disqualification by the race officials at Hackwood Park point-to-point on Easter Monday 2011.

The distraught 49-year-old claimed he heard a shout of 'Go Rowdy, go Rowdy' and mistook them for 'Go round it, go round it'!

340 NATIONAL KNOWLEDGE Aintree

Grand National course trivia:

'The Chair' jump was so named because a chair used to be placed there for a judge to sit on as he determined whether any horses had been beaten by a distance.

The Water Jump is the only fence less than 4ft 6ins high on the course

Valentine's is named after 1840 runner Valentine who tried to pull himself up there, but pirouetted over the fence and brook, running on to finish third to Jerry and Arthur

The Foinavon fence is named after the 100-1 shock 1967 winner of that name, the only runner not to come down or be interfered with there on the second circuit.

The Canal Turn is situated where the course meets the Leeds-Liverpool canal.

341 HEARTY CONGRATULATIONS

Hearty congratulations were offered to jockey Hywel Davies, who survived a fall in 1984 despite being so badly injured that his heart stopped seven times en route to hospital.

342 TO TELL OR NOT TO TELL

Useful chaser Tell Henry, a multiple winner from 2005-2009, was owned by a syndicate called Don't Tell Henry. Make your mind up!

343 NO PRESSURE, THEN!

Riding in a pony race when he was on the cusp of his teenage years, jockey Aidan Coleman, born in 1988, was unfazed when an owner came up to him and 'told me how many grand he had on his horse – I never let it get to me. I still don't,' he said – without revealing whether he'd won on that one! He hasn't always been a great judge – given the choice of Venetia Williams' 2009 pair of Grand National runners, he opted for 50-1 Stan who fell at the seventh while Liam Treadwell rode Mon Mome to a 100-1 shock win.

Coleman had ridden Mon Mome in 2008 when they were eighth and decided to get back on in 2010 – and fell at the 26th!

344 NOW DO YOU SEE?

Grand National runner Becauseicouldntsee, 16-1, fell in the 2011 Grand National. Like stable-mates from the Noel Glynn yard Gonebeyondrecall and Writingonthewall the name comes from the lyrics of Sean Keane's folk song 'Writing On The Wall'.

345 LET'S SEE McCOY DO THAT!

The Olympic Games of 500 and 496BC featured horseracing – but not quite as we know it. Author David Potter describes in his excellent 2011 book, *The Victor's Crown*, how there was a feature event for 'mares whose riders would run alongside them in armour for the last lap', holding the reins.

346 SPRAY THAT AGAIN!
Australia

When Brazilian jockey Wanderson D'Avila was disqualified from a race – he weighed in light on Short Trip at the Gold Coast Turf Club on February 19, 2011 – he came up with a unique defence. He had used a slimming spray which had prompted unexpected weight loss.

D'Avila's lawyers also launched a lawsuit against the makers of SensaSlim Solution for $12,500 plus loss of reputation. The jockey, who reportedly rode some 400 winners in his native country, apparently saw the product featured on Channel Seven's 'Today Tonight' programme in mid-February.

He reportedly alleged that during the programme the company said that when the product is sprayed onto a person's tongue it fooled the brain into believing they had eaten. It said SensaSlim 'sprayed away hunger'.

D'Avila purchased a bottle of SensaSlim for A$60. He sprayed the product onto his tongue and found that it did reduce his cravings.

Court documents said on the day of the race D'Avila admitted spraying the product several times more than the recommended direction. During the post-race weigh-in, he was 0.8 kilograms under his allocated weight. As a result he was disqualified and suspended from racing for one month.

He claimed that in 20 years of racing he had never weighed in light and attributed the weight loss to using the SensaSlim spray. He said he bought SensaSlim because it 'sprayed away hunger' but claimed it was not made clear to him that it would also 'spray the kilos away'. D'Avila claimed he had suffered professional embarrassment as well as loss of earnings due to the racing suspension.

The Aussie media was sceptical, one paper commenting: 'It is one for the would-you-believe-it sporting hall of fame, alongside Shane Warne's mum's slimming pills.'

The 35- year-old Avila, who has ridden in Britain, boasts an entry in the *Directory of the Turf* in which he lists one of his interests as 'swimming'. One wonders whether he meant 'slimming'!

347 NOT SO LUCKY, THEN! Wincanton

Wincanton racecourse employee Mike Cridge was on duty as a fence steward at the track's April 2011 meeting when he was knocked unconscious by a flying horseshoe which flew some twenty yards before hitting him on the forehead. He was air-lifted to hospital but later released.

348 DOWN AMONG THE DEAD MEN Redcar

When Channel 4 broadcaster and *Racing Post* hack Alastair Down commented that he wanted 'He never went to Redcar' engraved on his headstone, the track decided to tempt him to visit them. General manager Amy Fair managed it by naming one of the races on an April 2011 card the Alistair Down Gravestone Selling Stakes and inviting Down up to see the event and make the race presentation – an invitation he duly accepted.

349 HAUNTED HOUSE Newmarket

'This yard is full of history and Mat Dawson and Fred Archer are supposed to haunt it. I've been here every night of my life at 10pm for 44 years and I've never met them,' said trainer Sir Mark Prescott in March 2011, of the alleged co-dwellers at his Heath House Stables in Newmarket.

350 THAT'S RICH USA

Susannah Ricci is the wife of the improbably named, unfeasibly wealthy American banker Rich Ricci. The Midnight Club, who ran in her colours, trained by Willie Mullins, was a well fancied contender for the 2011 Grand National, but didn't win. Says Mr Ricci, co-chief executive of Barclay's Capital, and co-chief executive of Corporate & Investment Banking: 'watching my horses lose is like going to a job interview and then puking all over yourself.'

351 POTTY NAME

Alan Spence, owner of 100,000 euro yearling Hurricane Higgins, reportedly managed to get permission from the snooker star 'scribbled on the back of an envelope' to use his name just 'a couple of weeks' before the former World Champion died.

Betting slips on which Hurricane Higgins wrote messages to friends were due to be auctioned as this book went to press.

352 WEDNESDAY WINNER Hereford

Simon Gegg, owner of April 2011 Hereford winner Big Robert, insisted on trainer Matt Sheppard finding races for his runners on Wednesdays – as he had to spend the rest of the week looking after his 104-year-old mother.

353 FENCED OFF

Irish jump jockey Leslie Brabazon, who eventually turned to training, began riding winners in 1907. On one occasion he demonstrated his burning desire to secure a victory.

Set to partner a well fancied contender in a big race at a racecourse called Ballyhaunis, he walked the course on the evening before the meeting and saw a fence with an open ditch which he thought his mare would not fancy jumping and would probably pull up at.

Thinking things over, Brabazon went out at the dead of night with a can of petrol – and burned the fence to the ground.

Brabazon also contested a Flat race at the Curragh for which there was no winner. One horse swerved badly during the race and ran into a pillar, and was fatally injured. Brabazon finished runner-up to St Dunstan – which was objected to and disqualified – on Marble Hall – only to discover that as an amateur at the time he was not qualified to ride – and he was also promptly thrown out, leaving no winner.

354 SHARP SHOOTER

Kent trainer Philip Sharp lost a horse in an extremely strange manner when his hurdler Zimbabwe disappeared without trace after getting loose and finding his way on to a military firing range in January, 2010.

A year later Sharp was still pursuing a claim for £10,000 over the ten-year-old gelding's loss. He told the *Racing Post* in March 2010 that although the horse could be seen on CCTV, police were not permitted to enter the area by the military.

In early 2011, Sharp told me that Zimbabwe's remains were found on the shooting range and that he was pursuing a duty of care and public liability case.

355 FESTIVAL FROLICS Cheltenham

There were plenty of strange goings-on at the 2011 Cheltenham Festival, not least Henry Cecil making his first ever visit to the course (although it was suggested he may have been before in the dim and distant past) – and celebrating with a winner as his Plato won the charity 'bumper', run to raise cash for a cause close to Henry's heart, Cancer Research.

The final stages of the Ryanair Chase, won by Albertas Run, was almost the scene of tragedy as a protester clad in a bright orange jacket and brandishing a placard complaining about the sponsoring airline came close to bringing down runners.

That cut little ice with AP McCoy – 'If he'd brought me down I would have knocked him out', or Ryanair's racehorse-owning boss, Michael O'Leary – 'If someone's out there trying to generate some cheap publicity let them do it.' Pots and kettles, maybe?

The media became very excited when a woman racegoer arrived on the Wednesday wearing a hat made from a dead fox, which produced a reported comment from fur-specialising milliner James Faulkner – 'I find it very satisfying to make something beautiful from something gruesome.' It was not clear whether the racegoer had any connection with retail outlet Wear The Fox Hat, which was selling its wares in the tented village at the course.

Then there were the Animal Aid protesters carrying tombstone-shaped placards each bearing the name of one of the 32 runners to have died at Cheltenham over the last ten years, calling the track 'Britain's most notorious death trap for racehorses.'

Claiming to be the 'first social betting community', a new betting firm plugged their business by handing out condoms bearing the legend 'only gamble with Bodugi.com'. Binocular, the reigning Champion Hurdler, was withdrawn from the race a couple of days before it, over a scare that he might fail a drugs test if permitted to run.

Binocular's trainer Nicky Henderson was forced to scratch the horse from the feature event on the first day of the Festival when it became clear that he would fail a post-race drugs tests if he took part. The gelding, who was found to be suffering from an allergic reaction two weeks earlier, had been treated with a steroid, believed to be cortisone, which had failed to clear his system as expected.

Henderson later admitted that he had placed a bet – reported as £1,000 – at odds of 16-1 that his stable would not send out a single Festival winner. Long Run's Gold Cup victory scuppered the wager but *The Times'* chief sport correspondent Matt Dickinson asked: 'Is racing comfortable with the idea of a trainer backing against himself. Shouldn't there be a rule against fun such as that?' And Charles Sale in the *Mail* called it an 'astonishing admission.'

Henderson later had his knuckles rapped by racing authorities over the incident.

356 THAT BET'S AN ACCIDENT WAITING TO HAPPEN, MATE! Sussex

Betting shop proprietor Duncan Lillywhite was sitting quietly behind the counter of his branch in East Wittering in West Sussex in 2003, when suddenly 'a woman in a car managed to mount the pavement and come straight through the shop window, taking down the whole shop front in the process.'

The stunned Lillywhite 'sat shocked behind the counter, with the car parked in the middle of the shop' as racing coverage was broadcast onto his screens as though all was normal.

As Duncan started to come to terms with what had just happened, 'there's glass everywhere, we're comforting the woman, the police are on the scene, but one of my regulars came into the shop, picked up a betting slip and sat down, studying the form as if nothing was happening.'

357 GOOD HEAVENS, WOOD YOU BELIEVE IT? Goodwood

Until now I believed the only mystery of Goodwood racecourse's famous Trundle Hill, which traditionally provided a cheap, natural view of the track, was how I'd failed to back a winner there when taken for my first ever trip to the races, aged about 9!

But I now know that there is a much darker mystery connected with the place, revealed or, perhaps, rediscovered, by the magazine *Fortean Times* in its March 2011 edition.

Writer Peter Hassall, who had discovered a report of the incident from almost 30 years ago, told what happened early in the Second World War to a group of soldiers stationed there by an ancient hill fort.

It was a bright, moonlit night in 1940 on Trundle Hill, 'its bowl-like top giving it the appearance of a small volcano.' Four troops were stationed in a small, wooden shack, erected there by the Army, assigned to report any aircraft they spotted flying overhead.

One man was on duty, the other three resting in their bunks, when the soldier 'felt his hair rise and an inexplicable shiver sweep his body.'

His companions sat bolt upright. They decided to check that all was well outside but found they could not open the door which they discovered had been jammed shut by two large timbers. They finally managed to heave the door open.

'Lying at the foot of the wall of the hollow was a round ball, black and glistening, perfectly round, at least three feet in diameter. As they gaped, it began to move up the slope, to the top of the hollow. For a second, it paused on the very lip of the bowl, then disappeared, seeming to defy the laws of gravity.' They dashed to the spot where the ball had disappeared and saw it bouncing down the hill 'until it vanished in the lifeless gloom. For ever.'

There was a sensational incident at the track on March 20, 2010, when Kieren Fallon was punched in the face by owner David Reynolds, after partnering Elna Bright, who was struck into during the race in an incident which cost the favourite The Scorching Wind, owned by Reynolds, its chance of victory.

Fallon brushed off the incident at the time, dismissively observing: 'He came up behind me when I was unsaddling, but I'm all right – he hits like a girl.'

Reynolds, who admitted to losing a 'substantial gamble' on The Scorching Wind, claimed Fallon had impeded his horse.

360 MAN, TOURIE WAS TOUGH Australia

These days if a horse so much as breaks free before a race and runs a furlong or so before being caught, it will almost certainly be withdrawn.

Austin Dillon, a top Aussie jockey before the Second World War, recalled winning three races in one afternoon at Manangatang in 1922 on a horse called Don Tourie.

'I rode the horse and won the Maiden Plate, the Manangatang Cup and the Welter – we had brought him the day before by train from Ballarat, and the day after we walked him the 60 miles to Ouyen. The day after that it was 112 degrees in the shade and the horse ran second in the Ouyen Cup. He was a great horse.'

In those days Manangatang was, recalled the jockey, 'rough and ready – we didn't have anything like running rails. The track was marked out with red flags on bamboo sticks and usually ran between the trees and wherever the scrub was cleared.'

361 MAIDEN WINNER Maidenhead

When they raced at Maidenhead in September 1754, Driver won the Give and Take Plate, run over three heats – in which he was ridden by a different jockey in each. Thomas Brett fell off in the first, being replaced by David Newcomb, whose jockeyship was 'so poor' he gave way to Thomas Arnold, who won on the horse.

362 LOW ART Ludlow

They began racing at Shropshire's Ludlow racecourse on August 27, 1729. It used to have a Flat track, part of which is now incorporated into the jumps-only course.

The course acquired a bizarre link with Hitler when, in April 2009, 13 paintings by the German dictator were sold at auction there for almost £95,000.

363 WHEN THE SH*T HIT THE FANS! Jersey

Jersey used to boast four racecourses. Admittedly that was a few years ago – one of them was a point-to-point track at Plemont, which was still going in the mid 1940s, and another was a Flat-racing course at Les Quennevais in St Brelade by the Don Bridge railway station, where they raced twice a year. Recalled Jersey bookie Neville Ahier in 2010, 'The Germans used the stand as target practice during the Occupation, they made big holes in it, but it was still standing when racing resumed after the War.'

But they now have just the one course on the island, Les Landes, which is where jump jockey Richard Dunwoody added a unique achievement to his CV – he won their Derby.

A large holiday crowd at Les Landes was once 'treated' to the unedifying sight of a jockey in, er, soiled breeches after his weight-reducing tactics had, literally, back-fired on him.

Trainer Alan McCabe recalled the occasion when, in March 2009, he related what he described as the strangest and funniest thing he had seen on a racecourse: 'A friend borrowed a pair of breeches from a big-name jockey also riding at the meeting. He had a low weight to do, and had taken a substantial quantity of laxatives. While riding a vigorous finish he had an involuntary motion which resulted in one very messed-up pair of breeches. 'There was no hiding it when he dismounted.'

364 RACING MAY FLOURISH IN GUERNSEY Guernsey

Racing began to suffer from a lack of interest in Guernsey

during the late 1980s and it came to a shuddering halt in 1992, only to be resuscitated in 2005 when an estimated 4,500 spectators turned up to see the card.

Now, just once a year, on the first Monday in May, the golf course at L'Ancresse on the Channel Island of Guernsey is transformed into a racecourse. The track utilises railings purchased from Ascot when that course was being remodelled. 'The starter is mounting his rostrum' said the course tannoy when I was last there. I looked through my binoculars and saw him clambering unsteadily on to a collapsible stepladder he had brought along with him.

I went racing for the second time in Guernsey in May 2009. Fortunately, not only horses trained on the island qualify to race there – seeing as when I was there, there was only one horse trained on the island, and it was out, injured.

I looked at the on-course prices for the first race – which added up to 192% – and decided to stick to the sweepstake my party had organised for the afternoon.

Welsh trainer David Evans had sent a team of horses over and won three of the five races on the card – including one in which he had two runners, both apparently well fancied, until, with minutes to go before the race, a note appeared on the 'runners and riders' board that one of them would be carrying a mere 13lb overweight. The other one, reported by the local paper the next day to be owned by a Guernsey bookie, romped home by several lengths without appearing to break sweat.

There is an interesting link between Guernsey's modest but enjoyable L'Ancresse meeting and the Kentucky Derby. Mark Johnson was the course commentator at Guernsey – until in 2009 he was otherwise engaged calling the Kentucky Derby – so he was replaced in the Channel Isles by Lee McKenzie, who did the business nicely despite being stuck up on an exposed platform of scaffolding in the markedly chilly conditions.

By the time the last race came round there were a few brightly attired golfers queuing up, impatiently tapping their clubs against their golf shoes and hoping the course would be down in time for them to play around or a round.

In 2011 adverse weather conditions cut the card short – but minutes after the abandonment was announced, the bad weather cleared away and the sun came out – too late.

★

The island has a maximum limit on the number of betting shops, currently set at seven – the number of years one must have lived on the island in order to apply for a licence.

Betting shops there cannot open on Sundays, cannot advertise or provide any refreshments, and cannot offer betting machines. Any new ones opening, and all but one of those already trading, have to be first floor premises.

Oddly, although they cannot open on Sundays, they can still accept bets – as punters can also legally bet at dozens of pubs, corner shops and garages which have arrangements with bookmakers on the island and will pass the wagers on to them via the phone, from which it is quite legal to operate on Sundays!

365 MERTON MULTIPLES Australia

If you delve back into Britain's racing history you will occasionally find examples of horses running – and even winning – twice in an afternoon.

Merton racecourse in Victoria, Australia, held a meeting in January 1947 in which four of the six races boasted 16 or more runners.

But, explained Aussie racing writer Robert White, 'Closer inspection of the race card reveals that nearly every horse was entered in at least four – and sometimes five – races.'

366 OH MOE IS ME Moe, Australia

Having lost three late-2009 meetings because of rain, and having had to transfer their major event the Moe Cup to another track, Cranbourne, officials at Moe (an hour outside Melbourne) were confident that their January 2010 card would be dry. It was.

But then there were fears that the temperature would soar to an unhealthy 43 degrees centigrade.

So it was called off.

On the day, though, temperatures reached 'only' 39 degrees centigrade – still over 100 degrees Fahrenheit by my calculations – so it could have gone ahead.

367 MANE CHANCE France

It was May 2010 when I visited Le Lion d'Angers in France – where I saw several people suffering from the 'Angers' after backing losers, but there was no sign whatsoever of anything remotely resembling a Lion.

This was a very nicely laid-out track which featured the most entertaining cross-country chase any of us had ever seen, which involved the horses hurtling down what appeared to be a ski-run, then ascending the north face of the Eiger; taking sharp right-hand turns, then sharp left-hands, then doing a lap or two of the parade ring (I just may have been hallucinating when I saw that happen) before getting out their maps to trek off round the more distant reaches of Lion, or Angers, or wherever we were, before plunging into the water obstacle which seemed to intimidate the riders more than the horses.

Anyway, I backed the winner, so that helped make it one of the greatest racing spectacles I've witnessed.

But, as ever, tragedy is never far away from a racecourse, always lurking in a hidden corner, occasionally emerging to stun everyone and remind us of the price to be paid for enjoying racing.

Francois Doumen had a chaser running, Desert Jim, ridden by Hippolyte Huet. Coming to a fence on the first circuit Desert Jim and another horse took spectacular tumbles. The other horse rose and galloped off, minus rider. Neither Desert Jim nor Huet got up.

Desert Jim had died instantly. Huet was rolled on by one of the fallers.

The latest news I have been able to glean about Huet's condition was that he recovered the power of speech, but was paralysed from the waist down.

368 COMPOSER IN TUNE WITH RACING

Composer Sir Edward Elgar's (1857-1934) interests included sport. During the 1890s, he watched Wolverhampton Wanderers, while in later years his fancy turned more towards horseracing, particularly the jumps – he lived at various times in Worcester, Hereford and Stratford.

The story is told of the young composer William Walton who, finding himself unexpectedly alone in Elgar's presence, was overawed by the occasion and lost for words. Elgar broke the silence by asking Walton if he knew who had won the afternoon's big race. And other stories are told of Elgar curtailing important engagements so as to be off to the races.

369 ON THE BRIDLE Australia

Contesting the big race of the afternoon at Newcastle in New South Wales, Australia, during 1899, the horse Cromwell came to grief during the event – but his troubles had only just begun, reported the local paper:

'The whips of (jockeys) Tracey and Wilson were stolen after the lads had fallen. The bridle, too, was taken off Cromwell after the horse had fallen in the Cup, and there is no doubt that if the thief could have got Cromwell into his pocket before Mr James Mayo (the trainer) reached the spot, the veteran would now be deploring the loss of the gelding as well as the bridle!'

370 WELL DONE – YOU CAN'T COME IN! Newton Abbot

On May 17, 2010, trainer Karl Burke completed a 2,500-mile, £10,000-raising charity cycle ride, taking in every British track, when he pedalled wearily to Newton Abbot.

However, as he had been banned for a year for passing information for reward, and warned off as a result, Burke, who finished on his 47th birthday, was not allowed to set foot in any of the tracks he visited.

371 PHOCEANE HELL France

An October 2009 jaunt to France enabled me to see a rare, albeit not unique, racing phenomenon – horses competing in a race at Nuille Sur Vicoin (don't ask me, I don't have the slightest idea whereabouts in the country I was) which included having to run through a river – twice. Actually, by the time the horses had been shown the obstacle and asked to go through it prior to the race, it was four times – for those who made it to the final stages, anyway.

One or two horses made it obvious they didn't fancy the idea, and had to be, er, persuaded to go through the wet stuff by their sometimes equally reluctant riders.

It made for a great spectacle and I saw no horses injured or distressed as a result, although the same could not be said for all of the jockeys and, particularly so, as must have been inevitable as soon as I decided to back it – for the one I lumped on.

When in foreign parts my favoured betting technique is to opt for runners whose names mean something to me. In this instance my cunning plan was to back the horse with what appeared to be the rudest name on display. Which is why I was on Phoceane - which may not look very rude to you, but with a certain amount of imagination and inventive pronunciation, became very coarse indeed as I bellowed it out over the heads of the hopefully non-English speaking spectators.

It had some effect, clearly, because having had his doubts about the river on the pre-race introduction, Phoceane decided that although he would go through it during the race, he would do so only on the understanding that his rider didn't come with him.

So, as the field shaped up to ford the river, Phoceane cleverly bucked off his jockey and made his own, individually serene way through the flowing waters, sans jock.

All well and good, but Phoceane decided then to jump along with the field until they reached the farthest point of the course – and then set off in splendid isolation off through the surrounding, very rural countryside, never to be seen again during the remainder of the afternoon.

By now the, erm, medics – well, two blokes clad in fluorescent tabards and armed with a stretcher – had made their way over to the prone jockey. Once there they stopped for a fag and to discuss the situation – occasionally bending over to seek the opinion of the fallen horseman, who upon closer perusal of the racecard I discovered was not only the jockey, but also trainer and owner of Phoceane – and quite likely, also driver of his horsebox.

After several minutes in deep thought the stretcher bearers came up with

Hassall appealed to readers for any information or details they may have heard, read, or been told about the mysterious incident.

358 OPAL FRUITS Australia

This is what local racing historian Phil Percival told me about an intriguing Aussie track: '*A quaint racecourse in the little western Queensland town called Lightning Ridge. The course is just about in the middle of town, and at Easter they have their only race meeting of the year.*

They warm up on Good Friday with a rodeo. Not sure if some of the racehorses are part of the show, but there are plenty of the western 'brumbies', along with the western cowboys with their colourful shirts, jingling spurs and big hats (in the summertime it's 100 degrees in the water bags and the crows fly backwards to keep the dust out of their eyes).

Saturday morning to whet the appetite for the afternoon races it's a programme of goat races – they provide lots of entertainment, especially when a couple of old Billy goats take exception to each other and start fighting.

Then it is on to the horseracing, and some of the contestants do look remarkably like a few of the buck-jumpers that were throwing cowboys the day before, but it does show what a wonderful sport racing is.'

The Race Club was formed in 1909 'and in the early days jockeys used bits of a tree to add to their weight', secretary Denise O'Brien told me, adding: 'I believe we're the only straight track – 1,200 metres – in Australia. The meeting also promotes black opal, for which Lightning Ridge is famous, and a beautiful solid gold and opal bracelet is the trophy for the Lightning Ridge Cup.'

359 FACING CRITICISM Lingfield

On February 5, 1998, Lingfield's all-weather going, which for nine years had been uniformly 'Standard', was officially declared 'Slow'.

A racing oddity took place here in February 2008 when trainer Peter Grayson won a 5f maiden race with 40-1 shot Stoneacre Pat, having saddled six of the nine runners, and suggested to punters that his 20-1 chance Stoneacre Chris had the best hope of winning.

the illuminating insight that they might as well put the stricken cavalier on this piece of equipment and haul him back to the ambulance, which hadn't been able to drive over the bridge to reach him.

This they did, then drove him off – no, not to hospital as I had naively imagined might be the obvious course of action – but up towards the spectators and in close proximity to one of the track's alfresco bars. I can't swear to seeing them down a tumbler or two of the local vin blanc, but there is no doubt that they threw open the rear doors of their ambulance car and appeared to invite interested parties to come over and have a look at the presumably still breathing potential cadaver in the back.

There followed much shrugging of shoulders, waving of arms, prodding of prone body and baffled expressions, before someone did seem to decide to take the matter in hand and drove off with the fallen rider to, well, who knows where.

And as to what happened to the long departed Phoceane, I have no idea – and what's more, I can't really pretend that I could care less.

372 NON-RUNNERS ALLOWED? Newmarket

Twenty-one horses were withdrawn at short notice from racing at Newmarket on Friday, July 18, 2008. Had there been a sudden downpour or some other unexpected change in the going? Well, no.

Perhaps there was such bad traffic locally that none of the horses were able to make it to the course. No, that didn't happen.

However, Stephen Wallis, managing director of the course, believed he knew just why the horses had been withdrawn. According to trainer Mark Johnston, who reported it on his website, Wallis had explained that 'there was an explosion in the number of non-runners at their meeting on Friday, 18th July, because of owners and trainers declaring horses, with no intention of running, just to get tickets for the Girls Aloud concert.'

373 TRYING TIMES Navan, Ireland

'The Place of the Cave' is the translation of dual-purpose course Navan's Gaelic name, An Uaimh. They have raced at this track since 1920.

In December 1983 there was an odd incident at the course concerning what the *Irish Field* reporter of the time, Dave Baker, described as 'what appeared to be the most glaring example of non-trying that I have witnessed.'

Eleven days earlier Wee Mite had finished 20 lengths clear of Monanore. In the Dunsany Novice Chase, Wee Mite was 5lb better off than Monanore, yet was beaten by three lengths. Wee Mite had drifted from Evens to 15-8 pre-race.

'Wee Mite ran tailed off to beyond halfway,' wrote Baker. 'She did not seem to be asked for an effort until the last fence and did extremely well to get as close as she did.'

Racegoers were enraged: 'About two-thirds of the attendance rushed to the unsaddling enclosure and ugly scenes followed. The rider of the favourite had to receive a Garda escort. Some blows and kicks were exchanged at one point and a couple of crazy patrons even "had a go" at the horse.' Baker concluded: 'This is the sort of happening that brings racing into disrepute.'

374 ON THE OTHER HAND New Zealand

In 1974 New Zealand's prestigious Wanganui Cup, run under that name since 1880, acquired a new sponsor, a meat-packing company, who renamed the race the Tenderkist Cup.

Not everyone was best pleased and the local paper declared the race title was too commercial and would not be carried in their columns. Fine, responded the Tenderkist people, then we'll withdraw all of our advertising from your paper.

The Tenderkist Cup, whose title survived until 1992, was mentioned frequently in the local paper thereafter.

375 OF COURSE IT'S A MOUNTAIN! Australia

Mount Wycheproof Racecourse is named after what has been registered as, at 45 metres (some sources say 43m) in height, the world's smallest mountain.

Small it may be, but when the track was opened in 1891, it gave course officials a problem – as many racegoers preferred to sit on top of the mountain looking down on proceedings for free, rather than paying to get in.

The *Mt Wycheproof Ensign* reported in 1899, 'Buggy loads of people passed through the principal street on their way to the course, which is situated at the rear of The Mount, from the summit of which a full view of the course can be obtained by those who have scruples against paying for admission.'

376 ALL DAY AND ALL OF THE NIGHT France
South of Bordeaux, French course Mont-de-Marsan laid claim to the title of earliest rising racecourse in Europe in July 1993 when it staged the first race on the card at 8.45am.

I once attended a meeting at Naples where they still had a couple of races to run when I left at around 12.30am.

377 ROCKING THE DOWNS USA
Austin, Texas track Manor Downs, the smallest course in the state, is pronounced MAY-ner Downs, and is where legendary rock band the Grateful Dead played a gig in July 1982. Course owner Frances Carr Tapp, a rock promoter, toured on the road with the Dead until they stopped gigging.

In 1986 the course hosted a Farm Aid concert, staged to draw attention to the plight of America's small farmers, at short notice when the original venue for the show featuring Willie Nelson, Neil Young and John Mellencamp fell through.

378 PHILLIE FISTICUFFS USA
Spectators came to Philadelphia Park on January 8, 2010 to watch the racing – but were surprised when a boxing match seemed to break out.

Jockeys Erilus Vaz and Ademar Santos traded punches down the back stretch during the fifth race, with Vaz landing the first blow. Santos hit back, then Vaz used his whip. After the race Santos claimed that Vaz had 'veered' his mount, Divine Light, towards him three times before throwing a punch.

'I asked: Man, why you go like that?' Santos told the *Philadelphia Inquirer*. Answer came there none, as 'He hit me in the face – in the mouth.'

Santos claimed he struck back as a reflex action but did not make contact, which prompted Vaz's whip strike.

379 PUNCHING ABOVE ITS WEIGHT?
Punchestown, Ireland

Punchestown is an Irish track whose Gaelic name Baile Fuinse translates to The Valley of the Ash Trees. The course may have hosted 'the biggest crowd to ever attend a race meeting in the world' when, in 1868 the presence of the Prince of Wales drew a crowd 'reckoned to be 150,000', reported contemporary sources.

Punchestown has retained the spectacle of the old-fashioned style of racing over banks and walls with the Avon Ri La Touche Cup and the Ladies Cup at their Spring Festival – the former being won on seven consecutive occasions between 1995 and 2002 by Risk of Thunder – there was no race in 2001. The horse was owned by actor Sean Connery.

In 2010 in an unusual move, Punchestown the racecourse teamed up with Punchestowns the racehorse when the course offered to refund the cost of admission to its April festival if the horse won the RSA Chase at the Cheltenham Festival.

April 2010 saw the continuation of one of the greatest examples of one trainer dominating a particular race at a course – the La Touche Cup was won by L'Ami for Enda Bolger, taking his record in the event over the previous 13 runnings to an incredible 12 victories – missing out only in the 4m3f contest in 2008, having first won it in 1997 with Risk of Thunder.

In 2011, Denis Murphy-trained Another Jewle won the cup.

380 WOLVERHAMPTOFF?
Wolverhampton

Jockeys were told to pull up as they approached the stricken runner Sheila's Bond, who had suffered a broken leg on the second circuit of a 2m handicap at Wolverhampton in March 2011.

However, despite a flag man waving a flag, blowing a whistle and telling them to stop riding, some continued when a stalls handler reportedly said they should carry on.

The 17-2 chance Six Of Clubs passed the post first in front of Carnac, 4-1, and Prince Charlemagne, 8-1.

Eleven had started the race, with champion jockey Paul Hanagan, who was leading at the time, ceasing to race on 7/2 favourite Rare Coincidence because of the flag man, eventually coming in 94 lengths behind the 'winner'. Two other jockeys did not complete the course, but stewards allowed the 'result' to stand.

Fortunately for punters most bookies paid on the outcome and returned stakes on other horses.

BHA spokesman Paul Struthers claimed that 'stewards could not void the race because there were finishers' and Wolverhampton clerk of the course Fergus Cameron agreed, but Sheila's Bond's rider Kieren Fox said: 'It was as clear as day they were waving the flag, blowing the whistle and shouting "pull up".'

381 CAGNES YOU BELIEVE IT? France

Just a couple of years ago I went racing at French track Cannes – or is it Cagnes? (Cagnes-Sur-Mer, actuellement - pedantic Ed) – I'm never quite sure and neither are the local folk, because on the top of the grandstand is a sign saying Hippodrome Cote d'Azur.

You're in France so you expect a culinary treat from a racecourse restaurant, don't you? Sure enough, lovers of oysters get that treat because the first course is a dozen of the slimy things. I once saw renowned *Guardian* and *Observer* racing journalist, the late Richard Baerlein – the man famous for tipping Shergar with the words, 'now is the time to bet like a man' – tip two dozen of the beastly objects down his neck at a William Hill sponsorship announcement do. I don't like them, though – and nor do most of the 28 of us in the racecourse restaurant because we all send them back.

Next course will be better, though, won't it. Yes, if you are partial to the thinnest-sliced, most tasteless tuna you're ever likely to see or fail to taste, garnished with a slice of lemon.

Mm, at least there's a third course – beef. Possibly, beef, that is. Maybe some four-legged animal which once raced against other four-footed animals. Perhaps just an hour or two ago. The ones who ordered it well done got it just the cooked side of rare, the ones who asked for medium noticed it was still moving. It came in huge chunks the size of house bricks which crashed down into the stomach with similar impact to an edible house brick. As for the mushroom and/or spinach ravioli accompanying it – words fail me.

Pudding always comes up trumps doesn't it, though. Since you ask – not on this occasion. Cold, stodgy and of indeterminate variety. The whole thing cost us 60 euros each. Without wine.

We're English, though, so we leave the waiter a tip.

382 THERE'S ORAISON France

Oraison is a tiny course in the south of France, to which I repaired in the spring of 2000, accompanied by a modest picnic laid on by my host – modest, that is, for assuming you had the appetite of a Billy Bunter on a hungry day and the quaffing capacity of someone capable of quite copious quaffing.

The few locals who had turned up looked on enviously as I and a party of other apparently starved and parched Brits gorged themselves in the sun whilst listening to a somewhat incongruous musical soundtrack blaring from the course's tannoy system – *Music* by John Miles, *Oxygene* by Jean Michel Jarre, plus much from the likes of Status Quo, Gloria Gaynor, Barry White – someone had clearly just discovered a Greatest Hits of the 70s gramophone record.

The racing programme featured trotting but there were a couple of Flat races, the form to one of which revealed that a well-bred runner owned by Mme Andre Fabre had obviously been brought here to get a win under her belt, regardless of quality of opposition.

I teamed up with Middlesbrough fan Brian, to whom I had only been recently introduced, and we decided to land a coup. On the grounds that I used to work for boxing and betting big cheese Jarvis Astaire, we added Mistic Astair to make a straight forecast and bunged in a good proportion of all the francs (tells you how long ago it was!) we had left and headed down to the 'bet' window where the elderly gentleman behind the counter seemed shocked that there should be so much money in the world as he painstakingly counted our cash.

As our bet entered the tote system, so the attractive predicted odds of 16/1 beat a rather hasty retreat to half that price, to our chagrin.

We watched the race whilst waving bottles of the local rose around and occasionally sipping from them as the Fabre favourite duly cruised to a smooth win with Mistic Astair running on strongly from the rear to take second. The forecast returned 8.90 to the franc so we marched back, this time to the 'payout' counter, watched with great suspicion all the way by the locals who gathered round to gasp as vast quantities of the now ex-currency were loaded into our grasping hands.

One of the most satisfactory experiences I have ever enjoyed on a racecourse – well, apart from that time behind the grandstand when – well, enough of that for now!

383 NOT REALLY SO COMIC
New Zealand

In 1895 *The Sporting Times* carried an advertisement for a Maori race meeting taking place at Okoroire, New Zealand.

Spotting the ad, British paper *Racing Illustrated* had a little fun at its expense, exclaiming that the rules governing the meeting 'are quite comic enough to warrant reproduction here' and proceeded to do just that. I think the rules which caught the *Illustrated*'s eye were these ones:

- 'Don't bring any drink to these races. Well, there are plenty of courses who have that rule today – not to stop people coming in drunk, but so that they have to pay the inflated prices once a captive audience inside! On the day I wrote this, the *Racing Post* carried a letter from Rob Green of Nottingham, complaining of 'having had my carrier bag searched at several courses for food and especially alcohol, and seen signs at others stating "no drink to be taken in"'. Plus ca change, eh?
- Men who have taken much drink will not be allowed on this course. If any man disobey this rule he will bring the whip of the club down on him. It isn't clear whether that is a literal or metaphorical 'whip', but I don't envisage too many sober racegoers disagreeing with that action.

- No girls will be allowed to ride as jockeys. Hayley Turner might have
  something to say about this one.
- Jockeys must wear trousers in all events. Not clear whether this rule is
  related to the one directly above!
- No jockey must knock any other jockey off his horse, or strike any other
  jockey with his whip, or swear at or threaten any other jockey.
  Fair enough, such offences are not unknown today.
- 'Any jockey breaking these rules will be driven from the course if he does
  not pay 20s to the Treasurer.' All in favour?
- 'Persons allowed to see these races must not say rude words to the
  Stewards or swear at jockeys who do not win. 'No, I couldn't go along
  with that one!

★

Commented *Racing Illustrated*: 'It is not necessary to go back into the dark
ages to recall the time when the foulest sort of riding was common enough
in this country, especially in steeple-chases. The Stewards, when in evidence,
are sacred over here and need not fear "rude words", but now and again it
is unquestionable that the populace not only swear at jockeys who do not
win, but occasionally proceed to stronger measures.'

384 SORRY SRI ON WAY BACK? Sri Lanka

Nuwara Eliya is the highest town in Sri Lanka, where racing
dates back to 1840, and is also the location of the country's last
functioning racecourse, which during the mid-90s boasted a resident stable
of just three racehorses, which competed regularly against each other,
supplemented by a few other runners rounded up from nearby farms to fill
up the track's annual two-day season April.

In 2009 the course was still extant, albeit doubling up as a cricket pitch
for locals, with the correspondent of a tourism website reporting: *'A colonial
legacy, this is as far as I know the only proper racecourse in Sri Lanka.
Horseracing is big business in Sri Lanka – bookmakers make a fortune from
people betting on races held in England, and names such as Ascot and the
Grand National are well known. I'm not sure how often the course is used
for horses but there are plenty of ponies hanging about, cricket matches*

going on, a rubbish dump in the middle, and it's used as a shortcut through the town!'

However, by 2011 things were looking up as high profile companies came forward to sponsor the main races of the season, including the Governor's Cup, and a fashion show and giant screen were amongst the on-course attractions.

385 MUSICAL PHOTO FINISH
France

I added another unique occasion to my racing experiences when, in 2003, I visited a racecourse called Salon, in Provence, where they put on a mixed card featuring Flat racing and trotting.

But it was the first time I had seen a trotting race where the jockeys actually rode the trotters rather than sitting on one of those – whatever they call them – sulky things. And the interesting thing is that even when they are being ridden like that the horses still trot in that stylised manner. This means that gambling is more of a risk than it ever is on Flat racing, because almost invariably in every trotting race a relatively high percentage of the runners are disqualified for breaking into a run rather than a trot, so not only do you have to find the winner, you also have to hope the horse doesn't then get kicked out.

The trip also introduced me to a unique culinary delight. Offered a choice of a meat dish or a fish dish at the Salon restaurant I enquired of the waiter what variety of swimming creature it might be: 'Wolf,' he told me. So I had it. Wolfed it down, in fact. Very nice.

I also witnessed here an extremely entertaining set-to – the like of which I'd never seen before at the races – as the local band – several neatly uniformed chaps of a certain age – performed lustily in the intervals between races.

They then decided it would be appropriate to continue playing when the course announcer was making his, er, announcements. So, he shouted more loudly to make himself heard – which encouraged them to greater heights of brass bandy endeavour.

In the event the band, average age, I would say, around 73, claimed the honours in a photo-finish when, with the commentator beginning to get the upper hand as he urged spectators to get behind the young jockey who had just ridden a four-timer (he went on to become champion jockey a couple of seasons later), one of their members pulled out of his back pocket a secret weapon – sheet music, which he handed out to his colleagues, who then launched frantically into a rousing version of *Mambo Number Five*.

The commentator realized he'd met his match – and shut up.

386 MOROCCAN MAYHEM Morocco

It took some finding, but I was determined to do it – discover a 2007 Derby which Frankie Dettori wouldn't win.

So in mid-June of that year, following the Dettori dominance of the English, French and Italian Derbies, I headed for Morocco and the Souissi racecourse where the Derby was the fifth event on an eight-race turf card. It attracted ten runners to do battle for the first place prize money of 22,000 dirham – approximately fifteen hundred quid. Unlike the opening race on the programme, which was finished before it should have started – having been down to start at 1pm, but actually going off early and finishing at 12.59 – the Derby did go off at its proper time. Like all the other races, there was no commentary whatsoever, which made it a bit tricky to work out what was going on and demonstrated just what a breakthrough it must have been when the first commentaries were introduced to British racing.

Anyway, my optimism was justified and Frankie signally failed to ride the winner. The fact that he wasn't even booked to ride any of the horses and was probably thousands of miles away from the racecourse may have had something to do with this dismal failure by the diminutive Italian – but the Moroccan crowd realised that history had been made in the shape of a Derby not won by Dettori, and celebrated wildly. So wildly that one stable lad, who might just have had a bob or two on the winner, ran on to the track and began to strip off in his excitement. He was only just restrained by his pals from joining winning jockey Abdul Harrat on the back of the winner, Tantan, as they returned to the winner's enclosure.

But the Derby wasn't actually the most valuable race of the afternoon. That honour went to the sixth race, the Grand Prix de Sa Majeste, worth 100,000 dirham to the winner – about sixteen grand. A good-sized field of

14 faced the starter. But hot favourite Safety Meeting – whose Dad is a horse probably familiar to most British racegoers of a certain vintage, Kingmambo – seemed most reluctant to enter the stalls.

The horse was given as much time as it took to install him and he justified the support of racegoers by romping home in sensational style. His stable lad was even more ecstatic than the Derby winner's. He hurled all of the equipment he was carrying into the air, where it fell to earth, narrowly avoiding several nearby racegoers. He was then engulfed, screaming with joy, by hordes of well-wishers. He rushed to his returning equine hero and smothered the horse in pats and kisses before leading him into the grandstand area, right in front of the table where we were sitting enjoying the racing and the buffet laid on for our delight and edification. I must confess that one part of that last statement is not entirely accurate, but I have no wish to offend the good people of the Souissi racing establishment so I will not divulge which part, except to hint that it just might concern the food.

The horse demonstrated its delight by planting enough of the contents of its stomach on the floor, to demonstrate graphically just why this course is one of the most florally abundant I have ever experienced. Some members of the party with which I was travelling will have empathised with Safety Meeting's actions.

Revelling in the attentions of the crowd and the euphoric owner, a Mme M El Alami, who had been sitting amongst us without ever suggesting that we should all back her beast, the horse watched contentedly as the owner was handed the spoils of success in full view of, ooh, perhaps five per cent of the racegoers present.

But the best of my first exposure to Moroccan racing was yet to happen.

The last race of the day. I decided not to play. Everyone else got very excited about the fact that the favourite in the final event was owned by a member of the Moroccan Royal Family – descended directly from Allah, they are, if I understood correctly the explanation of the guide who showed us around the city of Rabat. I think I did, after all, he did invite all 26 of us into his house which boasted, he declared proudly, 'a very big toilet.'

So, concluded everyone else, the Royal runner must be a certainty. My misgiving was based on the fact that if every horse with a Royal owner were to win every race they contested, even the most slow on the uptake Moroccan punter might soon figure that something was amiss in the conduct of the sport.

The Royal horse, Rubiszo, won the race.

Much celebrating and hilarity abounded, reduced only a fraction by the stern admonition of our own private Tote operator that he would not be able to pay out on the last for a few minutes. This was the same Tote operator who had introduced clients to the bizarre rule that only bets placed in multiples of six dirhams would be acceptable. So that instead of, for example, one hundred dirhams, he would insist that only 96 be staked. And would then discover that, frustratingly, he didn't have the four dirhams change immediately to hand. Odd, huh?

The few minutes dragged on for a few minutes more, then Tote man gestured the punters over. One or two of them had a strange expression on their face as they returned to our table. Well, how much did you win, then? I asked. 'Er, apparently, nothing. He's given me my money back.'

The trickle of punters treated this way became a stream. No-one had been given any winnings. The race had been voided, went one rumour. The winner was so heavily backed that no-one had bet against it so the win dividend was the equivalent of refunded stakes, went another.

That rumour was scuppered by the undeniable proof that many people had indeed bet against the Royal runner. And that there appeared to be no punter riot going on amongst the slightly, shall we say, more robust element of the crowd.

Whatever the explanation, Tote man had now become 'former Tote man'. He'd disappeared. Just about at the same time as my companions had realised that if everyone backing the winner was only getting their money back and/or the race was void, anyone backing a loser must also be refunded.

But our coach was waiting, Tote man had done a runner and no-one else on the racecourse seemed to be able to speak English, or understand what they were being asked. And most people had only gambled a hundred or so dirhams which they were not going to be allowed to take out of the country with them, anyway.

I know what I reckon was going on, but I do not wish single-handedly to end the apparently flourishing diplomatic relationship between Morocco and England by explaining it in detail.

So I won't go back there in a hurry.

387 CHELSEA GIRLS ON TOUR America

I attended the 2008 Breeders' Cup partly because the previous year's Breeders' saw us almost washed away in a monsoon of biblical proportions at New Jersey's Monmouth Park, so better US weather was almost guaranteed, and duly supplied; and partly because legendary sportswriter Hugh McIlvanney had told me that Santa Anita was the most beautiful racecourse in the world and that I must see it.

He's not far wrong – although I'd have to say Guernsey's L'Ancresse might give it a run for its money, albeit Guernsey boasts fewer mountains to encircle its track.

At Monmouth Park I'd set a new personal record of 19 consecutive losers, most of them ridden by Frankie Dettori. I'm not one to hold grudges (sorry, don't know what came over me, there. Actually, I really am one to hold grudges - sometimes for years and years, but that's another story, so let's pretend for the purposes of this book that I'm not.)

Anyway, seeing as I wrote a book about Frankie and he was kind enough to help me out with it, I will always owe him a small debt of gratitude. So I stuck with his mounts on Day Two at Santa Anita, deciding that he and Sixties Icon were a banker bet in one of the early races, the so-called Marathon, run over that marathon distance of, er, one and a half miles.

The horse's trainer, Jeremy Noseda, clearly agreed with me, because before the race he'd got great US jock, Jerry Bailey, to give Frankie the lowdown on the track, and after the race he told the media something along the lines of 'if jockeys listened to the instructions given them by trainers they would ride more winners'. Frankie evidently didn't listen, or if he did, he didn't hear. He gave Sixties Icon what I judged to be a stinker of a ride and never looked like winning.

Mr Noseda got his revenge by jocking Frankie off the horse a few weeks later. I got my revenge by backing him again in the next race, to ensure that he continued his Breeders' Cup losing run - which he did when he led close to the line only to be collared by a strong finisher.

Frankie's luck was clearly out so I decided to look elsewhere for betting material.

You will almost certainly recall that Frankie then went and produced vintage displays to win two of the biggest races on the card, in the process proving the old adage that if you get value in the price, the horse seldom wins.

I had backed American equine hero Curlin at 3/1 for the Classic before flying out. He was backed down to 4/5 and shorter on course, only to be left trailing by Frankie's mesmerising performance on Raven's Pass.

Every Brit bar one in the place was bellowing Frankie home. I maintained my dignified composure, and only booed Frankie enough to attract the attention of one or two law enforcement officers.

Around me the British press pack appeared to be parking their traditional neutrality at the starting gate and were high-fiving and back-slapping each other. Yes, of course, it was a great story for them to write about but I have the smallest hunch that they may also have been demonstrating that their financial futures had just been declared healthy regardless of credit crunches – as they had clubbed together in an effort to win the big accumulative Pick Six bet on the day – and had gone and scooped the pool.

Oddly, they seemed unwilling to reveal the extent of their financial good fortune but I heard later that a few of them trousered (skirted, frocked? Well done to my colleague, Kate Miller) decent five-figure sums. I even – through gritted teeth – congratulated one or two of them, who didn't appear to care what I thought.

I haven't yet seen the good journo friend of mine who had told me two races before the end of the card that he was wondering whether to bother paying over his contribution to the bet, on the grounds that they had no chance of winning, so he might just as well save himself the expense.

I'd also bumped into another pal there, from the sports desk of news agency Reuters, who was combining the Breeders' Cup with a round-the-world trip-of-a-lifetime, which he had organised himself.

It wasn't going well. He and his wife had arrived at their carefully chosen hotel in Washington only to discover no sign of the leafy grounds and tempting swimming pool which had looked so alluring online when he booked. Instead, there were fire-escapes and barred windows at the front of the building, which apparently hosted many of the more dubious elements of the city's low-life population and made them fear for their safety.

Still, they'd been kept optimistic via thoughts of the lovely place they'd booked in Las Vegas, where they would be based for the Breeders' Cup.

And no disappointments this time – it lived up to all the claims made on its behalf as they walked up to the check-in.

Except that the reception desk had no record whatsoever of his booking, and point blank refused to give them a room. They had to wander round town until they found somewhere which deigned to take them in!

388 STALIN'S STALLIONS Moscow

US-born Kathleen H. Mortimer, nee Harriman, was described as an 'heiress, journalist and philanthropist' by *The Times* when she died aged 93 in February 2011, having worked in Moscow with her father, who was US Ambassador there.

She must have made a success of the job, as when she left there in 1946 it was with two thoroughbred stallions, Fact and Boston, given to her as a parting gift by Soviet Prime Minister Joseph Stalin.

389 LEAVE IT OUT! Epsom

Musjid, the 9-4 favourite for the 1859 Derby, duly obliged by half a length, with the judge placing 20-1-shot Ticket-of-Leave second – a decision which sparked a considerable row when connections of 22-1 outsider Marionette claimed that their colt had finished second.

An enquiry was held two days later, with the judge accepting that he had been mistaken, and an official announcement made: 'The stewards hereby declare Marionette to be the second horse in the Derby Stakes and that Ticket-of-Leave was placed second by mistake. Beaufort. H.J. Rous.

Bizarrely, however, Ticket-of-Leave was demoted entirely out of the first four.

There was a sub-plot to the race, with Alfred Day, who rode 4-1 third favourite Trumpeter, eventually placed third, allegedly pulling his horse in order to facilitate victory for Marionette on whom he stood to win £30,000 in bets.

390 BUSY SQUIZZY Australia

Towong Turf Club, which races at a track alongside Murray Valley Highway in New South Wales, seems inordinately proud of the fact that one of the highlights of its history is that it was raided by infamous Melbourne gangster Squizzy Taylor.

It happened on the course's Cup Day in 1927 when the notorious underworld figure arrived literally mob-handed, caused an argument in the betting ring, then simply walked into an apparently deserted course secretary's office and made off with a suitcase stuffed with the equivalent of £280 gate takings.

The club held its first meeting in 1871 and is proud of the fact that the legendary Phar Lap made his racecourse debut here, finishing last. Well, almost – in fact, the horse Towering Inferno, who played the part of Phar Lap in the movie, was brought to the track to recreate the great horse's first-time-out flop, which actually happened at a different country track.

391 BEVAN BUNNY Towcester

Best known for its policy of free admission (other than Easter Sunday and Boxing Day) since 2002, Towcester was one of the five tracks at which Hugo Bevan used to be clerk of the course.

A budding artist, Bevan recalled the occasion when a 'beautiful nude model' posed for him in his studio near the course. Next day, 'late for an appointment and putting his toe down on a straight stretch of the nearby A5' he was pulled over by the police. A female officer got out of the car and approached his vehicle: 'Oh, it's you, Hugo – don't you recognize me with my clothes on?!'

Bevan also had a part-time job as a public relations man for now defunct Playboy Bookmakers in which guise he took a bevy of their famous bunny girls to Sandown racecourse where 'I was called to one side by a senior Jockey Club steward who told me that bunny girls and racing don't mix. I told him that if they put extra numbers on the gate, it was a good mix.'

392 DEAD HEAT? Guatemala

A race in Guatemala proved fatal in December 2008, reported news agencies at the time:

'At least 17 people were killed after a drunken row over a horse race between Mexican and Guatemalan drug traffickers spilled into violence, police say.

Gun battles erupted in the Guatemalan town of Santa Ana Huista, close to the Mexican border, after a disagreement over the winner of the race.

More than 100 soldiers were sent to the area to restore order. Police said the dead included both Mexicans and Guatemalans, some with previous convictions for trafficking.

"They had been drinking at a local rodeo, and they were drunk, when they started insulting each other during a horse race and the shooting started," police spokesman Donald Gonzalez said.

393 TABY TIP FROM HORSE'S MOUTH Sweden

My wife and I arrived at Taby racecourse, ten or twelve miles outside of Stockholm, on a glorious sunny Sunday afternoon in September 2003. We were on a long weekend to celebrate our wedding anniversary and were traveling with the Horse Racing Abroad company, whose representative, Scarlett, was taking us for a look round one of the barns used by a trainer based at the course, prior to racing.

En route to the barn, a fellow traveller, John Gloak, and I were lagging slightly behind the rest of the field, and as we passed three yearlings who were happily skittering around in little paddocks, John tried to attract the attention of one of them, calling him over. When the colt responded, John said to him: 'What do you fancy in the third, then?'

Now, surprisingly to me – as I didn't expect the horse to understand anything other than Swedish, he looked at John and began to paw the ground excitedly – once, twice, thrice – nine times, in fact.

'So,' said John, 'That's number nine, then.' Number nine in the third was called Indian War Hero.

Naturally, having little knowledge of the form at Taby – I ended up backing Sagittarius because that's my star sign, and everything ridden by jockey Madeleine Smith because the nubile actress of that name had once been my main – sorry, only – reason for watching Hammer Horror films – we decided to plunge our Kroner on our tip straight from the horse's hoof.

Scepticism all round from the assembled racegoers in the splendid Grandstand restaurant where we gathered and dined - with a charming little Union Jack on each table. When the horse showed odds of around 12-1 on the tote I must admit my resolve wavered a little, but John and I duly went in hard, each-way. The horse came second – paying just under 7-2 for a place. Not a bad tip, eh?

394 LEFTY YANK USA

Races took place at Sportsman's Hill, Kentucky, towards the end of the 18th century, organized by local settler Colonel William Whitley, who is now remembered at the site by a plaque, erected as recently as 1993.

In 1975, on Independence Day, a descendant of the late Colonel, Martha Scott, organized a commemorative race meeting – an event that continued for a few years before ceasing.

Sportsman's Hill could have been the start of the tradition that saw American racetracks almost unanimously racing left-handed on dirt.

Whitley's abhorrence of all things British meant that when he organized races he was mindful that the Brits usually did it right-handed on turf, so deliberately opted for a different direction and surface.

The plaque at the site declares; 'A fervent patriot, he built the track to contrast with the British ones, using clay instead of turf and running races counter-clockwise. Racing here ended with the Civil War.'

395 GROWING UP QUICKLY
Salisbury

Jockey Philip Robinson had been narrowly beaten on Thorganby at Salisbury in 1978 – his first ride outside of his former jockey-turned-trainer father Peter's yard.

Returning home, his father took the wheel of the car to drive them up the M3 only to suffer a seizure whilst driving – Robinson, still a learner driver, somehow managed to grab the wheel and knock the wildly careering vehicle out of gear and bring it to a halt on the hard shoulder. But despite his efforts at resuscitation his father died. 'That made me grow up very quickly.'

396 ALL WHITE? Lambourn

Nicky Henderson's five-year-old of 2010, The White Admiral, is reportedly a rare example of an 'albino' horse, of which the Lambourn-based trainer quipped: 'We can't have him in the strong sun for too long because he'll burn, and when it snows I'll be petrified of never finding him again should he get loose!'

However, it is a matter of dispute as to whether there is any such thing as a true albino horse. The White Admiral is listed as 'White' rather than 'Grey'.

397 END OF NON RUNNERS USA

Pictures of racehorses in action painted prior to the 1870s look odd to us today – mainly because the artists had no real idea of what happened to a racehorse when it was running.

But then English-born photographer Eadweard Muybridge (real name Edward Muggeridge), working in the US, revealed the truth about equine motion when he took a series of photographs of a horse which, as it moved, tripped a series of wires triggering a row of cameras which took successive shots showing at last how they ran in close-up.

Racehorse artist Degas immediately incorporated Muybridge's discoveries into his work.

398 EXCUSE ME, ER, HAVE YOU SEEN MY DRESS? Ascot

Royal Ascot does, of course, have a rigorously enforced dress code, but in September 2010 Ascot clerk of the course Chris Stickels remembered the Royal meeting at which 'the lady arrived in the racecourse reception looking for lost property – because she had lost her dress. Needless to say it hadn't been handed in, and she was provided with an overcoat to go home in.'

399 WHEN 11-2 BECAME 11-1 Kempton

Three members of staff at Turf TV were reportedly fired – one for gross negligence and the others for gross misconduct – after the opening show for a race at Kempton in August 2010 was 11-1 for Henry Cecil's Wafeira, followed by 8-1, 7-1, 6-1, 9-2, with an SP of 4-1 favourite.

It later emerged the opening show should have been 11-2. The horse won.

Turf TV claimed: 'there was no evil intent. It was just a mistake followed by a foolish attempt to cover up that mistake.' A *Racing Post* report quoted a Turf TV source as saying that it had been the result of 'a cock-up, followed by stupidity.' Others in the racing world were not convinced.

400 WHAT DECIDED FRED NOT TO CARRY ON Leicester

If Fred Winter hadn't only recently announced his forthcoming retirement from the saddle, declaring, 'It's the bit between the starting gate and the winning post that doesn't appeal to me any more', what happened during his ride in Leicester's £173 3m Quorn Chase in 1963 might well have made up his mind to pack in this unpredictable game there and then.

It was just a run-of-the-mill four-runner chase and Fred was on the even-money favourite Carry On who was actually carrying a hefty 12st 4lb and giving away at least 9lb to his opponents.

At the very first fence the field was reduced to three as Norwegian – ridden by David Nicholson – took a tumble. Four fences later Kilvemnon unseated his rider and in the process brought down King Fin, leaving Fred and Carry On in splendid isolation.

They continued without incident for a further four jumps when Carry On landed in the water jump, depositing Fred on the bank.

As Carry On removed himself from the water and Fred caught his breath he also caught Carry On, remounted and headed towards the next fence, only for the horse to refuse and then finish up in its ditch instead of jumping it. At this point Carry On was reportedly led back to the paddock.

By now David Nicholson had caught early faller Norwegian, who had set off back towards the racecourse stables, and they went back to the first and started again. Until two fences later when the jockey pulled his mount up. Carry On was now remounted, and rejoined the race.

Kilvemnon and King Fin had also got going again and the former actually took the lead from King Fin three out, until Carry On cruised up to take over approaching the last and prevailed from 15-2 King Fin and weakening third-placed Kilvemnon, 100-30. Fred must have been relieved to start training shortly afterwards.

Average time for such a race was 6m 18.5 seconds – this one took 12 minutes, 52 and a half a seconds to complete!

401 ALMOST LEGLESS ON HONEYMOON
Minorca

Jump jockey Dougie Costello was left nearly literally legless during his September 2010 honeymoon after marrying Aimee Mercer and flying out to Minorca.

Costello, 27 years old, had been so wrapped up in the wedding preparations that he paid scant attention to the 'buckle-rub' on his leg following his last ride before the ceremony.

But when the happy couple arrived on the Mediterranean island he realised his leg had become far worse, swelling up from ankle to knee – 'the pain of it, because of the pressure, was unbelievable. It was worse than a fracture.'

He sought treatment and was immediately hospitalized when a doctor told him that he had come very close to having the leg amputated – 'he made a cutting movement with his hand – I'm sure he wasn't joking.'

Costello, who had cellulitis, was in hospital for a week before returning home.

402 'I WAS ON HIM!' Chepstow

The lad spotted showing his mates a mobile phone picture in a Chepstow racecourse bar in October 2010 may well have been telling them of the recent 5-1 winner, Escort'men – 'I was on that one, you know!'

And he would have meant it – because shortly after the Paul Nicholls-trained, Ruby Walsh-ridden runner had returned to the winner's enclosure following a £25,000 handicap hurdle, the unidentified racegoer had wandered into the enclosure and attempted to mount the horse.

Dressed in a red top, he got an arm over the horse's back and was about to haul himself on board when he was spotted. Ruby Walsh lifted his whip towards the man who immediately fled, but was later spotted in a bar and then escorted from the course.

'When seen in the bar he was shouting "Ruby, Ruby, Ruby"', explained Chepstow managing director Richard Holland. 'I expect this youth has had too many beers and was trying to show off to his friends. We don't want his type here.'

Walsh commented, 'Some idiot came from nowhere and attempted to get on the horse.'

403 CASHING IN Senegal

The World Encyclopedia of Horse Racing insisted that there was racing taking place in Senegal as recently as 2001, claiming that racegoers would 'festoon winning jockeys with notes. The riders return with money in their mouths, their boots and anywhere else it will fit.'

I imagine that doesn't happen any longer – or our jockeys will have been fighting to get out there – however, they do seem to be racing there still, reported www.startafrica.com – 'The new management of the National Management Committee of horse racing on Thursday announced the opening of the new season for Sunday, February 6, 2011 at the track Thies. This first day will gather five categories at the Racetrack City of Thies. But all will start over short distances, no more than 1500 meters, in order to prepare horses to face the rest of the season. As for participation, it is requested from each horse a sum of thirty thousand francs cfa'.

404 HOGG ROAST Australia

It was the equivalent of Frankie Dettori getting legless and losing his Derby mount on the way to Epsom.

Australian jockey F. Hogg was entrusted to make sure top big-race contender Alice Hawthorne, the best horse in Melbourne during the 1850s, arrived fit and well to contest her next big race – at the Geelong Carnival meeting in 1856.

Hogg set off a few days before the April 15 date of the race but became somewhat distracted en route, got drunk, and completely lost the mare for two days and two nights in the bush.

To his huge relief he was reunited with the great mare in time to get to the course, but she ran unaccountably (to connections) badly and could finish only fourth in the feature race of the Carnival, the Town Plate. Sent out to contest another event, run in heats, she managed only last and fourth places.

Her overall record was 52 wins in 71 starts but it seems unlikely that Hogg was ever on board again.

405 OKAY, SO HOW GOOD'S YOUR SERBIAN, THEN? Serbia

The history of racing in Serbia stretches back to the early 19th century. Unfortunately political upheaval in more modern times led to the dissipation of the industry and it has become a case of building the sport back to its former glory.

I made contact with a Serbian gentleman called F. Alexander Bozanic, who glories in the title of 'Handicapper For Flat Gallop Races'. In response to my request to know how many racecourses there are in Serbia, he responded in February 2010: 'As far as I am a bit bussy (sic) and will need a bit of time to collect the dates abou (sic) you are interested I will be able to write you back concerning the interest of yours earlier then (sic) next Saturday. Please inform me does this suit to you.'

I must say that F. Alexander's English, quaint though it may be, is different class to my Serbian. He accompanied his thoughtful missive with a photograph of himself looking very dapper, and well turned out in a neat flat cap, clutching a brolly and certainly properly clad in what racecourses have taken to calling 'smart casual' gear.

Alex sent me a massive missive in April 2010, revealing a history of racing in the country, photographs of the tracks and details of the six currently active courses:

'At this moment active race organizers are: Belgrade, Sabac, Pozarevac, Vrelo, Kragujevac and Cacak Racetracks.'

Who knew that? Not me, for sure – and with that my fantastic correspondent signed off in his own, inimitable style:

'If you consider that it is something more neccesary or to get expressed in diferent fashion please inform me to try to adjust.'

Here is an extract from Alex's history of racing in Serbia:

'The history of races in Serbia in fashion of modern world with Thoroughbred bloodstock strated in 1820 in city named Shabac when first race was at distance of round 6 000m (about 3.72 miles).

In 1863 first complete season was establishe by Duke Michael Obrenovic with fascilty of that time named as Belgrade Racetrack (Hipodrom Beograd). The governing Racing Authority was established in 1888 by cavalry officer of Serbia captain Milisav Kurtovic.

The authorty was later in 1947 changeded in to Horsmanship Federation of Yugoslavia and after spliting of Former Yugoslavia it becomed just Horsmanship Federation of Serbia. First winner of former Yugoslavian/ Srbian Tripple Crown was Fantast (ch.c., 1929 in Yugoslavia, by Fointainblue (USA) – Cendre De Bois (FR), St Bris (FR)) from male line of Matchem trough branch of Solon.

I'll spare you the rest.

406 HOWZAT? Wales

England cricketer Ted Arnold was the owner of Bubbly, a beaten odds-on favourite at Tenby in Wales in January 1927.

The winner was Bubbly's stablemate Oyster Maid, who just happened to be owned by Arnold's professional punter pal, Ben Warner.

The 100/6-shot had been the medium of a huge off-course gamble.

'The result concealed the biggest and most bitterly resented betting coup National Hunt racing has ever known,' declared one Dick Francis, who should know about such things, later, and after this many bookies refused to stand at the track again.

407 FEELING A LITTLE SHEEPISH? Australia

'Kickback' is a problem on many racecourses, particularly those which have all-weather tracks, and jockeys have to wear masks to prevent swallowing unpleasant particles thrown up by the horses in front.

At Tambo Valley in Australia there is a different kind of kickback, which encourages jockeys to go hell for leather from the off. Racing writer Robert White reveals why: 'Jockeys have learned that it is no fun running into the tail of the field – who wants sheep dung thrown into their faces?'

The course generally stages one meeting a year – for the rest of the time the course, situated on private land at Swifts Creek, Victoria, is grazed by the owner's sheep!

Adds White: 'It is one of the most primitive racecourses in the State – and therein lies its charm.'

408 AS PLAIN AS, ER, A PIKESTAFF? Cheltenham

But for an unprovoked and grisly attack during which his nose was literally bitten off by his assailant, Bob Clarke would never have become a racehorse owner.

However, using the money he received from the Criminal Injuries Compensation Board, he purchased a racehorse. He contributed £1,000 to the cost of Wannaplantatree and got back £5,000 when the horse was sold on.

But his second go was the £4,500 cost of Lady Rebecca, who went on to win three successive Cleeve Hurdles at Cheltenham from 1999-2001, and totted up prize money of some £170,000 in winning 13 of 19 career starts.

'The whole thing was meant to be. None of it would have happened if that guy hadn't bitten off my nose,' said Clarke.

409 ME DRUNK? WASH YOUR MOUTH OUT! Listowel

Teetotal jump jockey Davy Russell failed a breath test when he arrived at Listowel racecourse in September 2010.

Russell, who said, 'I haven't had a drink for 15 years and that was the only drink I've ever had', was permitted to wash his mouth out and take the test again – and passed. The mouthwash he had used that morning had apparently contained enough alcohol to casue a positive result.

Relieved, the jockey partnered Mister Two Fifty in a chase, fell and fractured a leg.

410 PHAR OUT Australia

A notebook used by the trainer of Australia's greatest racehorse, the New Zealand-born Phar Lap, was claimed to have proved the true reason for the champion's mysterious 1932 death in California.

The five-year-old gelding, winner of 37 of 51 starts including the 1930 Melbourne Cup, died just two weeks after winning the valuable 1932 Agua Caliente Handicap in Mexico.

Racing fans were appalled by the news and many theories for the horse's premature end were advanced, with poisoning by US gangsters, whose illegal gambling syndicates were holding huge bets on the horse to win future races, emerging as the most popular.

However, trainer Harry Telford's notebook, which came up for sale at auction in April 2008, revealed the ingredients of the pre-race tonics he would regularly give the horse – arsenic, strychnine, belladonna, cocaine and caffeine.

The Melbourne Museum purchased the notebook, which contained 30 'recipes', for some £18,000, and auctioneer Charles Leski commented: 'It's the first confirmation in writing that ingredients we think of as poisons were actually used by Harry Telford. 'In strictly measured doses, mixed with other feed, presumably these served the purpose of being a stimulant, and didn't adversely affect the horses.

'But if Phar Lap had been unwell in the trip over to America, or been in the hands of more than one person in the US, it's possible the dosage wasn't strictly adhered to, and it appears he overdosed on a concoction considered good for him.'

Telford did not travel to the States with Phar Lap, his assistant Tommy Woodcock going instead, and Woodcock reportedly admitted on his deathbed in 1985 that the horse may have consumed an excessive quantity of one of his tonics, with 2006 tests on a strand of the animal's hair suggesting he had ingested large amounts of arsenic.

The Melbourne Museum already contained Phar Lap's hide, while his skeleton was held by the Museum of New Zealand – and his massive 14lb heart at Canberra's National Museum.

411 NATIONAL DISGRACE Aintree

With the 2008 Grand National about to start, course commentator Richard Hoiles, accompanied by his assistant Nicky Leeson and a cameraman, was concentrating hard as the runners milled about – only to be shocked as eight drunken stag party revellers invaded his commentary box at the top of the County Stand.

Having already expressed concern about a lack of security earlier in the afternoon, Hoiles decided that least resistance was the best course of action. 'We thought trying to kick them out would be more likely to antagonise them, so we bluffed it and said they could stay to watch provided they did not say a word. We concentrated on the ones who were less drunk to keep the ones that were more drunk quiet,' said Hoiles. He was able to get through the commentary with no-one outside of the box suspecting what had happened.

In May 2011 Hoiles made an uncharacteristic error when calling Hawkeyethenoo, winner of the 28 runner Victoria Cup at Ascot, 'Horseradish' – the favourite. Hoiles tweeted an apology, adding 'Gutted. I am paid not to make mistakes'.

412 HILLARY'S TRAGIC LOSER Kentucky

As the only woman in the US Presidential race, Hillary Clinton thought it would be a smart move to pin her colours to those of the only filly contesting the 2008 Kentucky Derby.

Addressing a crowd in Jeffersonville, Indiana, former President Bill's wife told them she was sending in her daughter to place her bets. 'I hope that everybody will go to the Derby on Saturday and place just a little money on the filly for me. I won't be able to be there this year – my daughter is going to be there and so she has strict instructions to bet on Eight Belles.'

Racing authorities were delighted at the exposure. Eight Belles ran very well to finish runner-up to Big Brown, but was euthanised on the track minutes after the race when she collapsed with two broken front ankles.

Political commentators were not slow to draw parallels with Ms Clinton's bid for the White House. And she was even predictably castigated by Peta – People for the Ethical Treatment of Animals – for daring to tip a horse.

They obviously believed the tip and the horse's tragic death were cause and effect. This is the bizarre letter they sent to Hillary:

Dear Senator Clinton:

As a high-profile political figure with the esteem of many women, I regret to say that your public support of horseracing – and specifically betting on Eight Belles – makes you culpable in her destruction. I ask you now to publicly condemn races like the Kentucky Derby. Eight Belles ran for her life and was fiercely whipped as she came down that final stretch when she was no doubt in a great deal of pain. We cannot call ourselves a civilized nation if we allow any living being to endure such abuse.

Races like this are the equivalent of child sweatshops. These are not even seasoned horses: they are young fillies and colts whose joints are not formed enough to endure such a grueling race. Despite this, they are pushed beyond their limits. The Triple Crown and other major horse races have become the graveyards of too many horses who were called champions. For example, Go For Wand, who went down in the 1990 Breeders' Cup Distaff and then stumbled up and tried to keep running with her broken leg dangling; Union City, who fractured a leg in the 1993 Preakness and was destroyed; Prairie Bayou, who that same year suffered a compound fracture in the Belmont Stakes and had to be destroyed; George Washington, who was euthanised after breaking his leg while running the Preakness (sic – that happened at the Breeders' Cup) last year; and of course Barbaro, the 'poster horse' of the racing industry's failures and excesses, who despite efforts could not be saved from the injuries sustained during the 2006 Preakness. Barbaro's injuries were terrible – fractures of his cannon bone, sesamoids, and long pastern as well as the dislocation of the fetlock joint. These are just a few of the horses we hear about – they are the winners, the horses who run the big races. Hundreds of horses meet the same painful, deadly fate every year in the horseracing industry.

A racetrack is not a place for a fun day out, and we are writing to Chelsea on that score. Attending the Derby is as despicable as attending a dogfight. For most – not a few – of the horses you see will not end up put out to pasture on a beautiful ranch but will be sent overseas to be slaughtered for someone's dinner plate. At some point, all horses stop winning.

PETA takes no position on whether you win or lose the race you are in, but we call on you to publicly reject betting on such hideous spectacles of domination over wonderful animals who deserve more than pain and death for human profit and amusement.

Very truly yours,
Ingrid E. Newkirk
President

413 HOOKED ON RACING

Jockey David Probert enjoyed fishing in his spare time – until he managed to hook himself through the hand whilst angling – and was forced to miss several scheduled rides during 2010.

Having fully recovered by September of the same year, Probert decided that golf may be a safer pastime to indulge in – only to dislocate a finger when his tee shot went wrong.

Explained the jockey: 'I took a swing, but hit the ground, not the ball. The impact knocked the little finger on my right hand out of its socket.'

The golf tournament had been organized by Probert's trainer Andrew Balding, who commented drily, 'He probably should just concentrate on his riding.'

414 FUNNY YOU SHOULD BRING THAT UP Brighton

Trainer David Evans' stable jockey Cathy Gannon rode a winner for him at Brighton – only to be sick as she passed the post in front.

'I think it may have been the thought of me kissing her that did it,' declared the Wales-based handler.

415 REALLY MOTORING Beverley

Still an apprentice at the time, 2010 Champion jockey Paul Hanagan recalls a ride at Beverley when a runner got loose at the start whilst still blindfolded.

'The horse went straight through the rails, went flat out into the car park and fell head over heels on top of a car – my car! Luckily the horse was fine, but my first car, my pride and joy Peugeot 106, wasn't.'

416 TRAMORE – OR LESS? Ireland

All 14 jockeys riding in the Newtown Handicap Chase at Tramore on New Year's Eve, 2007, which involved three circuits of the track, rode a finish at the end of the second circuit. Not only that, course commentator Jerry Hanlon called it as though it was the end of the race – and the judge announced victory for Boher Storm from Doc Charlie and Mr Aussie as riders began to return to the unsaddling enclosure.

At this point, five of the jockeys suddenly realized their mistake and began to race on, this time with Alberoni, Dream Believer and Ballysheedy finishing first, second and third – but the subsequent stewards' inquiry ruled that the original 'result' would stand.

Eventually, nine of the jockeys were handed five-day suspensions and ordered to forfeit their riding fees.

One of the jockeys, Andrew McNamara, who was not fined or banned, later explained: 'Suddenly everyone started riding a finish. I was roaring that we had another circuit to go and others were roaring that we didn't, and it would make you doubt yourself.'

417 COLOURFUL IDEA Carlisle

Carlisle racecourse had a mixed reaction when it introduced coloured number cloths in March 2010.

Similar to greyhound trap numbers, the course designated red for number one, white for number two, through to lemon-coloured number 20. Each cloth also carried the number as well as the colour.

In August 2008 racing at Carlisle had been delayed when a racegoer refused to stop shouting at jockeys – until he was handcuffed and taken away by police.

418 NO HALF WITT California

He was the youngest trainer in the game when he took out his first licence in 1931 and when he saddled his final winner in 2006, aged 95, he was the oldest ever to do so.

Noble Threewitt finally retired from training in February 2007 when he was 96 – after which the Californian stalwart was honoured with a 'Noble Threewitt Day' in Arcadia, where the Santa Anita racetrack is housed. He died in September, 2010, aged 99.

Threewitt played the role of a jockey in the 1934 Paramount Studios movie *Goin' To Town*, during the making of which he met actress Mae West.

Threewitt said he was in a hurry the morning he entered Correlation for the 1954 Florida Derby, which he won, and signed his name '3WITT', an abbreviation he stayed with for insignia on stable belongings such as stall webbings and feed tubs.

In 1984, when he was 73 and not winning as many races as in the past, Threewitt told the *Los Angeles Times*, 'I got in a slump and then I guess everybody started noticing my age. But I'm no dumber or smarter now than I've ever been.'

Down to five horses at the beginning of 2002, Threewitt told *Thoroughbred Times*, 'I think the reason I'm almost out of horses is that I've outlived most of my good owners.'

419 BURYING THEIR HEADS IN THE GROUND Wanganui, New Zealand

In 1877 Queen of the Vale, owned by Mr J D Powdrell, became the first winner of the Wanganui Derby. Winning jockey John Belcher recorded his reaction in his diary – 'Mr Powdrell wanted to know how much he was in my debt for winning the Derby. I said "Nothing". I was only too pleased to ride the first Derby winner, but he insisted on my taking a cheque for £10. Before closing time I think the cheque had melted nearly all away.'

Wanganui racecourse received a generous but bizarre offer from the local Borough Council in 1921 – two ostriches 'to run in the middle of the track'. The course reluctantly turned down the offer 'on the grounds that they would be a danger to horses.'

420 ARKELL NEARLY BROUGHT DOWN Chepstow

Edward Arkell, acting clerk of the course at Chepstow, turned up at the track in the early hours of the morning in July 2008 to check the going. He'd forgotten his keys and was unable to get in, so had to shin over a wall – only to be spotted by a passer-by who called the police.

421 BOOKIES BET WITHOUT BAR! Ayr

Bookmakers at Ayr threatened to go on strike in October 2010 – because a bar at the track was closed!

The on-course layers were outraged when they discovered that a bar, from which many of their customers usually emerge to place a bet, was closed for a private lunch.

'No-one could have access to the Tatts' or paddock bookmakers,' said Bert Logan, a track bookie for some 30 years. 'We were fed up with the lack of consideration from the racecourse towards the bookmakers and there was a strong will from the bookmakers to say "We've had enough, we are going home".'

Eventually, the bookies did operate, even though 'we would have no customers but I felt I should take a bloody nose commercially.'

Elspeth Walters was delighted to win with her first runner as an owner when the judge ruled that her Eternal Ruler had just prevailed in a photo finish at Ayr in October 2010.

The judge who ruled in her favour was former jump jockey Fraser Perratt – Elspeth's brother!

422 PAUL'S CHARITABLE GESTURE

Newly crowned 2010 champion Flat jockey Paul Hanagan donated all his earning from the last fortnight of the season to two charities – Alder Hey Children's Hospital and Jack Berry's 'northern Oaksey House'.

423 GOING TO POT Newbury

Trainer Roger Charlton was unable to witness his five-year-old Clowance's victory at Newbury in October 2010 – he was confined to stables with a slipped disc, after endeavouring to move one of wife Clare's hefty flowerpots which decorate the Beckhampton yard.

424 HAVANA LAUGH? Cuba

Writer Norman Deplume is a frequent visitor to Cuba. Under the title of 'World's Worst Dumps: 22' – he wrote an article for readers of *The Oldie* in November 2010 about the island's capital, Havana, in which he wrote of his observation there of 'the ubiquity of old men with depraved countenances in the company of nubile young women with deprived countenances.'

'We were told the women were jockeys, or jinateras,' he said, at first assuming 'they must be discussing tactics for the 3.30 with their trainers.'

Not so, he then revealed, in fact 'they were talking to their mounts – flea bitten and ready for the knacker though they so transparently were.'

425 TWO COUNTRIES DIVIDED BY A SINGLE LANGUAGE USA

In his 1951 publication *The Argot of the Racetrack*, the University of Louisville's David W Maurier listed an alphabetical list of American racecourse words and phrases of the day, which make for fascinating reading:

Attack of the slows – imaginary disease from which a racehorse is said to be suffering when he bogs down during a race.

Bastard plate – type of heavy racehorse shoe.

Bloomer – horse that makes excellent showing in the morning workout but cannot run well in a race.

Boat race – fixed race.

Chalk eater – favourite backer.

Cold horse – horse whose owner has no intention of letting it win the race.

Come on – mantout's accomplice who sets him up with suckers who buy his worthless information.

Don Alonzo – horse which sulks – apparently named after a horse of that name which, apparently, sulked.

Dope – information on a race.

Dust – a horse given any narcotic or drug pre-race.

Finger – horse.favourite.

Freemartin – filly in a pair of twins.

Get ring in one's nose – lose everything betting.

Grifter – professional gamblers and big-con men.

Have a bucketful – said of horse fed just before a race to cut his wind and decrease his chance of winning.

Have one in his boot – when a betting ticket is given to a jockey to carry in his riding boots for luck.

Hop head – horse given a drug before a race.

Juice – protection money paid to police by gamblers and bookies on the West Coast.

Leaky roof circuit – small-time racetracks.

Leg locking – of a jockey – to ride close to another and place his leg in front of the other's leg in such a manner as to hold him back.

Lobhorse – pulled to keep him out of the money.

Meet eater – ungenuine horse.

Midnight handicap – race whose outcome is decided the night before it is run.

Mortal lock – a sure thing.

Nine of hearts – horse with no chance.

Pagoda – judges' stand at the track.

Peep – horse finishing third.

Plant – racetrack.

Rail bird – amateur clocker following morning workouts at the track.

Sawbuck – ten-dollar bill or bet.

Spark a horse – to use a hand battery to galvanise a horse.

Sponge a horse – insert a sponge into a horse's nostril to cut off part of its wind.

Stooper – racetrack hanger-on who makes a living by picking up and cashing in discarded winning betting tickets.

Suicide club – jump jockey fraternity.

Take a run-out powder – said of a welshing bookie.

Wrinkleneck – racing old-timer.

426 SNOWED UNDER Swindon

Trainer Donald Geary Snow found himself in the Bankruptcy Court in Swindon in October 1935 – and he blamed his plight on 'a run of bad luck', and because he had had 'an abnormal number of horses beaten a short head', oh, and the Ogbourne-based handler had been 'further handicapped by having to charge unremunerative training fees.'

And then, perhaps more importantly, there were his gambling debts – which he estimated at 'about £4,000'.

He had an excuse, though – 'A trainer's life is nearly all gambling. Few trainers make a living without having an occasional bet,' he explained, overlooking the obvious riposte that clearly he had more than the occasional bet and wasn't making a living out of it.

The Official Receiver listened with interest, then pointed out that this wasn't actually the first time that Snow had turned up at the Bankruptcy Court.

On the last occasion, he mentioned, the Court had found that 'he had been guilty of rash and hazardous speculation, extravagant living and gambling.'

His present failure, elaborated the Receiver, was 'largely due to the fact that he had borrowed from one money-lender to pay another.'

Crestfallen, Snow admitted that perhaps it was true that he 'had lived extravagantly.'

427 CHEST A QUICK ONE, THEN
New Zealand

Racing writer Oliver Scott, editor of New Zealand paper *The Truth*, recalled his days covering the sport at Wanganui racecourse, reminiscing, 'It seemed that all racing writers had to be elderly, and even bearded. The Press Room had a unique piece of furniture. It was a huge wooden sea chest, into which was stacked, before the meeting opened, a plentiful supply of liquor. It seemed a bottomless chest, for the day of its exhaustion never came.'

428 BY GEORGE!

Jump jockey George Williamson enjoyed an astonishing few days during 1899.

Having won the Grand National on Manifesto, despite at one point finding himself virtually on the ground, with his feet literally touching the turf after a bad mistake by his mount, Williamson passed on the after-race celebrations, accepting a £2,800 'gift' from delighted owner Mr Bulteel, and then catching a train for London.

Once in the capital he then joined a boat train, heading for Prague, where next day he won the main chase of the day and finished third in a Flat race.

Next stop was Budapest where he won the Hungarian Grand Steeplechase on the very next day, then he headed to Turkey where he won another race worth £2,000.

English and Irish jockeys dominated jump racing on the continent in those days and Williamson was eight-time champion Austrian-Hungarian jump jockey, maintaining a house in Hungary and becoming something of a personality there when he married an Austrian countess.

The couple were later divorced after his bride was spotted 'entering a Parisian hotel with a foreign looking gentleman' according to unparalleled chronicler of jump racing in those parts, John Pinfold, who points out: 'Not that Williamson was entirely innocent himself. One season he appeared on the Budapest racecourse with an elegant new girlfriend on his arm. On seeing her the crowd started singing the well known music hall song, 'Daisy, Daisy, give me your answer, do' – as she was Daisy, Countess of Warwick –

the woman about whom the song had been written, and the former mistress of King Edward VII.'

The affair turned sour when Daisy left him for the president of the Hungarian Jockey Club, Count Elemer Batthyany, who made sure that he had the 'lady' to himself – by making sure no-one could book Williamson (the first, and thus far only, man to win both the Grand National and the Velka Pardubicka) to ride their horses in Hungary. This drove the jockey back to England, where he died, single, in 1937.

429 300-1 BACKER BAXTER Wetherby

Owner Alan Baxter landed a 300-1 bet on his debut-making Maoi Chinn Tire over hurdles at Wetherby in October 2010, as the horse returned an SP of 200-1 and tote odds of 223-1, making him the longest-priced British winner in almost five years, since 200-1 Arctic Blue at Chepstow in March 2005.

430 BLEEDERS' CUP Kentucky

The 2010 Breeders' Cup nearly became the Bleeders' Cup when, on day one, jockey Calvin Borel floored rival rider Javier Castellano in the winner's enclosure at Churchill Downs, following the opening race in which Castellano's mount Prince Will I Am was disqualified after interfering with a number of rivals including Borel's mount, A. U. Miner.

The post-race punch-up was shown live on television as triple Kentucky Derby-winning Borel squared up to Castellano, telling him: 'I'll kill you in one second,' before releasing a flurry of punches.

'He was very aggressive and tried to hit me in the face,' said Castellano later.

431 TALKING HORSE?

The Henry Daly-trained seven-year-old jumper Possol, a six-time winner, was reportedly the first horse to open up a Twitter account and begin tweeting to his 80 followers in October 2010, telling them at one point that he would 'refuse to run on anything else' other than good ground.

432 HAPPY NEW YEAR, MAC London

Returning from Cheltenham's 2009 New Year's Day meeting, John and Jenny – aka The Booby – McCririck were shocked to discover that their London mews home had been ransacked.

Devastated, they began checking what had been stolen when John's phone rang. He answered it and, bizarrely, found himself talking to a man who claimed to have carried out the burglary.

'There was no shouting,' said John, 'I was very calm and found myself saying things like "how many bottles of champagne did you take?"'

The burglar told him he'd been looking for Mac's shotguns – which he denies owning.

'I told him the jewellery he took wasn't worth anything but that it was of great sentimental value to my wife. He said he would give it back and would call again to tell me where he would leave it.' He didn't.

'He also told me it could have been worse and that he hadn't taken my racing awards – which was true.' He did though, steal two Flat screen TVs, several hundred pounds in cash and gold shirt studs.

433 WINING ABOUT SIR ALEX Old Trafford

Chelsea manager – well, he was when I wrote this – Carlo Ancelotti was delighted when he took his team to Old Trafford for the first time – and managed a 2-1 win.

'As is the tradition, a few minutes after the final whistle we (he had assistant Ray Wilkins with him) went to Sir Alex Ferguson's room to drink the usual glass of wine. We walked in, and silence reigned. He sat there staring at a television screen; the set was tuned to a horse race, his greatest love.'

Ancelotti and Wilkins stood around awkwardly 'without saying a word'.

Finally, at a loss, 'we drank a glass of wine, to our own health. Bye-bye.'

434 WINNIE THE FIXER?

Winston Churchill was a keen racing man and a useful rider, very active in the late 19th century. He raced in a March 1895 steeplechase – 'the animal refused and swerved – very nearly did he break my leg' and a few days later, contested the 4th Hussars Subalterns'

Challenge Cup, adopting the name 'Mr Spencer' to do so, and finishing a very creditable third. 'It was very exciting and there is no doubt about it being dangerous' he told his brother, Jack. 'I had never jumped a regulation fence before, and they are pretty big things.'

However, this race had a fascinating postscript – it was declared void with allegations being made that the winner was actually a ringer and that 'all those in the race must have been in on the plot.'

The horse was an outsider and a publication called *Truth* declared: 'The coup resulted in the defeat of a hot favourite by the last outsider in the betting.'

Churchill was outraged at these allegations, and urged his mother to take legal action on his behalf – but the matter was allowed to drop.

435 BATTLING TO BACK A WINNER Caen

During the June 1944 attack on Caen, which was code-named Operation Epsom, after the racecourse, and which coincided with the running of the Derby, British troops and officers really embraced the spirit of the theme, according to historian Catrine Clay.

In her book about German soldier-turned Manchester City goalkeeper Bert Trautmann, she writes: 'They put up boards in the midst of battle listing the runners and riders and took bets, then listened to the results on the wireless.'

436 CRYING SHAME! Churchill Downs

Jockey Mike Smith burst into tears after the sensational late charge by Zenyatta failed by inches to land her 20th win in 20 races, in the 2010 Breeders' Cup Classic.

Blaming himself for leaving the mare with too much to do after they had come out of the stalls slowly and soon dropped many lengths behind the field, Smith admitted: 'It's my fault – she should have won. I truly believe I was on the best horse today. If I had to blame anyone I would blame me. It hurts more than I can explain, just because it was my fault.'

Zenyatta, whose exploits had entranced US racegoers more than any other horse for many years, went off as odds-on favourite against a star-studded field of colts, but was just held off by Blame, a 5-1 chance, partnered by Garrett Gomez who then had the strange experience of trying to encourage the crowd to cheer his winner when they only wanted to commiserate with the loser.

John McCririck commented: 'In defeat Zenyatta ran her greatest race.'

437 WHO LIVES IN A PLACE LIKE THIS?
Lambourn

Legendary rock guitarist Pete Townshend of The Who – who once wrote a hit record called 'You Better You Bet', literally moved into the world of racing in autumn 2010 when he bought a 41-year lease on Lambourn's Ashdown House – the property from where 1855 Derby winner Wild Dayrell was trained.

Wild Dayrell was named after a 16th-century landowner who reportedly killed a new-born baby by throwing it on a fire and who was said to haunt Littlecote, the estate where the horse was born, following his death in a fall from a horse.

Wild Dayrell was the first foal born at Littlecote and so excited was the butler there, that he insisted on moving the fragile infant around in a wheelbarrow. Wild Dayrell's progress to Derby triumph was not straightforward – attempts were made to sabotage the horsebox taking him to Epsom – but Townshend apparently moved in without a hitch.

438 STEED BY NAME, STEED BY BREEDING!

Best known during his acting career as John Steed in the ground-breaking sixties TV show 'The Avengers', Patrick Macnee, now a veteran in his late eighties, was born the son of a racehorse trainer, Daniel 'Shrimp' Macnee, who trained at Aston in Berkshire until 1932 and who sent out decent horses like Aid, winner of seven consecutive races, and nine-times winner Salford, while his Glen Mazarin won four Flat races and five chases.

Patrick, born in 1922, became a very good rider because of his proximity to horses whilst growing up and remembers: 'with Robert Wagner, the famous star, riding on horses into Trafalgar Square on Thanksgiving Day at 7.30am. That was a great moment for me.'

439 HACKED OFF

Gold Cup and Champion Hurdle-winning trainer Kim Bailey was bucked off of his hack when he was training at Preston Capes in Northamptonshire – with terrifying results.

And Bailey has harboured a suspicion that maybe the incident was not entirely accidental.

'I think the staff always had a price on my head and took mischievous delight in trying to get me off,' he told Alan Lee of *The Times* in December 2010. 'In Lambourn days I had tack falling off and bridles disintegrating. I don't know why this happened but I had one foot stuck in the irons and got dragged 300 yards. It was utterly terrifying.'

As a result of the fall, Bailey now has three fused vertebrae in his back – 'I have no lift in my left leg and it brought an end to my cricket-playing days.'

440 FISHING FOR BUSINESS

When the self-styled 'world's oldest bookmaker' Morry Peter died in 2009, aged 99, fellow layer Leslie Steele recalled one of his stunts – 'To promote his place betting, he nailed a large plastic fish on the top of his board with the slogan 'Plaice Only'.'

441 SHELTERED LIFE? Market Rasen

There was a report in the *Market Rasen Mail*, following race day on Easter Monday, 24 April, 1905, saying that a 'Mr Cottingham had accidentally been jumped upon' (whether by competitor or mounted spectator I do not know) and that he was 'recovering in the Cottage Hospital at Market Rasen'.

The report says he was 'sheltering' behind the hedge. As you do.

442 SOFA, SO ... ER, BAD Exeter

En route to the races at Exeter during a very cold and icy spell in December 2010, former leading point-to-point jockey Tim

Mitchell was delayed by an unusual traffic hazard – 'While I was driving here I hit a sofa in the middle of the road.'

Despite always needing to watch his weight due to having the stature of a second row forward as opposed to a jockey, Tim Mitchell was one of the outstanding riders of the 1990s. He went into the final day of the 1997 season level-pegging with Andrew Dalton and Julian Pritchard, but was robbed of the chance to claim a well-deserved championship victory when Umberleigh was called off due to waterlogging, his rivals managing a winner apiece at Garthorpe to share the title.

443 ARE YOU SURE?

Harvey Smith, former showjumper and husband of Bingley-based trainer Sue, told the *Racing Post Weekender* in November 2010, 'I have never bought a record in my life and I've never read a book, either.'

Mm. In 1972 *V For Victory* was published, purporting to be Harvey Smith's autobiography.

444 FRANCOME'S DRIVING FORCE Cornwall

Former champion jump jockey John Francome has always been driven to excel in whichever field of activity he has participated in.

Perhaps the driving ambition stems from his early experiences behind the wheel – 'One day my father was knackered and had a job to do in Cornwall, so I drove him from Swindon while he slept,' he told the *Racing Post*'s Julian Muscat in December, 2010, adding, 'I was only 12.'

445 MIXED-UP KID? Cheltenham

Sam Twiston-Davies is a Cheltenham Festival-winning jump jockey who has certainly been mixing it with the best since arriving on the scene. But it is difficult to believe that he is not genuinely mixed-up himself – about his hair colour.

Someone who uses the word 'Ginger' to sum himself up, who claims that if he were to have a tattoo it would say 'Ginger' and who, invited to a fancy dress party, would go as 'a carrot' might reasonably be expected to believe the colour of the thatch adorning his head is, er, Ginger.

But not so. Asked by the *Racing Post* in December 2010 to 'tell us something about yourself that only you know', he declared: 'I'm strawberry blonde, not ginger.'

446 HOLE LOT OF TROUBLE Soviet Union

Optician-cum-jump jockey Andy Orkney claims to be the first (modern-day, at least – in 1857 all seven races on a card in Moscow were won by Brits) British rider to win over fences in the Soviet Union – but when he did it in Georgia in 1991 the course was, to say the least, a little different from what he was used to. 'It was a mile and three-quarter steeplechase – and the third fence was a hole in the ground – you wouldn't want to ride one first time out over that. We (two other Brits were with him) had two rides each, and I rode a winner on one of mine.'

447 PREGNANT MOMENT Leicester

Jockey Lawney Hill, a trainer and punk music fan these days, rode her first winner in March 1995, partnering Green Archer to victory in a 3m chase at Leicester whilst carrying a little additional weight – she was four months pregnant with son Joe.

On another occasion Ms Hill injured her arm when she fell during a point-to-point race at Higham, and was being stretchered off when the owner ran across the course to find out how she was – only to suffer an asthma attack – 'so I was kicked off the stretcher, and they grabbed my gas and air for him.'

448 JOCKEY'S ROYAL ROLL

Top amateur rider Sam Waley-Cohen famously declared he would retain that status when he told Alan Lee of *The Times* 'I've never earned a penny from racing and I never will. My approach is to have fun but having fun is winning races.'

Waley-Cohen's day job is running Portman Healthcare, the dental company he founded, but he is likely to be remembered as a footnote to

Royal history both for coming to the rescue and lifting up a yellow hot-pant clad Kate Middleton who had taken a tumble whilst roller-skating (during an event to raise money for a cancer charity set up in the name of Sam's brother Thomas, who died from the disease in 2004), and for apparently reuniting that Queen-to-be with King-to-be Prince William after they split up in 2007.

'We were skating together at the roller-disco and funnily enough I was wearing our second racing colours (orange) under my (very pink) jacket,' explained Waley-Cohen.

Oh yes, and there was the small matter of riding Long Run to win both the King George and Gold Cup.

449 JACQUELINE'S TRAGIC QUEST Newmarket

It was a harsh enough decision by stewards to disqualify 66-1 first-past-the-post outsider, the Henry Cecil-trained Jacqueline Quest, in the 2010 1,000 Guineas for interfering with French filly Special Duty, but when put into the context of owner Noel Martin's life it was downright tragic.

Martin was left a quadriplegic when in Germany in 1996 his car veered off the road and hit a tree after a block of concrete was thrown through his windscreen by two racist thugs. Needing constant care, Martin and his long-term girlfriend Jacqueline planned a suicide pact when she was diagnosed with cancer, but she died before they could carry out the action.

Martin's interest in racing – sparked at an early age by his father, who gave him 2/6d (12.5p) to back a horse with (it won) – saw him buy Baddam, who, trained by Ian Williams, won twice at the 2006 Royal Ascot meeting.

Then he bought Jacqueline Quest, and had told himself that if she won the 1,000 Guineas he would take a trip back to his native Jamaica before travelling to Switzerland to end his life.

Martin dealt with the blow philosophically, telling *Racing Post* reporter Peter Thomas 'My main problem in life is not being able to walk from the age of 36 and watching my wife die and not being able to touch or hug her. Losing a horserace is trivial and I know what reality is. If you settle for reality and truth you'll be all right.'

450 KEEP OFF THE GRASS Oxfordshire

Five-year-old thoroughbred Pandora's racing career was over before it began – as she was allergic to grass.

The mare, bought in 2007 by Oxfordshire veterinary nurse Emily Pearce, would gasp for breath and break out in painful boils whenever even a blade of grass touched her coat.

Eventually, Emily came up with a protective 'overcoat' for her, which consists of a layer of high-tech breathable fabric with a see-through mask covering and protecting her eyes.

She eats a special mixture of sugar-beet and soya oil, and has to take 15 anti-histamine tablets each day.

'She looks silly but it is the only thing that helps her,' said Ms Pearce, who paid £2,600 for the 15.2-hand animal, of whom a vet treating her said he was aware of only two other similar cases, neither as acute.

451 (MY)SORE LOSERS India

A record ten thousand spectators turned up to see India's prestigious 2010 Poonawalla Mysore Derby – which produced an eventful start. Just as the starter pressed the button to send the field off, 7-2 second favourite Immense acted up, unsettling 5-4 favourite Sun Kingdom and causing jockey Vinod Shinde to dismount from his own horse, which was next along in the stalls.

So, Immense unseated his rider as the stalls opened, Sun Kingdom's jockey stayed on board only for a few paces while Shinde's mount Bucethalis set off with no jockey on board. With the two best fancied horses out of the running, Fist Of Rage came home first of the six remaining runners – to the great displeasure of many in the crowd.

'Racegoers refused to accept this result at face value, and decided to take the law into their own hands,' said an eyewitness. 'They expressed their displeasure by smashing the Club's property including TV sets and furniture. Extra battalions of the local police were summoned, and discipline was ultimately restored.'

The stipendiary stewards repeatedly viewed the tapes, before talking to the three jockeys involved, and the starter. The stewards of the Mysore

Race Club eventually declared the race 'Null and Void', and all bets were refunded.

452 DEAD HEAT? WHAT DEAD HEAT? China

Chinese racing authorities virtually did away with dead heats when re-launching racing there in Wuhan, 600 miles south of Beijing. As betting is officially illegal a free competition rewards anyone selecting a winner with a small reward – typically a free bus pass.

In order to assure there is always one winning selection the photo-finish separates horses by determining individual race timings accurate to one ten-thousandth of a second, resulting in a December 2010 winner clocking 2m 43.7891 seconds, compared to the runner-up, which trailed behind in 2m 43.7931s.

The racecard at Wuhan also features 400-metre sprints, the type of race suggested by many in Britain only to fail to receive official support.

453 NAP OF THE DAY Fontwell

Jockey Anthony Freeman was well on time to ride Wishes Or Watches at Fontwell on November 5, 2010, but failed to weigh out in time to partner the horse.

Stewards called the jockey in only to hear the excuse that Freeman had been so early that he decided to take a nap in his car – and fell sound asleep.

454 ASTONISHINN Australia

Melbourne Cup-winning jockey Blake Shinn admitted to backing a horse other than that which he had ridden in an August 2010 race at Randwick.

Shinn, who partnered Viewed to victory in the 2008 Melbourne Cup, admitted, strangely, 'I'm very embarrassed and disappointed because it does affect the image of racing' after being told during an inquiry by chief steward Ray Murrihy, 'Here we have one of the best jockeys in Sydney, a Melbourne Cup winner, having Aus$2,500 on the head of another horse in a race that you're riding in.'

Shinn's mount, Diamond Jim, finished fourth, the one he backed, Giresun, second. Shinn was suspended for 15 months for this and other offences.

Outspoken At The Races pundit Matt Chapman called in his *Weekender* column for jockeys to be allowed to bet: 'Wouldn't it be easier to regulate jockeys if they had to supply stewards with account details? Wouldn't it be better for stewards to be in the know if a jockey is betting? I think punters would warm to a jockey backing themselves. Just think of the excitement if before each race, ATR and RUK revealed jockeys' bets.'

455 ARMED POLICE STOP RACING Ghana

With passions running high between the racing fraternity who were keen to keep racing on the traditional racecourse in Accra, Ghana, and the developers hoping to get permission to turn the track into a hotel complex, the major event of the year, the Independence Day meeting scheduled for March 2008, failed to happen when armed police arrived to prevent the races taking place.

The row was continuing in May 2010 when a local report explained: 'The project has only been delayed by the refusal of families of jockeys and horse owners to move from the old racecourse but, all things being equal, the horse racing fraternity would soon be moving to new grounds being constructed free of charge by Cascade, as part of their commitment to promoting tourism in the country. It will cost the company $2m.'

One of the reasons why racing seems to have fallen out of favour may be explained by an article in the *Accra Mail* in 2001: 'Horse racing is one area in sports which has suffered neglect from the Sports Ministry over the years, especially since the allegation some years back that Alidu Kora and his Medium Mortar Regiment gunners planned firing their big guns from that location in their bid to topple the PNDC government.'

★

The Queen visited the Accra races in 1961 and a fascinating photograph taken then shows her filming the racing through a cine camera.

456 AKA 'YOU TIGHT BAS*ARDS'!
Tasmania

When the good folk of Cornwall in Tasmania were invited to subscribe towards the costs of a new racecourse, not all of them were too keen to shell out.

However, thanks to the sacrifices of a few, a course was duly laid down around two cricket grounds and it was all systems go for the opening meeting in March 1830.

Local paper the *Launceston Advertiser* was on hand to record the occasion, which it did with one or two pointed, but neatly phrased observations:

'It is difficult to imagine from whence the numerous vehicles and their elegantly dressed inmates could have sprung we regret that many persons of respectability should have attended sports they were not liberal enough to subscribe to. They, at least, had their amusements at something less than cost-price, and, as is too much the case, when others pay the piper, they seemed to enjoy themselves.'

457 THEY MADE 'EM TOUGH BACK IN THE DAY

When jump jockey Tom Scudamore suffered a kidney tear with a haematoma and was out of action for a while in January 2011, he took a call from his grandfather, Grand National-winning former jockey Michael Scudamore, telling him that he, too, had suffered such an injury.

'He told me quite abruptly that he had managed to carry on riding through it. He admitted that the passing of blood was quite concerning – but there was no time for being soft and that whisky eventually solved the problem.'

458 CHALKING THINGS OVER Wiltshire

Everyone loves a white horse – including the Alton Barnes white horse in Wiltshire, carved into a hill in 1812. The horse's originator was Robert Pile, of Manor Farm, Alton Barnes. Mr Pile paid £20 to John Thorne, also known as Jack the Painter, to design the white horse and have the work of cutting it carried out. Thorne designed the horse, and sub-contracted the excavation work, but before it was finished Thorne took off with the money, and Pile had to pay out again. Thorne was eventually hanged, for criminal behaviour.

459 GRAND SECOND, BUT SAND FIRST
Aintree/Sedgefield

Don't Push It finally give Tony McCoy the Grand National winner he craved in April 2010, as he beat Denis O Regan into second on Black Apalachi. Somewhat miffed to have missed out, O'Regan won a National of his own two days later when he stormed to victory in Sedgefield's 'Sand National' – riding a camel.

460 ...GENUINELY TUBED GELDING Australia

Mac's Glory may well be unique in the annals of Australian racing history – the only horse produced by artificial insemination to race there.

It happened in May 1981 at a small country course called Gatton in Queensland (where they still race today). The local paper's David Argus reported on the horse's 20-1 debut:

'The three-year-old gelding is Australia's first test tube galloper'.

Owners Dulcie and Kevin McLennan from Wacol had been reluctant to put their pet on the turf. 'This is only the second time I've been to a racecourse,' said Mr M.

The couple had been asked by vets from CSIRO, the Australian Commonwealth Scientific and Research Organization, if they could artificially inseminate their mare, thoroughbred Susan's Glory. 'We thought it would be a good idea, but never at any stage did we think it would go this far,' said Mrs M, adding that when the Australian Jockey Club registered Mac's Glory they told her it would be a 'once only.'

Reluctant to name Mac's donor sire, Kevin said that he had once beaten famous Aussie horse of the early 1970s, Gunsynd, but declared, 'That's all I'm allowed to say.'

Mac's Glory, ridden by Ken Steepe, missed the break in his 800-metre maiden race – and finished last. Said renowned Australian racing historian Phil Percival, 'I am certain this will not happen again.'

461 SHE NOSE, YOU KNOW! USA

Perhaps it was inevitable that the finish to the $41,000, ten-runner seventh Flat race at Monmouth Park in August 2010 would be fought out between 2-1 favourite Mywifenosevrything, and 6-1 chance Thewifedoesntknow!

Track commentator Larry Collmus pretty soon realized what was about to happen and declared, as they battled it out, 'They're one and two – of course they are!'

Finally, three-year-old filly Mywifenosevrything, trained by a woman, Jane Cibelli, got the better of Thewifedoesntknow, trained by a man, Eddie Broome.

Within a week 69,000 people had watched the race-call on YouTube.

462 HORSE SEMEN ON THE NHS

Louise Tomkins, General Manager at Hammersmith Hospital NHS Trust and later interim director of operations for Ealing Hospital where she managed a budget of £57m, defrauded hospitals of over £200,000 to pay for the running of a stud farm she was involved with, the Benson Stud.

Tomkins, reported *The Times* in January 2011, used fraudulent methods to make payment, amongst other things, for the importing of thoroughbreds and horse semen from world-class stud farms in European countries, which was used to inseminate four of her mares.

'The deliveries were disguised in invoices as human semen for hospital fertility treatments,' explained the paper.

463 GRUBBING ABOUT San Francisco

A San Francisco-based bookie and gambler of the early 1940s, at the Golden Gate Fields track where he had a reserved table in the restaurant, Eddie 'Bozo' Miller had an unusual talent – he could eat vast quantities of food.

So much so that before he died, aged 89, in January 2008, the *Guinness Book of Records* acknowledged him as the 'world's greatest trencherman', based on his ability to, for example, eat 27 2lb chickens in succession, winning a $10,000 wager in the process; drink more martinis than a circus lion; quaff two litres of whiskey in less than an hour, and gobble 63 apple pies in an hour.

464 NOT ABANDONED WAS, WELL ... ABANDONED Australia

A huge horse hunt was launched in Alice Springs after the town's leading racehorse escaped and teamed up with a herd of wild horses roaming the outback in January 2008.

The owners of the aptly named gelding Not Abandoned desperately tried to track down their missing galloper, thought to be learning bush survival skills with some local 'brumbies'.

As soon as his disappearance was discovered, the syndicate of six, led by Stephen Smedley, chartered a helicopter to scour the bush. When that failed, the group began sending photographs of the 12-time regular winner at local track Pioneer Park to local farmers. Then they posted a reward for him.

'He's brought everybody a lot of good times, and we're very keen to get him back,' Mr Smedley said of their winner of some of the Northern Territory's biggest races, and with A$215,000 in prize money to his name.

'He was having a break at his trainer's property when it was discovered that he'd somehow got out.' Mr Smedley said some motorcyclists had passed through the property not long before and it is believed they may not have properly latched the gate shut.

'The eerie thing about it is that there were other horses in the paddock with him.'

Tracks indicated that all the horses had left the paddocks but the others, excepting Not Abandoned, returned to it.

'We sent a helicopter up to look for him and, in all honesty, we thought that he'd probably be spotted dead somewhere, as he's a racehorse, not used to being allowed to run wild. Thankfully, that didn't happen, and we now think he's somewhere in the bush with the brumbies (wild horses) that run around the hills outside Alice Springs.'

Not Abandoned's plight gripped Alice Springs, with the town's papers,

TV and radio stations chronicling the seven-year-old's mysterious disappearance.

I contacted course officials in 2011 to check whether Not Abandoned ever turned up, but it appears that he did not.

465 LIMP DECISIONS Warwick

In February 2008 jump jockey Christian Williams took a crashing fall at Warwick from his mount Allistathebarrista. He was able to walk back to the weighing room where he prepared for his ride in the next race, Big Buck's.

Channel 4's Nick Luck interviewed 23-year-old Williams: 'I asked him if he was okay to ride after the fall and he said "Yes, the doctor says it's all right". By the time we finished the interview he was very pale and when he limped over to get on the horse he couldn't manage it.'

In fact, he couldn't even get his swollen foot into the stirrup and he was replaced, with permission from the racecourse executive, by Liam Heard.

Trainer Evan Williams later confirmed, 'He has broken his leg just below the knee – the tibia bone.'

Astonishingly, in November 2010, Williams took another terrible fall which resulted in an initial mis-diagnosis – when Beshabar was brought down two out by the fall of Chicago Grey in a novice chase at Cheltenham. It was first thought he had only broken his left arm but after observation at Cheltenham General Hospital it was found that he had sustained two breaks to his left arm and also fractured his right arm.

466 SUB NORMAL GAMBLE? Towcester

It is not unusual to hear connections of a gambled-on winner expressing total bafflement over the source of the money which forced the odds of their horse to collapse like a demolished building, but the explanation, reported in the *Racing Post* of January 13, 2008 suggested by trainer Sean 'this isn't a gambling yard and I didn't back him' Regan, after Blinded Bythelight, his winner in a Towcester bumper on Boxing Day 2007, was backed down from 25-1 to 3-1, albeit returning 9-2, was a corker:

'My brother's in the navy and he's my biggest fan. He said everyone he works with was going to back the horse. He works on a submarine – there's only 80 guys, but if they all put a tenner on it, that could do it, couldn't it?'

Ever get that sinking feeling about anything?

467 CONOR O'FALLRRELL Taunton

Betfair punters matched £20,000 at 1.01 as conditional rider Conor O'Farrell jumped the last hurdle at Taunton in February 2011 and cruised eight lengths clear on the run-in to claim a 9-2 victory on David Pipe-trained Arrayan. Except that he didn't, instead becoming unbalanced on the run-in and somehow slithering off his horse to the floor.

'I cannot believe it, my foot slipped out of an iron,' O'Farrell moaned afterwards. 'I had the race won.'

468 NUN BETTER Galway

Irish betting shop manager Aoife Mulholland, who ran one of her father John's Galway branches for a year, made a slight career change via 2006 TV talent show *How Do You Solve A Problem Like Maria?* – and won herself a starring role in the London Palladium smash hit show *The Sound of Music*.

469 BY GEORGE, MP IS GRAND NATIONAL WINNER'S SON Norfolk

George Freeman became the Conservative MP for Mid Norfolk at the 2010 General Election and he brought a unique pedigree to Parliament – becoming almost certainly the first ever son of a Grand National-winning jockey to take his place in the House of Commons.

For Freeman's dad, Arthur, was a 30-length winner of the great race in 1958 when he was handed the ride on Mr What just a week before the event and proceeded to romp to an 18-1 triumph – after which the Tom Taaffe-trained eight-year-old raced 33 more times but failed to score another win. Arthur also rode for the Queen Mother, and in the same year as his National victory he also won the King George Chase on the Peter Cazalet-trained 7-2 chance, Lochroe.

Although his older sibling Edward rode as an amateur, George, the youngest of three brothers, never threatened seriously to follow in his father's stirrups, despite doing a little riding as a child. Due to family circumstances, George did not really get to know his famous father well until he was a teenager, but he was so proud of his dad's achievements in the National and other big races that he made a point of buying the *Lett's Sporting Diary* every year to see his name printed amongst the Grand National winners recorded therein.

And George's paternal pride was demonstrated when he ensured his father's feat would be recorded in *Hansard*, the official record of parliamentary speeches, when he spoke during the levy debate: 'I grew up in and around Newmarket in a racing family. As some of the more senior Members of the House who follow the sport may know, my father stormed to victory in the 1958 Grand National on a brave Irish gelding called Mr What. My uncle served for many years as chairman of the then British Bloodstock Agency and my brother trains in north America.'

George doesn't get to the races as often as he might like but on the 50th anniversary of Arthur's National win he was invited to Aintree along with other members of his family where he met Peter Scudamore and many other racing celebrities.

470 I'LL DRINK TO THAT New Zealand

A dim view was taken by some of a punt on a horse by police and road safety bosses in March 2005.

But Land Transport New Zealand reckoned the $1,000 it spent on naming rights to a racehorse called Don'tdrinkanddrive was just the ticket to make gamblers think twice about drowning their sorrows at the racetrack. And for punters who still didn't get the message, Don'tdrinkanddrive's highway patrol livery racing silks would jolt their conscience.

The two-year-old would retain the name throughout its career, doing its bit for road safety by recording three wins and four second places in 19 outings, after which another horse was then bought and named Don'tdrinkthendrive.

471 JUSTICE NOT SEEN TO BE DONE AS RACING TAKES PRIORITY Australia

Bookie Colin Peter 'C P Speed' Myers started out on the Queensland circuit in Australia in the mid-1950s. Making a big impression locally, he was invited to be the only bookmaker at the Tower Hill meeting, which traditionally permitted just one layer to operate.

Accepting the offer, Speed was alarmed to be called up for jury service at the same time.

'I had to go to court and argue that I had to be released to go to a race meeting because I was to be the only bookmaker, and if I didn't turn up there probably would be no race meeting.'

Proving that Australia really is a different country, the magistrate excused Speed from his jury duty and the meeting went ahead. 'Usually, at these meetings half of the bookies' profits were shared with the club. Coming to the last two races I was losing and thinking if things didn't improve I would have to face the club and tell them I couldn't pay,' said Speed.

He needn't have worried – he recovered to make a profit over the two days of the meeting.

472 SARAH'S BOOB Belmont Park, USA

Bizarrely enough, the state of possible US Presidential candidate Sarah Palin's breasts became the subject of speculation when she went to the races at Belmont Park in June 2010.

Reported one excited website: 'Sarah Palin watchers have taken a break from asking whether the former Alaska Governor plans to run for President in 2012 by speculating instead on whether she has had breast implants. The internet chatter over Palin's alleged boob job began after photos appeared of Palin stepping out in a form-fitting white T-shirt at Belmont Park racecourse in New York on Sunday. Palin and her husband Todd were there to watch their horse First Dude come third in the Belmont Stakes race.'

Columnist Ken Layne of Washington gossip website wonkette.com commented: 'Sarah Palin sure looks like she was trotting out some new work at the horse races on Sunday'.

473 WELL, WELL – IT'S THAT SINKING FEELING
Truro

Useful colt Manrico was standing happily in his stable in top late 19th-century trainer William Day's yard when the floor suddenly gave way, pitching the startled animal into a disused well which had been previously covered up.

The *Racing Illustrated* magazine of April 1895 reported that despite his 'perilous predicament the horse was extracted, practically uninjured, after a sojourn of some hours in his uncomfortable quarters.'

The magazine then detailed a similar episode which rivalled, and perhaps, exceeded Manrico's ordeal: 'A colt, the property of Edward Lemin of Truro, in October last fell down a shaft four fathoms deep, where it remained for one month before it was discovered; it was taken up alive and unhurt though in a very emaciated state and is now perfectly recovered. It was impossible that it could have received the least food or water whilst it was in the shaft!'

I wonder whether this latter tale was an early April fool gag!

474 LOSING A ONE-HORSE RACE
Reefton, New Zealand

There was only one horse entered for the 1899 Jockey Club Handicap at Reefton in New Zealand – Speculator. And he lost. Reported the *Otago Witness* newspaper: *'The Starter went to his place; the horse did not arrive; the advertised time for the race had passed, and the Starter dropped his flag and sent an imaginary field galloping down the course. The consequence was the Club saved the stakes, owing to the jockey, after the manner of his kind, not coming up to time.'*

475 WEIGH OUT PROTEST
Ballarat, Australia

In 1867 Exile, which had won the race the year before, completed the Ballarat Cup double at the Australian track of that name, but tragically collapsed and died just after passing the winning post.

In an act of supreme sportsmanship, the owner of the runner-up, Nimblefoot, protested and objected to the winner on the grounds that winning horses had to be ridden back to weigh in.

Stewards dismissed the scandalous complaint.

476 CANCER PUNTER IS £10,000 WINNER FOR FELLOW PATIENTS Buckinghamshire

A cancer patient, who won £10,000 by betting that he would survive longer than his doctors had predicted, died just days before he was set to to win a further £10,000 by staying alive until June 1, 2010.

But the winnings he would have collected purchased a vital piece of equipment with which Harefield hospital, where he was treated, was able to progress its fight against the disease that killed him.

Jon Matthews, 59, who lived near Milton Keynes, Bucks, was diagnosed as being terminally ill with mesothelioma in early 2007. His doctors told him he was unlikely to survive until the end of the year.

A keen racing fan and punter, Jon contacted William Hill in October of that year to ask whether they would be prepared to take a bet from him that he would still be alive not only on June 1, 2008 but also on June 1, 2009 and June 1, 2010.

Jon won the first two, collecting winnings of £5,000 from his bets of £100 at 50-1 each time, but he died when within days of a third win, this time of £10,000 after betting £100 at 100-1. Hills donated the £10,000 Jon would have won to fund a vital ventilator needed by the hospital where he was treated, which was in place by early 2011.

I had never been asked to accept a bet of this nature before in over 30 years at William Hill, but as Jon approached me directly and was adamant that it would give him an additional incentive to battle his illness, I decided to offer him the wager he wanted. Never had I been so pleased to pay a winning client £5,000 on two occasions – and I was very sad that he didn't quite make it to win his third bet and felt it would be an appropriate gesture on our part to offer the money to the hospital where he had been treated and of which he spoke so highly.

477 AL CAPONE, GUNS DON'T ARGUE ...
Chicago

The first president of Chicago's Sportsman's Park racecourse was a known associate of legendary gangster Al Capone.

Edward J O'Hare, also a lawyer, was in place when the track opened in May 1932.

Capone's 'mob' had controlled an illegal greyhound track in the early 1930s, the Hawthorne Kennel Club, very close to the site of the new track, whose president was indeed dogged by problems after taking the somewhat ill-advised decision to 'inform' on Capone. O'Hare was gunned down in 1939.

478 BUSHWHACKED
Homebush, Australia

A charge of manslaughter was brought against jockey John Gilligan after an incident during an 1847 race at Homebush in Australia, which resulted in fellow rider George Marsden falling from his horse and later dying in hospital.

At the inquest, reported by the Queensland-based *Moreton Bay Courier* in February 1847, jockey 'Higgerson', who also rode in the race, blamed Gilligan for 'drawing his mare across the one (the) deceased was riding.' But two witnesses disagreed, blaming Marsden who, they said, 'acted foolishly in attempting to pass inside Gilligan's mare.'

The jury 'carefully considered' the evidence and were of the opinion that 'George Marsden met his death in consequence of coming in contact with a post on Homebush Course, and that John Gilligan, having pressed Marsden on the off side, was the occasion of his striking the post.'

The jury also recommended that Gilligan should 'not be allowed to run races for the future.'

Gilligan faced a charge of manslaughter, was acquitted, but never rode again.

479 BEAT THAT, SONNY Warwick

Sonny Somers is one of the few horses to have won a race at the great age of 18, usually believed to be the oldest winning age on the turf.

But a hurdler called Cigar won a race at Warwick on March 20, 1832 aged 19, according to a record of the event in the *New Sporting Magazine*.

A report of the contest declared that Cigar was 'well known as having figured in the bloody fields of Waterloo' and that although 19 years of age when he won the three-runner (10 sovs each) 2m hurdle, 'he took his leaps and won the race in very gallant style.'

480 POND LIFE South Africa

It sounds as though there were fun and games at a meeting held in Cape Town, South Africa in September 1797 to judge by this *London Morning Chronicle* report – 'This gay scene was attended with only two accidents. Lord Macartney's groom in running had his left leg broke from his horse falling. And Mr Maxwell, his lordship's secretary, had a narrow escape of his life, having tumbled into a pond, coming from the Ball.'

481 LUCKY BEGGAR? Epsom

You'd have thought the talented Tom Walls, a noted actor and movie star, would have been happy enough to become a Derby-winning trainer when his April The Fifth won the big race in 1932 – but after the victory he started complaining about the number of begging letters he had received.

'He says that he received 4-5,000 letters and that quite 3,000 of them were begging appeals, the demands for assistance varying from a humble 10 shillings (50p) to £1,000,' reported the *Irish Field*. 'Had he acceded to all he says he would have had to pay out something like £150,000.'

482 HOW NOW – SURELY THAT'S NOT A BROWN COW! Reading

In 1791 three of the runners in a race at Bulmershe, Reading – Straggler (whose rider, John Halladay, suffered life-threatening injuries), Britannia and Andromeda – were brought down after colliding with a cow lying on the course.

In 1806 on the same track Langton, hot favourite for the second running of the Bulmershe Gold Cup, looked sure to win as he challenged along the straight – only to collide with a large coach-horse being ridden right across the course by a spectating gentleman's coachman.

483 KNIGHT OUT FOR HOMING HORSE Berkshire

Trainer J E P Rogers brought his Blue Knight from Cheltenham to contest a handicap chase at Maiden Erlegh in Berkshire's spring meeting of 1904.

The horse fell on the second circuit, unseating his rider and running back to the paddock, where he tore around the enclosure before jumping a high, spiked iron fence behind the grandstand, which saw him now in a park.

He then jumped some oak palings to get on to the Wokingham Road, where he knocked down a policeman who attempted to stop him. A labourer, Alfred Dell, also had a go at bringing Blue Knight's charge to a halt but was also hurled to the ground for his pains.

Blue Knight galloped on past the local tram terminus and made his way back to the stables in Crescent Road – where he had been staying since his arrival from Cheltenham.

484 WATERED DOWN Bogside

Jump jockey Avril Vasey almost drowned in the water jump at Bogside racecourse when he was thrown by Hereford Lad during a 1929 race – fortunately for him, fellow rider Bilby Rees was also dumped by his mount and spotted that Vasey was lying prone face down in the water. Rees quickly rescued Vasey.

485 EACH-WAY BET?

Wealthy US breeder Harold Harrison was in his 80th year when he donated the proceeds of his sale of a $3.9m Kris S. colt at the 1999 Keeneland September yearling sales to fund the building of a church in his native Georgia.

He died in April 2001.

486 THE RACE WAS IN THE BAG Del Mar

Racegoers at Del Mar, USA, were shocked when a man ran on to the track during a 1995 race and hurled a gym bag at filly Toga Toga Toga.

487 THERE WILL NOW BE A SHORT INTERMISSION New England

More than 10,000 excited racegoers flocked to the opening meet of new racecourse Rockingham Park in New Hampshire back in June 1906.

Legendary gambler John 'Bet-A-Million' Gates and partner Augustus Belmont II had arranged the 21-day meet, planning for every eventuality. Well, except for one pretty important one.

It appeared to have slipped their minds that betting on horses was illegal in the state.

On the third day of the meet, Pinkerton detectives duly arrived to close the track. However, they continued to race, albeit without any legal betting – which demand, of course, was satisfied 'underground'.

With the help of writer Damon Runyan, legislators finally relented and permitted pari-mutuel betting, enabling 'The Rock' to re-open in 1933 after a 27-year gap which may give hope to those who'd like to see Great Leighs reactivated.

Five years later the track was hit by a hurricane which blew track announcer Babe Rubinstein's commentary box clean off the roof. Happily he wasn't in it at the time. The winds also lifted jockey Warren Yarberry off Singing Slave at the eighth pole during one race.

Also during 1938, a mysterious 'Lady in Red' appeared. A woman, always dressed in red and always frequenting the track on a Saturday, wagered huge sums of money on the favourites, and often created minus pools for the track. One day she was said to have lost $10,000 on a race.

There was another 'time out' of four years after fire destroyed the grandstand in 1980, so the track's proud 2011 boast of 'Celebrating 105 years' was maybe slightly over-egging the pudding!

488 NET RESULT Tulsa, USA

A giant net hangs between Fair Meadows racecourse in Tulsa, USA, and the neighbouring sports stadium. It 'keeps foul balls from landing on the track's final turn' reported the *Thoroughbred Times Racing Almanac*.

489 MOCCASIN'S A SHOE-IN Canada

Between August 14 and September 1, 2001, every one of the horses ridden by jockey Tim Moccasin was something of a shoe-in as he booted home a record 14 consecutive winners at Marquis Downs in Canada without a single slipper up.

490 RACING TO NUMBER 11 Westminster

Labour's Shadow Chancellor Ed Balls is clearly not a man who spends all of his time pondering what he would do with the nation's finances should his party win a future general election, giving him one of the top jobs in Cabinet.

But his mind is clearly constantly racing, as on February 6, 2011 he took time out from his arduous duties to tell anyone who cared via Twitter that he had 'Just played Totopoly (my first ever eBay purchase) for the first time for over 30 years – just as good as in the 1970s.'

Expect him either to gamble the national debt on the National if and when he takes over or to put up all state resources for sale on eBay.

491 BOOKIE'S ODDS-ON LOSER West Ham

In November 1895, London bookmaker John Edward Headley was attacked by a group of conmen or, as they were known at the time, 'rampers', who had tried to con him by backing a horse 'entered in two races on one day after it had won the first race and then demanding money, though the horse lost the last race'.

In a survey of the world's most cunning schemes to defraud bookies this one would figure somewhere near the bottom of the list.

When, unsurprisingly enough, Headley told the cheats to sling their hooks, they resorted to violence. One of them, James Finch, produced a knife and threatened to 'rip Headley up'. Police duly summoned Finch to appear at West Ham Police Court.

It appeared Finch was 'bang to rights' and the only speculation was about how severe a sentence he would get.

But when Headley told the court that he was 'in fear' of the defendant, and had been unable to pursue his trade as a result of the attack, sitting magistrate Mr Baggallay shocked those present by commenting: 'A very good thing, too', reported *Racing Illustrated* magazine.

Baggallay then announced, 'I dismiss the summons. The business carried on by the complainant is a curse to society and so long as he carries it on he must protect himself.'

Surely no-one could take such a dim view of bookmakers in today's enlightened times – I don't think I'd bet on that, though.

492 COME ON MY, ER, SON? Chicago

Five-year-old mare Martha Maxine won 18 races worth over $400,000 on the harness racing circuit in and around Chicago until, in April 2009 after a race in Pennsylvania, a routine test for steroids revealed the horse had an 'elevated' level of testosterone – further tests indicated that the horse 'has normal female genitalia, but also has testicles inside HIS abdomen.'

Martha Maxine was examined by New Jersey veterinarian Dr Patricia Hogan. Hogan works with harness horses and thoroughbreds and is respected in both sports and is married to a top trainer, Ed Lohmeyer. She determined that Martha Maxine had ambiguous external genitalia, indicating an intersex condition. It was eventually determined that Martha Maxine was a male pseudohermaphrodite.

The Erv Miller-trained Martha Maxine was classified as 'intersex' and permitted to continue racing, contesting 'colt'-only versions of 'filly' races he/she had previously won. Said Miller, 'The only thing I ever noticed was that she was a very muscular mare. When you think you've seen everything in this business, something else comes along.'

493 NOT TO BE CONFUSED WITH EACH OTHER

George Moore (1923-2008), the Aussie jockey who rode 119 Grade One winners before becoming a very successful trainer, shouldn't be confused with **George Moore** (24 February 1852 – 21 January 1933), Irish novelist, short-story writer, poet, art critic, memoirist and dramatist whose 1894 novel *Esther Waters* features plenty of racing action including a description of the 1888' Stewards Cup, and is still in print.

Hadden Frost, the jockey son of former jockey Jimmy Frost, actually SHOULD be confused with **Hayden Frost**, the jockey son of former jockey Jimmy Frost – as the former is his given name according to his birth certificate, but the latter is what dad Jimmy meant to write on it when he went to register the birth!

When **Gordon Richards**, the subsequent trainer of Grand National winner Hallo Dandy and top chaser One Man, weighed out for his first ride as an apprentice jockey, there was some confusion because **Gordon Richards**, the multiple champion Flat jockey, later Sir Gordon, was still in his pomp. The clerk of the scales suggested the younger Gordon should place an initial between the Gordon and the Richards to avoid confusion with the great jockey. Thus he became G W Richards.

Young Flat jockey **Stevie Donohoe** should not be confused with ten-time champion Flat jockey **Steve Donaghue** (1884-1945).

Up-and-coming Flat jockey **William Carson** probably should be confused with his grandfather, the former champion Flat jockey-turned-TV presenter who we must now address as **Dr William Hunter Carson OBE**.

In 2008 the eighth-placed finishers in the eccentric annual Hayes Golden Button Challenge, Quality and rider **Katy Price**, attracted considerable media interest – but the Katy Price in question was not the cosmetically enhanced owner of a similar name **Katie Price**, alias glamour model Jordan, but a 29-year-old mobile phone shop proprietor whose business is based in Hay-on-Wye. Acknowledging that her name provokes regular comments, Katy said: 'The only reply to that is, 'mine are real'.'

I'd be surprised if there were any similarities between **Kerrang** the heavy metal music radio and TV stations and magazine, and the Victoria, Australian racecourse **Kerang** – although with the Aussies, you're never quite sure. The biggest event on the Kerang social calendar is apparently their Boxing Day races. I learned from the track itself that, 'The country hospitality and warm welcome are clearly evident when you enter the Kerang racecourse and a relaxing day at the races is guaranteed.' So, turn up the volume to eleven, and rock on down to Kerang!

In March 1946, the owner/trainer of useful Plumpton course specialist hurdler, M&B, needed a late replacement jockey for the horse and opted for top rider **Don Butchers**. After calling Butchers out of the jockeys' changing room, he was surprised when the rider asked if it was okay for him to carry 1lb overweight as he couldn't claim his 5lb allowance. He'd actually called out **Bob Butchers**, Don's young, claiming nephew. Neither Butchers eventually rode – Bill Heavey deputising and winning.

Miss Suzy Smith, East Sussex-based trainer of Material World and Golden Bay, amongst others, is not to be confused with **Mrs Sue Smith**, West Yorkshire-based trainer and wife of show jumping superstar Harvey Smith, even though both sent out jump winners on February 28, 2011.

494 GHOSTLY GALLOPINGS

Mahalaxmi racecourse in India (which was modelled on Australia's Caulfield course) is reportedly haunted, due to graveyards in its vicinity and the death of jockeys and horses on the turf.

Irishman Richard 'Boss' Croker, who owned 1907 Derby winner Orby, died in 1922 and his spectre was said to haunt the stables at Glencairn estate near Leopardstown where his horses were trained

Not strictly speaking a ghost, the possibly mythical 'Beast of Bodmin Moor' was spotted in December 2007 by trainer Becky Kennen (sober at the time) who was out exercising one of her horses on the moor when 'I watched the Beast until it disappeared over a hill, then galloped in that direction hoping to get another view. As I was nearing the top of the hill, a llama came flat out in my direction and nearly knocked me from the saddle'

Prestbury is very close to Cheltenham racecourse and is claimed to be one of the most haunted villages in the UK, with horses often part of the hauntings, notably at the Prestbury House Hotel, which has a ghost of a young girl walking in the garden, and also sound of horses' hooves can be heard, as the building next to it used to be a stable

American horseracing has a Halloween tradition, with the annual Gray Ghost Handicap at the Meadowlands in New Jersey, run over 1 1/6 miles on the turf. This race is usually held on Halloween night but when that is a Sunday night it will usually be run on Halloween Eve. It is restricted to grey horses only and the trophy is presented by the winners of the Halloween costume contest

Carol Parker, her husband and her three children used to live at Tillingdown Farm, close to the A22, by the Caterham by-pass, within the area of sightings of a famous ghost. 'We lived there in the early 1970s, when it was a horseracing yard,' she told www.cobraworkshop.co.uk. 'I don't remember seeing anything unusual in that area, however the farm was a different matter. The "tied cottage" we lived in was spooky, we were always hearing and seeing things. There was a room at the top of the house that I hated going into. We'd hear footsteps outside the windows at night, but never found anybody about. Our sitting room door would be 'thumped' at the same time every evening. Toys would be moved. I would regularly see a figure, out of the corner of my eye, but when I turned and looked there was nothing there. I was so scared, I used to sleep with the light on. Our nearest neighbour was a cottage about 200m away where the stable lads lived. They too had many strange happenings, things repeatedly being moved within moments of being put down, bags, coats, tools. We heard that a man had shot himself outside our house.'...

Former trainer Tom Jones, who died in December 2007, shared his house, remembered friend and fellow trainer Charlie Brooks, with 'a loving wife, a properly eccentric housekeeper, and a ghost that left £1 coins in strange places.'

Racing Post writer Rodney Masters lives at the Lambourn Place estate in Lambourn which is on the site of trainer John Humphreys' yard from the end of the 19th century. Masters reported that the site is haunted – naming one Henry Hippisley, who apparently 'spent an infamous life oppressing the locals and defrauding charities', as the most likely candidate for the roving spirit said to remain there.

Irish trainer Gordon Elliott and partner Annie Bowles went to look at a derelict house on land which had come up for sale close to his Capranny stables in September 2010. For some reason they went in the evening, remembered Bowles: 'It was hard to see much by the moonlight, we crept up the creaky old stairs and just as we were about to enter the first door off the landing, the faint sound of a radio or television showed me a totally different side to Gordon – that of complete terror – we didn't hang around to find out who or what was living in the dilapidated old house and we won't ever be returning to find out, either.'

495 STRANGE QUOTES

'Tony McCoy looks between his legs and sees Richard Johnson hard at work,' declared a race **commentator** who shall remain nameless in late 2010.

'My first wife – she said 'I do'.' Trainer **Keith Goldsworthy**'s answer to 'What's the worst thing anyone's said to you?'

'I was so drunk I fell off the weighing-room scales.' Former jockey **Jimmy Duggan**, now ten years sober and running an equine health company in California

Owner **Alec Wildenstein** was a little miffed after Dominique Boeuf finished only third on his Vallee Enchantee in the 2004 Coronation Cup, but was philosophical: 'We weren't unlucky, she was ridden by an arsehole who didn't follow instructions'

Racegoers at a December 2005 Punchestown meeting were slightly taken aback to hear a pre-race **course announcement**: 'The colours will be correct but two horses will be carrying number eight saddlecloths'

'He was mad. He used to carry round a Luger and threaten to shoot people' Trainer **Bill Turner** on his former employer, trainer Ricky Vallance.

'Rats, I hate rats. They are the only things I fear', admitted **Ruby Walsh** in February 2011

'I am going to receive treatment from a female doctor. She is vague about her methods, but I know she first massages you for a long time with (horse) placenta fluid.' Arsenal striker **Robin Van Persie** on treatment for his injured ankle, reported by Sky News, in November 2009

'A Hungarian National Hunt jockey'. Bizarre response by comic **Paul Merton** to the question 'How would you like to be remembered?' posed during a February 2011 edition of the Radio show 'Just A Minute'.

'If you make it through the streets to the track without being shot at or kidnapped you get looked after like royalty.' A glowing endorsement, or a warning, depending on your point of view, from Denman's jockey **Sam Thomas** about the delights of racing at South Africa's Turffontein

'He was a natural, we might yet see him racing on a real horse.' **Mick Fitzgerald** discussing footballer-turned-TV pundit Chris Kamara's performance on a racehorse simulator in March 2011.

'At first we were a bit like two strange dogs sniffing each other's bottoms.' A somewhat unsettling image suggested by **Luca Cumani** to explain he and Kieren Fallon's relationship when they teamed up

'If you want to be the man you've always wanted to be, you have to take this bet. Your comfort zone has been broken and whatever happens you will never turn back.' Bookie **Ben Keith** of Star Sports speaking in March 2011 on taking his first six-figure bet.

'You pulled that, you corrupt ****,' shouted a punter to a taken-aback **Lee Mottershead**, after the *Racing Post* journo had had his first ever ride in a charity race on Paul Nicholls' Goblet of Fire which he was relieved and delighted to have piloted into a respectable fourth place. Unruffled, he told his critic, 'I think you'll find it was incompetence rather than corruption.'

'There are plenty of jockeys who are frightened to death of horses.' Jockey-turned-trainer **David Bridgwater** in March 2011 not, I think, including himself in that analysis.

'Britain's most notorious death trap for racehorses.' A reminder of how others see us, perhaps, from **Animal Aid**, describing Cheltenham as the 2011 Festival got underway.

'It wasn't a horse that kicked me – I fell off the starter's rostrum. My leg went through the ladder and my shin snapped – luckily it was my left leg, and AP's car is an automatic, so it was the right one to break.' Tony McCoy's chauffeur **Arnie Jones** doubles up as a stalls handler but is unlikely ever to hanker after the position of racecourse starter after breaking a leg at Ascot.

496 UNFORTUNATE FATALITIES

Death by Grandstand! When Bogside racecourse's new 2,000-capacity grandstand was officially opened at an 1896 meeting, the *Glasgow Herald* reported that 'a compositor named Peter Hughes, overcome perhaps by excitement, fell down and immediately died.'

Bridge collision. Trainer Sue Bradburne's gelding Safin, a ten-year-old chaser part-owned by BBC racing's Cornelius Lysaght, died when the lorry transporting him in September 2010 collided with a low bridge. The vehicle was written off and falling partitions inside caused the horse's legs to be seriously gashed. Despite treatment he could not be saved.

Chance ride is killer. Amateur jockey James S Taylor thought his big break had come when he got a chance ride in the opening race on the card of the 1866 West of Scotland Grand National meeting at Houston, when Richmond's nominated rider failed to turn up. Richmond stumbled and fell during the race, throwing Taylor, and twice rolling over the stricken rider. The damage he sustained to his spinal cord led to his death nine days later, having never regained consciousness.

Fatal crossing. In February 1941, a car was leaving the track at Plumpton, via the level crossing exit, whilst a race was in progress. One of the runners, Roman Chief, partnered by jockey Sean Magee, collided with the car whilst actually endeavouring to jump it, sadly sustaining fatal injuries.

Delayed death. Cornelius Kenneally, a promising 16-year-old Irish jockey, fell in a 1956 Chepstow race. His mount fell on him and he was paralysed. When he passed away some 48 years later in June 2004 the Deputy Cotswold coroner, Sally Scanlon, said that the condition which killed him, chronic renal failure, was linked directly to the effects of his fall.

Death by frog. The president of Australia's Nerang Jockey Club, the Honourable J.C. Appel, met a tragic end in 1929 after drinking tank water polluted by a dead frog.

If it had to happen. John Clark, 48, long-serving jockey at Thistledown, Cleveland, who won over 900 races worth over $5m, died in May 2001 whilst taking a shower in the jockeys' room.

Best to check first, probably. The December 18, 1895 edition of *Racing Illustrated* recorded the demise of Mr Thomas Harpur, Irish owner and rider of racehorses, 'who, whilst handling a gun, which he believed to be unloaded, unfortunately shot himself.'

Fluid situation. When US all-time great Man o' War (20 wins in 21 races) died in 1947 he was the first racehorse to be embalmed. It took 23 gallon bottles of embalming fluid – humans needed two. Heavy rain meant gravediggers took three days to dig his final resting place in his paddock. 'Big Red' was buried in a 6ft x 9.5ft x 3.5ft oak casket lined in owner Samuel D Riddle's yellow and black colours. A 10ft wide, 6ft deep moat surrounded the plot. Up to 2,000 attended the funeral. Thirty hornbeam trees – one for each year of his life – were planted along the walkway to the site in Lexington, Kentucky.

Bugles were played by men of the Man o' War Post of the American Legion as the horse – an honorary colonel of the First Cavalry Division of the US Army – was buried. In Tokyo, 3,000 members of that Cavalry Division paid their respects with military honours. To coincide with the 3pm funeral racecourses throughout the US held a minute's silence.

He was originally interred at Faraway Farm, but, in the early 1970s, his remains were moved to a new burial site at the Kentucky Horse Park, where his grave is marked with a statue by American sculptor Herbert Haseltine.

Suicidal plot. Five men were charged with conspiring to administer drugs to racehorses during 1958 and '59, following a three-month investigation. One of those charged was 32-year-old jockey to Sir Gordon Richards' stable, Bert Woodage, who was arrested in the paddock at Salisbury after finishing unplaced on the Richards-trained Bosphorus.

All were charged, between January 1958 and August 1959, with conspiring to administer drugs to 'affect performances in diverse horse races and thereby cheat and defraud owners of horses and such bookmakers who should make bets on the results of said races.' They were alleged to have conspired with Bertie Rogers, a former head lad who made a 'lengthy' statement to detectives, and hours later committed suicide.

Death by chocolate. Controversial and colourful racing journalist Jeffrey Bernard, whose life became the subject of hit West End show *Jeffrey Bernard Is Unwell*, was accused of many things during his life, but only after it finished in 1997 was he accused of being a killer. And his apparent victim was another major racing figure – flamboyant racecourse tipster and early version of John McCririck, Ras Prince Monolulu. Bernard was sent in 1965 by *Queen* magazine to interview the ailing personality at the Middlesex Hospital. 'Bernard took along a box of Black Magic chocolates,' explained his biographer Graham Lord. 'And when Monolulu proved to be too weak to help himself, Bernard pushed a strawberry cream into Monolulu's feeble mouth. The 'Prince' tried to swallow it, coughed and starting choking. A nurse sent Bernard out and drew a screen around the bed but it was too late. Monolulu had choked to death.'

Flooding. Racing became involved in the wider tragedy as lives were lost in Queensland, Australia as massive floods swept the region in 2011. A former steward at Seoul racecourse in South Korea, James Perry, 39, had arrived in Australia to become chief steward of harness racing in Toowoomba. He, his wife and nine-year-old son found themselves in the floods and became trapped on the roof of their 4x4. The other two were plucked to safety but there was no trace of Perry or the car when they returned to save him.

Topdog. When Sir Peter O'Sullevan's beloved dog Topo, 12, died in late 2010, Brough Scott was amongst those who planned to find him a replacement – but the Grand Old Man wasn't interested – 'I'm not going to live long enough and that would be so unfair on my pet'.

497 THAT'S NO COINCIDENCE ... IS IT ?

On the day that the Pope arrived in Britain on September 16, 2010 for a controversial state visit, astute punters noticed that a horse called **Man of God** was running at Lingfield, and made the appropriate investment – duly thanking whichever deity they favoured as the horse, ridden by reigning champion Ryan Moore and backed to 11-8 favourite, proved a winner at that most heavenly of tracks, Yarmouth.

Only nine days earlier, as the 70th anniversary celebrations and commemorations of the blitz kicked in, naturally a horse called **Blitz** was a winner – also at 11-8 – at Lingfield, partnered by George Baker.

A September 2010 Hands and Heels race at Bath was won by a jockey called Matthew **Cosham.**

In October 2010 a race was sponsored at Cheltenham by **Ruby Walsh**'s new autobiography – and, of course, Ruby won it on Aiteen Thirtythree.

On the same card, jockey **Dominic Elsworth** returned for his first ride after 14 months out, winning a £50,000 chase on Edgbriar – at 14-1.

On the very day the Royal Wedding between Prince William and Kate Middleton was confirmed – November 16, 2010 – punters were able to cash in on the 8-1 victory at Fakenham of **Tocatchaprince**...

And on the day of the nuptials, April 29, 2011, **Royal Wedding** was a fairytale winner at 4-1 of a handicap chase at Fontwell.

Returning to the saddle after more than five months out through injury, a week or so before Christmas 2010, Robert 'Choc' Thornton's fears that he had perhaps begun to slip off the racing radar were eased when he landed his first comeback winner at Towcester – **De Forgotten Man**.

Edward William 'Wizard' Thompson was both clerk of the course and controversial handicapper for the Chester (Tradesmen's) Cup from the early 1840s – he died on the very morning of the 1873 running of the race.

Jockey Robby Albarado was thrown from his ride at Fair Grounds in the States in January 2011, and had to have surgery on a broken right heel. The horse was called **Mollys Missb'havin**.

Coincidence punters looking for a winner at Kempton on September 22, 2008 spotted that in race four, the 4pm, **number four** was drawn four, was quoted at 4-1 and was ridden by Jimmy Fortune. No, not fourth – it won.

The last winner jockey Michael Martinez rode was called **Stormin Proud Papa**. Three races later, in September 2010, the 24-year-old Southern California rider took the fall at Golden Gate Fields which severed his spinal cord and left his brain bleeding. Nine days later his fiancée, Charlotte Garcia, gave birth to their daughter, Merari.

Laurel Park racecourse in Laurel, Maryland, was established, spookily enough, by James Laurel Jr. It was known as Laurel Park when it first opened its gates on 2 October 1911 under the management of the Laurel Four County Fair.

498 WHAT'S IN A NAME?
Winner of the 2007 Classico Jockey Club el Peru at Monterrico in Lima was **Tracatrantracatran**.

US jockey Victor Molina was suspended for a month and fined $1,000 at Philadelphia Park for kicking his horse **Yes Yes Ohyes** in June 2007, after TV viewers spotted him doing it and rang in to complain.

Pot8os, sired by the immortal Eclipse in 1773, was thus named by an illiterate stable lad.

There can hardly ever have been a better named jockey than the Aussie female currently riding there who goes by the name of **A. Beer**.

Having persuaded his boss at the Halsion company to buy a horse and name it **Halsion Chancer**, Chris Powell celebrated its 3-1 debut victory at Lingfield in February 2007 by having the horse's name tattooed on his chest.

A rarity in those days, leading jump jockey and 1871 Scottish Grand National winner Maunsell Richardson had a nickname, and was known as **'The Cat'**.

While a more contemporary figure, the ever so slightly irascible and volatile trainer Barry Hills, glories in his **Mr Combustible** nickname – so much that he once trained a horse of that name

Apparently a certain BBC radio commentator who shall remain – oh, what the, its **Cornelius Lysaght** – is known, they tell me, to friends, as Semtex, on account of his explosive temper.

And then there's trainer **Nigel Twiston-Davies** who, according to Claude Duval of *The Sun*, that indiscreet chronicler of the racing scene, is known to fellow local handler Kim Bailey as 'TFFFN' – which, according to Bailey, stands for The Fat Farmer From Naunton.

Big Knickers pulled up.' Worcester commentator Iain Mackenzie told racegoers in October 2010 during a novice hurdle race.

The winningmost rider in British point-to-point history is **Richard Burton**.

A contender for best racing name of 2011 appeared as early as January 2 when Zed Candy won at Southwell under the eye-catchingly monickered **Pernilla Hermansson...**

Fontwell's clerk of the course was obviously born to work in racing – he's (Mister) **Ed Arkell.**

Chairman of Tasmanian racing in the 1950s was **Mr O. Layh.**

Having raced in Britain as **The Bas*ard** the horse was exported to race in Tasmania only for the authorities to ban that name and insist it be changed to The Buzzard.

A gale hit the October 1848 Brighton meeting, blowing away one of the tents serving as bars – the one run by **Mr Careless.**

Waggle Bum – the pet name her husband David Stait called – probably still does – Jenny Pitman. By the way, anyone know why she's still known as Pitman and not Stait?

A trainer in Brisbane during the Second World War had the impressive name **Pompy Conquest** – his stables were close to those of another neatly named handler, Roley Wall.

Despite what many from abroad believe, in actual fact there is no **'Durban'** track as such in South Africa – but the name is often used to describe Greyville, the course in Durban, Natal, while Durbanville is in Cape Town. Greyville, situated just below the ridge of Durban and on the edge of the city centre, has long been a night racing venue.

Yavapai Downs is an Arizona racecourse, two hours north of Phoenix where they run at a 5,400ft elevation.

Racing around the Queensland, Australia, circuit in the 1980s, Sandra O'Sullivan-trained **Pyfo's** name stood for 'pull your finger out'.

Don't you just have to love an Aussie race meeting known as **Gundagai-Adelong**, which proudly declares that it 'is best known for its Snake Gully Cup', which is run in mid-November each year.

Rattleyurjewellery, a son of champion sprinter Royal Applause, made his debut in September 2010, named in honour of the Beatles' 1963 Royal Variety performance appearance prior to which John Lennon told the audience, including the Queen: 'Would the people in the cheap seats clap your hands – and the rest of you, just rattle your jewellery.'

After a poor run of results as a rider (breaking a collarbone and suffering concussion), and as a trainer with no wins at all in a year, Mrs Adrian Wintle announced in early January 2008 that she would be reverting to her maiden name of **Hannah Lewis** – and promptly both rode and trained Shareef to win at Tweseldown point-to-point.

What could owner Mr Buckworth have been thinking of when naming his 1727 Bulmershe Heath, Reading winner, **Wanton Willy**?

Perhaps the same as Mr Boot, whose 1731 winner there gloried in the name **Ruff Country Dick**.

A racehorse with over $300,000 prize money to her credit died in March, 2001 in Ocala USA of injuries sustained during a severe thunderstorm. She was named **Lucky Lady Lauren**.

A nervous bookie standing at meetings on Australia's Gold Coast in the 1960s, who was reluctant to take bets on well fancied springers in the market, would tell punters 'I've already laid it'. He quickly acquired the nickname of **'The Hen'**.

America's Pimlico racecourse is known as **'Old Hilltop'**, a nickname dating from the time that trainers and racecourse 'faces' would gather on a small rise on the infield, removed in 1938.

He died aged 94 in February 2011, but grand old **Cloudesley Marsham**, one of the first racecourse commentators in 1956, gloried in one of the turf's great names – and even had handicapper Cloudesley named after him. Mind you, the ancestor after who he was named had an even more impressive nomenclature – Admiral Sir Cloudesley Shovell.

Great Falls is a Montana Downs, USA racecourse which just might have the least appropriate name in world racing.

499 STUFF WE THOUGHT WE KNEW, BUT DIDN'T

Everyone thought the first running of what became known as the **Scottish Grand National** was in 1867 when the West of Scotland Grand National was run at Bogside – but racing historian Paul Davies has now uncovered evidence that from 1863-66 there was a West of Scotland Grand National run at a course 14 miles west of Glasgow, outside the village of Houston, which was the origin of the race we know today – in the 1866 running all six runners fell at least once, but Antiquary was remounted to win.

Everyone knows that the authorities in **Iran** could be no supporters of gambling and racing – yet there is racing in Iran at a course called Gonbad-e Qabus where thoroughbreds, Turkmen and Arab-Turkmen horses compete.

Everyone knew racehorses would always beat athletes in **man v horse** challenges – until 20-time winner and popular former chaser Beef Or Salmon took on Tipperary hurler (not hurdler) Shane McGrath at Limerick over one furlong in October 2010 when the 5-2 human outsider defeated the 1-4 Timmy Murphy-partnered slow-starting favourite, to raise cash for Tracy Piggott's charity Playing for Life and the Jockeys' Accident Fund.

Everyone knows that jockeys should pack it in before they reach their late fifties – except that no-one seemed to have told **Josef Vana**, who won the 2010 Velka Pardubicka, arguably the world's toughest chase – his seventh victory as a jockey and eighth as a trainer – at the age of 57 on Tiumen, winning for the second straight year – and he shouldn't even have been alive to do it, as in 1994 his heart stopped after a fall.

Everyone knows the shortest distance we race over is 5f – but it wasn't always thus – Tosson won the last 4f race run in Britain – at Hurst Park in May 1912 – and there are many who would like to see such **'bullet races'** brought back, not least, I believe, *Racing Post* editor, Bruce Millington.

Everyone knows that you couldn't run a hurdle race over 4f – but clearly no-one knew that Brighton races held such a race in October 1848, in which two of the three runners failed to make it past the first hurdle, leaving Worcester to come home in splendid isolation.

500 STUFF WE JUST DIDN'T KNOW ANYWAY

Zenyatta's trainer **John Shirreffs** is a Vietnam veteran who says he would have become an English teacher but for racing.

Zenyatta's favourite drink was Guinness.

Legendary TV and racecourse commentator **Graham Goode** (first commentary at Worcester on April 8, 1967) bowed out of the business at the end of 2010, declaring himself 'taken aback' that his application to become a racecourse steward had been turned down by the BHA.

TV personality, nun and art critic **Wendy Beckett** confessed in the *Sunday Telegraph* magazine in 2010: 'When I stayed in hotels while filming my documentaries I sometimes watched the TV and found immense pleasure in the horseracing.'

Lester Piggott announced his (second) retirement on September 10, 1995 – in the *Mail on Sunday*.

Harry Beasley rode his own horse Pride of Arras to win the Maiden Plate at Punchestown in 1923. Beasley, part of a famous Irish racing family, was 72 at the time, and would ride on over jumps until 1924 when he and the same horse finished unplaced in the Irish Grand National. He even rode in a Flat race aged 83, beating the record of American jockey Levi Barlingume who was 80 when he rode on the Flat at Stafford in Kansas in 1932.

Paul Hanagan, Liverpool fan and 2010 Champion Flat Jockey, was presented with his trophy by former legendary goalscorer Ian Rush on the famous

Anfield pitch prior to their game with bottom-of-the-table Wolves. Liverpool promptly lost 0-1.

Joe Osborne rode Alice Whitethorn to win Punchestown's 4m Kildare Hunt Cup in 1925, again in 1926 and in 1927 when she carried a massive 13st 3lb.

Empyrean won two chases on the same afternoon at Wye racecourse in September 1935.

Three-time champion jump jockey **Terry Biddlecombe** estimated he was concussed more than one hundred times during his career.

Who knew **Rod Stewart** was a racing man? Well, he certainly was in 1997, as he and partner Rachel Hunter were on hand at the Otago Racing Club's 1997 Gold Cup day at Wingatui, New Zealand to see his Blooming Lucky live up to its name in the big race, after which the animal was draped in a tartan horse blanket, reflecting Rod's national allegiance.

Clyne Valley racecourse near Swansea closed in October, 1927. The site was bought by the local corporation and the track disappeared under 30 feet of compressed rubbish.

Trainer **Henry Cecil** is an avid collector of perfectly painted lead soldiers, which are displayed in a cabinet in his study.

Trainer **Jessica Harrington** was part of the Irish equestrian team at the 1984 Los Angeles Olympics.

A new drug for Parkinson's disease just might turn you 'into a **gambling transvestite'** revealed a *Metro* newspaper report in November 2010, reporting how 60-year-old Pete Shepherd 'suffered delusions of grandeur' and 'was out day and night at racecourses, betting shops, casinos and brothels' as a result of taking Cabergoline to ease his symptoms.

Independent racing writer Chris McGrath was an undergraduate at Brasenose College, Oxford, at the same time as **David Cameron**. As well as crediting himself with teaching the PM 'everything he knows', McGrath recalls: 'I used to subscribe to the *Racing Post* when I was at college and David Cameron would come searching for my copy every time his father had a runner'. Oh, tight, too, then?

Still on a political theme, the late **Robin Cook**, at one time Foreign Secretary, was a keen racing man. And so, now, is his son Chris Cook, who rejected life as a lawyer to enter racing journalism, editing *Racing and Football Outlook*, before joining *The Guardian*. His conversion to racing had come at the 1984 Grand National won by Hallo Dandy, which he watched from Becher's Brook. 'It had a startling effect on me and I was completely hooked'.

The world's first **hydraulically powered odds board**, which displayed all the betting stats and dividends and moved up and down between races to avoid blocking racegoers' view of the action, was proudly unveiled at America's Delaware Park in May 1951.

Brash bookie **Barry Dennis** would have been a long-distance lorry driver had the betting business not worked out.

Trainer of hunter chasers including the very useful Special Portrait, **Mark Hughes** doubles up as a bin wagon driver.

Winning the opening race on the first ever card run at Plumpton, on February 11, 1884, **Cowslip** surely set a record by winning twice on the same afternoon by a combined distance of 70 lengths when, after a 40-length triumph in the first, the four-year-old then turned out again a couple of races later in a chase – winning by just 30 lengths.

When the Bolsheviks came to power in **Hungary** in 1919 one of their first acts was to order that the Budapest racecourse be turned over to growing potatoes.

Tony McCoy's wife Chanelle reckons her 2010 BBC Sports Personality of the Year husband would give up racing to become fictitious trained assassin Jason Bourne.

With yards to run to complete the course in the **2009 Grand National** the last finisher in the race was brought down by course stewards – well, it was a man wearing a suit and a horse's head outfit.

The *Wiltshire News* reported in early 2011 that 'A horse had its **mane plaited** by a mystery person on Saturday' – no indication as to whether this was a racehorse, but it must have been a quiet newsday.

28-year-old jump jockey **Alan Crowe** went out to ride at Tramore in early January 2011 with the back of his silks bearing the legend 'Lookin 4 Luv', courtesy of his valet, Paul Fox. Crowe admitted, 'I am single at the moment, so who knows.'

In 1985 jockey **Steve Cauthen**, in Australia for a holiday, was offered the opportunity to ride at a Flemington meeting by the Victoria Racing Club – but declined in favour of a round of golf with local jockey Midge Didham. On March 6, 2010, a freak storm hit **Flemington** in Melbourne, and left the track covered in 2cm of ice.

When **Fontwell** was used for the filming of the Dick Francis story *Dead Cert*, starring Judi Dench and her husband Michael Williams, the script called for a particular horse to fall, but despite hiring one that was a poor jumper, it persisted in jumping perfectly well whenever it was on camera.

Christina Odenberg, who became Sweden's first female Bishop in 1997, was a champion amateur jockey, and when she retired in 2007 she began training.

Probably the first appearance on a British racecourse of pool betting was when bookmaker Richard Dunn operated a **pari-mutuel machine** at Wolverhampton in 1873 – the Tote took their first bets in 1929.

Singer-songwriter and master guitarist **Richard Thompson**'s 1972 song 'Angels Took My Racehorse Away', from his album of that year 'Henry The Human Fly', is a masterful composition with a strong racing theme: 'Well the angels came to see me today/Said 'We've taken your racehorse away'/ And I believe it was that bookmaker from Crail/I believe that he put one in her pail'.

New Zealand claims to have been the first country to broadcast **radio commentaries** of racing – starting in 1926 when the Canterbury Jockey Club's winter races were heard via station 3YC.

Peter Scudamore is a huge Guns 'N Roses fan.

The then **Edward, Prince of Wales**, raced under rules for the only time on December 7, 1923, finishing third on his own Phaco in a Sandown 'bumper'.

Scottish National-winning trainer Andy Crook, whose Ryalux won that particular event, retains longer-lasting memories of talented but temperamental sprinter **Ubedizzy**, who savaged him in Newmarket's unsaddling enclosure, costing Crook a finger.

Punters at South African track **Kenilworth** in late January 2011 knew their fate when in the big race, the J&B Met, Paddy O'Reilly came out of the stalls still blindfolded. Unlike the soon-to-be-changed rules in Britain, the Springbok runner was quickly deemed a non-runner and stakes were refunded. Because the race sponsors were a whisky company, under-18s were banned from the course.

Jump jockey **Robert 'Choc' Thornton**'s superstitious ceremonial throwing away of his racing breeches following a disappointing run of results in January 2011 resulted in – falling at the first; finishing third and fifth, and pulling up at the last in his next four rides.

1873 Derby winner Doncaster, who also won Ascot and Goodwood Cups, was sold for £14,000 in 1875, a sum described then as 'astounding' but which translates today, according to moneysorter.co.uk, to a mere bargain £1,129,428.57.

Grand National-winning jockey **Liam Treadwell** would love to 'become a professional surfer'

A leading **Aussie owner** of the late forties and early fifties would celebrate each big win by giving away 'one shilling' pocket money to every child who came to his factory – he had to stop when 'hairy-chested "boys"' began muscling in to the queues.

Festivals are not a modern-day phenomenon. In 1866 Reading's **King Meadow** track added Saturday to its usual Thursday-Friday meeting to make it a three-day festival. It didn't prove popular, however. One of the odder races at King's Meadow's 1855 meeting had been one in which owners rode each other's horses, something the local paper called a 'curious anomaly' as Mr Elwes, owner of the runner-up, rode the winner.

The bizarre 1947 attempt at US track Portland Meadows to enforce specific jockey silk colours for specific race **draw positions** was doomed to failure while Narragansett Park's similar experiment of matching jockey caps with 'post' positions was equally short-lived.

Kurtsystems, a company based in Turkey, has devised two rail and car systems designed to **automate** the training of racehorses, in which a vehicle driven by the trainer wraps around the horse as it runs at a regulated speed, and, in the other, an elevated rail system with a train of box cars drop down around the horses, enabling up to 50 to be exercised simultaneously.

Irish trainer **Willie Mullins** has a secret, unfulfilled ambition – 'I fancied myself as a film director'.

Another Irish handler, **Gordon Elliott**, grudgingly admits to being a huge fan of Aussie soap opera 'Home And Away'.

A top jump jockey from the forties to fifties, **George Slack** remembered riding at Huntingdon in those days as like 'riding in a maze. You rode from one meadow into another and at times you could not see the next fence which could be round a bend and in another field'.

Desert Orchid's jockey, **Colin Brown**, learned to knit before he was ten.

After winning a race at Toulouse in March 2011, jockey Jean-Bernard Eyquem became embroiled in an **exchange of insults** with fourth-placed rider Gloria D'Isere, which eventually continued in the weighing room and the female changing room into which the Frenchman went to confront the Spanish jockey, resulting in his suspension for three weeks.

All four runners in a novice chase at Towcester on March 17, 2011 failed to finish. It was the first time it had happened since new rules had been introduced forbidding jockeys to remount, and it became the first race to be **voided** for that reason.

PR consultant **Max Clifford**'s favourite building is a tea stall on Epsom Downs, he told the *Independent* in March 2011, which he discovered whilst flying a kite there and going with his father to the Derby.

It was reported in May (not April, you'll note) 2009 that Seattle artist **Kim Graham** had invented 'Digitigrade Leg Extensions', complete with hooves, which 'enable the wearer to walk and prance more or less like a horse'. Said Graham: 'Level surfaces are easy. Sharp inclines are difficult and stairs are downright touchy. No, you cannot roller skate in them.' Don't believe it ? Check out Ms Graham's website, www.kimgrahamstudios.com, which pictures her 'wearing' the legs.

CH 4   1980's

JOCKEY OF WINNING HORSE BEING INTERVIEWED IN WINNING ENCLOSURE. DONCASTER.

INT " CONGRATULATIONS ON YOUR WIN ON "GRAND LASS' I BELEIVE YOU ARE FAMILAR WITH THE HORSE."

JOCKEY " OH YES! I RODE HER MOTHER TOO "

BIBLIOGRAPHY

ANCELOTTI, Carlo; with Alciato, Alessandro: *The Beautiful Games of an Ordinary Genius* (Rizzoli, 2010)

ASHFORTH, David: *For the Good of Racing* (The Tote, 2004)

BAUMGART, Kenneth: *Delaware Park* (The History Press, 2008)

BEAVIS, Jim: *The Brighton Races* (Jim Beavis, 2003)

BEAVIS, Jim: *The History of Fontwell Park* (Jim Beavis, 2008)

BEVAN, R.M: *The Roodee* (Cheshire Country Publishing, 1989

BURT, L G & FLEMING, B D: *Racing on the Coast 1885-1985*,(Hawera Star Print, 1985)

CAMPBELL, Robin: *All Bets Are Off* (Gomer (2004)

CLAY, Catrine: *Trautmann's Journey* (Yellow Jersey Press 2010)

COATES, *Austin: China Races* (OUP, 1983)

COLLINGS, John: *Gold Under Their Hooves* (CVRP, 1987)

DAVIES, Paul: *Cartmel Races* (TCR, 2006)

DAVIES, Paul: *The Scottish Grand National* (TCR, 2010)

DAVY, Colin: *Ups and Downs*, (Collins, 1939)

DUNWOODY, *Richard: Method in my Madness* (Thomas Brightman, 2009)

EACOTT, Bill: *A History of Racehorse Training at Epsom* (CW Eacott, 2009)

EDWARDS, Eric: *Friars Wash Point to Point Races* (Flamstead Society, 1996)

ENNOR, George& MOONEY, Bil: *The World Encyclopedia of Horse Racing* (Carlton, 2001)

GALTON, Barry: *Bunyips, Phantoms and the Magic Millions* (CQU, 2001)

GAY, Derek: *Taunton – The Complete Record* (TCR, 2007)

HALPENNY, M R: *British Racing and Racecourses* (Holmes & Sons, 1971)

HEWITT, Ian: *Sporting Justice* (Sports Books, 2008)

HOLMES, Nigel: *Ladies That Ride* (Nigel Holmes Enterprises, 2008)

HOLT, Richard & MASON, Tony: *Sport in Britain 1945-2000* (Blackwell, 2000)

HUDSON, Noel: *Catherine the Great to Wordsworth* (Huntingdon Steeplechases Ltd, 1985)

LEMON, Andrew: *The History of Australian Thoroughbred Racing* (3 vols, Various)

LEWES: *The People of: Lewes Remembers Racing And Race Days* (Lewes U3A Publications, 1994)

LORD, Graham: *Just The One* (Sinclair-Stevenson, 1992)

LUCAS, Jean: *Market Rasen Races* (Sporting & Leisure Press, 1989)

MATHIEU, Paul: *The Masters of Manton* (Write First Time, 2010)

MAYNARD, John: *Aboriginal Stars of the Turf* (Aboriginal Studies Press, 2002)

MAURER, David W: *The Argot of the Racetrack* (American Dialect Society, 1951)

McCAIN, Ginger: *Red Rum: A Racing Legend* (Weidenfeld & Nicolson, 1996)

McNAMARA, Ed: *Cajun Racing* (DRF Press, 2008)

MORRIS, Tony & RANDALL, John: *Horse Racing: The Records* (Guinness, 1990)

MOUNTIER, Mary: *The Racing Scene in New Zealand* (McGregor, 1987)

NASH, Stewart: *Plumpton; Illustrated History 1884-2000* (Plumpton Racecourse, 2000)

NASH, Stewart: *Plumpton Racecourse; The Complete Record* (TCR, 2009)

NICKELL, Patti: *Horse Lover's Guide to Kentucky* (Eclipse Press, 2009)

NORMAN, Matthew: *You Cannot Be Serious* (Fourth Estate, 2010)

O'CONNOR, Brian: *Add A Zero* (Hachette Books, 2008)

OLIVER, W C S: *From Then...Till Now* (History of Tasmanian Racing) (Privately Printed, 1986)

PINFOLD, John & PECHEROVA, Kamila: *The Velka Pardubicka And The Grand National* (Helios, 2010)

PITT, Chris & HAMMOND Chas: *When Birmingham Went Racing* (CC Publishing, 2005)

POLLARD, Jack: *Australian Horse Racing* (Angus & Robertson, 1988)

PREBBLE, G.K: *Horses, Courses and Men* (Ashford-Kent Ltd, 1972)

RUCKLEY, Harry: *Oswestry Racecourse* (Shropshire Books, 1989)

RUSSELL, Campbell: *Triumphs and Tragedies of the Turf* (John Long, 1930)

SHUBACK, Alan: *Global Racing* (DRF, 2008)

SIMPSON, Chris: *A Brief Guide To European Jump Racing* (TCR, 2005)

SMITH, Raymond & COSTELLO, Con: *Peerless Punchestown* (Sporting Books Publishers, Dublin, 2000)

SOLE, Laraine: *Wanganui Jockey Club* (1999)

STAWELL, Jessica: *The Burford and Bibury Racecourses* (Hindsight of Burford, 2000).

STEVENS, John: *Knavesmire* (Pelham, 1984)

SUTCLIFFE, Nigel: *Reading: A Horse-Racing Town* (Two Rivers Press, 2010)

THOROUGHBRED TIMES' STAFF: *Thoroughbred Times Racing Almanac* (various years, TTB)

TYRREL, John: *Chasing Around Britain* (Crowood, 1990)

TYRREL, John: Racecourses On The Flat (Crowood, 1989)

WALMSLEY, Michael & SMITH-BARANZINI, Marlene: *Horse Racing Coast to Coast* (Bow Tie Press, 2006)

WARNER, Dave & BRASCH, Nicholas: *Horseracing's Hall of Shame* (Harper Sports, 2000)

WHITE, Robert: *Courses For Horses* (Five Mile Press, 1985)

WINDMILL, Robert: *Geelong Racing* (National Library of Australia, 1988)